ENJOY YOUR PRECIOUS LIFE

CHRIST CAME TO BRING JOY

ENJOY YOUR PRECIOUS LIFE

Spiritual Joy through Faith and Will-Training

Father John Catoir, JCD

ST PAULS

Library of Congress Cataloging-in-Publication Data

Catoir, John T.
  Enjoy your precious life : spiritual joy through faith and will-training / John Catoir.
    p. cm.
  ISBN: 0-8189-0937-4
  1. Spiritual life—Catholic Church.   I. Title.

  BX2350.65.C38 2003
  248.4'82—dc21

                                          2002074505

The author wishes to acknowledge with gratitude permission from the Estate of
Dr. Carl Sagan to reproduce the correspondence in Chapter Two of this book.

Produced and designed in the United States of America by the
Fathers and Brothers of the Society of St. Paul,
2187 Victory Boulevard, Staten Island, New York 10314-6603
as part of their communications apostolate.

ISBN-10: 0-8189-0937-4
ISBN-13: 978-0-8189-0937-5

ISBN-10: 0-8189-0538-7   Volume 1: Enjoy the Lord
ISBN-10: 0-8189-0594-8   Volume 2: God Delights in You
ISBN-10: 0-8189-0937-4   Volume 3: Enjoy Your Precious Life
ISBN-10: 0-8189-0938-2   3-Volume Set: Trilogy on Joy

Printing Information:

Current Printing - first digit   3   4   5   6   7   8   9   10

Year of Current Printing - first year shown
                       2007   2008   2009   2010   2011   2012   2013   2014

*In loving memory of
my parents, Kitty and Jack,
who gave me the precious gifts
of life and faith.*

Biblical Abbreviations

OLD TESTAMENT

Genesis	Gn	Nehemiah	Ne	Baruch	Ba
Exodus	Ex	Tobit	Tb	Ezekiel	Ezk
Leviticus	Lv	Judith	Jdt	Daniel	Dn
Numbers	Nb	Esther	Est	Hosea	Ho
Deuteronomy	Dt	1 Maccabees	1 M	Joel	Jl
Joshua	Jos	2 Maccabees	2 M	Amos	Am
Judges	Jg	Job	Jb	Obadiah	Ob
Ruth	Rt	Psalms	Ps	Jonah	Jon
1 Samuel	1 S	Proverbs	Pr	Micah	Mi
2 Samuel	2 S	Ecclesiastes	Ec	Nahum	Na
1 Kings	1 K	Song of Songs	Sg	Habakkuk	Hab
2 Kings	2 K	Wisdom	Ws	Zephaniah	Zp
1 Chronicles	1 Ch	Sirach	Si	Haggai	Hg
2 Chronicles	2 Ch	Isaiah	Is	Malachi	Ml
Ezra	Ezr	Jeremiah	Jr	Zechariah	Zc
		Lamentations	Lm		

NEW TESTAMENT

Matthew	Mt	Ephesians	Eph	Hebrews	Heb
Mark	Mk	Philippians	Ph	James	Jm
Luke	Lk	Colossians	Col	1 Peter	1 P
John	Jn	1 Thessalonians	1 Th	2 Peter	2 P
Acts	Ac	2 Thessalonians	2 Th	1 John	1 Jn
Romans	Rm	1 Timothy	1 Tm	2 John	2 Jn
1 Corinthians	1 Cor	2 Timothy	2 Tm	3 John	3 Jn
2 Corinthians	2 Cor	Titus	Tt	Jude	Jude
Galatians	Gal	Philemon	Phm	Revelation	Rv

CONTENTS

"Lord, to whom shall we go? You have the words of eternal life."
(Jn 6:18)

"I have told you all these things that my Joy may be in you,
and your Joy may be complete." (Jn 15:11)

❦

"Do you want to know one of the best ways to win
people over, and lead them to God?
It consists in giving them Joy, and making them happy."
St. Francis of Assisi

"The greatest honor you can give to Almighty God is to live
joyfully because of the knowledge of His love."
Blessed Julian of Norwich

"Christ came to bring Joy... Joy is the keynote message of
Christianity, and the recurring motif of the Gospels... go
therefore and become messengers of Joy."
Pope John Paul II

"Adult life is not driven by instincts, but guided by the will.
Mental health is possible through will training."
Dr. Abraham Low

"Joy is the music of the soul."
St. Augustine

"Enjoy your precious life."
C.S. Lewis

INTRODUCTION

This book marks the completion of my Joy Trilogy. The first one, *Enjoy the Lord*, was written in the 1970's; the second, *God Delights in You*, in the 1980's. This one, *Enjoy Your Precious Life*, was written in 2001.

I wrote the series to help Christians understand that they have a vocation to live joyfully. The very idea of the duty of delight may seem daunting, and for some even beyond human strength, but with God all things are possible. If I can encourage one reader to enjoy life a little more, becoming a saint in the process, I will have succeeded.

Here is the basic outline of the Trilogy:

Book one: *Enjoy the Lord.* (Since God loves you, why not enjoy His Love?)

Book two: *God Delights in You.* (He not only loves you; He delights in loving you.)

Book three: *Enjoy Your Precious Life.* (You were created for Joy. Jesus came to bring you Joy. Love and Joy go hand in hand. True love involves the will to bear discomfort for the sake of the beloved. This takes discipline and will training.)

I realized that I had been used as an instrument of the Holy Spirit when hundreds of letters of appreciation began flowing in from all over the world. One lady, whom I never met, bought over six thousand copies of *Enjoy the Lord* to give away to her friends and family.

That little book has been translated into French, Italian, Spanish, Dutch, Korean, Filipino, and two Indian dialects. Ten years later, hundreds of thousands of copies had been sold, and I felt the urge to write another book on Joy. This time I called it *God Delights in You*. Some people liked it even more than the first one.

In this final volume of the trilogy, I have tried to go beyond the material covered in the other two. The faith issues involved in our personal relationship with God are the essential basis for spiritual growth. Knowledge is power. But one needs to act on that knowledge before it bears good fruit. Jesus called us to obedience.

The *New Catholic Encyclopedia* defines Joy as a pleasant state of quiescence in which the will rests satisfied. You can surely feel joyful when you achieve some goal you diligently pursued. Graduating from high school or college can bring you human joy for awhile, but the thrill passes.

Spiritual Joy is Joy with a capital "J." It is God's life abiding in you. It is an awareness that lasts. It is something added to any other happiness you might be feeling at any given moment. When you kneel down and thank your Maker for all His graces, you will experience a Joy that the world cannot give.

You were made for this Joy. All you need to do is open your heart to the Lord, and obey Him. **"Do not merely listen to the word, and so deceive yourself. Do what it says"** (Jm 1:22). Faith in the Lord involves doing what He asks. Joy follows obedience, and obedience takes will training.

The Supreme Commandment is a command, not a suggestion. Love takes courage as well as faith. What I have tried to do in this book is to help you realize Christ's wish for you, **"that your Joy may be full."**

You are His child. He wants to share His happiness with you. He gave His life for you. On the night before He died Jesus clarified how He wanted you to experience Joy, **"I have told you all these things, that my Joy may be in you and your Joy may be full"** (Jn 15:11).

You do not have to be perfect to experience spiritual Joy. The saints were not saints twenty-four hours a day. God gives freely to all His children, and those with the eyes of faith know enough to claim Joy as their birthright.

We are all saints in training. The Holy Spirit is alive and well in our midst. Doing the best you can is often not enough to qualify for heroic sanctity, but it is enough to enable you to persevere in God's love.

Jesus came to liberate us from our shoddy egos. He wants us to be happy. All He asks is that we make a reasonable effort to be followers of His word. If we make a sensible effort to love God and neighbor we will flourish. Jesus said, **"My yoke is easy, my burden light"** (Mt 11:30). Once you know this, submitting to the Lord can become a joyful adventure.

It is important to realize that you are responsible for your own happiness. Since spiritual Joy is the basis of true human happiness, you can begin to take responsibility for achieving this Joy.

True human happiness, and deep spiritual Joy are both God's gifts. Those who obey Him by living a meaningful life experience abundant Joy.

If you apply your mind to the task of living joyfully, in His Holy Will, you will find the fullness of Joy of which Jesus speaks. He wants to give you His Joy. Learning to draw from His Bounty is an art that takes time to develop. No one can escape the pain of life in the process of learning to live in His Joy. Jesus suffered and so will you. The saints all suffered and carried heavy crosses, and yet, by the grace of God, they exuded an inexpressible Joy.

Striving to be like the saints is essentially the same as striving to be a loving, joyful person.

We all realize that Christ doesn't want us to put ourselves first. Living selfishly, at the expense of others, is taboo for the Christian. Unbridled selfishness is a sin, and the mindless pursuit of worldly pleasure is pure folly. Wise men and women know that this kind of worldly happiness always disappoints. It is a poor substitute for true Christian Joy. Christ wants us to attain this Joy by loving one another. Joy is the by-product of a loving spirit.

Deciding to strive after Joy does not weaken one's spirit of altruism. We were made for Joy. It only enhances our generosity of spirit. Christ promised an eternity of Joy to those who follow Him. Altruism is the basis of our Joy.

If you are feeling a tinge of suspicion about being encouraged to enjoy your life more, I want to assure you I have no intention of deceiving you. I will not present a counterfeit Jesus who will leave you complacent in a world sadly in need of healing. Jesus calls you to a life of heroic service and sacrifice. He wants you to love your neighbor.

In the Gospel of St. Matthew, Jesus says: **"When I was hungry did you give me to eat?"** (Mt 25:40). The formula is simple: cling to God, and think of others. In the process, don't put yourself down, for you must also love yourself.

Love is patient, it implies enormous self-control. Most people reproach themselves needlessly for feeling impatient, but impatience is universal. All the saints felt the pain of impatience. Many of them felt like exploding in anger when others abused them. Jesus felt this way at times. Remember how He overturned the merchants' tables in the Temple.

Life often drives us to rage. No one is perfectly patient; however, we still have to live with our thoughts and feelings day in and day out. Some of us deal with our anxieties better than others. This takes self-discipline. If you are not yet skilled in this ability, do not be discouraged. Self-reproach can be overdone, and if it becomes a habit it will kill your spirit of Joy.

Just laugh at yourself for being human, and carry on with courage. Accept yourself where you find yourself, and be grateful. The Lord will heal you. **"Ask and you will receive"** (Mt 21:22).

Trust the Lord, but at the same time take responsibility for projecting a joyful presence. You can decide to be more joyful right now. Jesus came with a radical message. He came that your Joy may be full. He turned the values of the world upside-down.

Why not let Him turn your life around too? He can perform great miracles; He can transform your life in the wink of an eye. He came to create something new. His aim was to make us into a people of peace and Joy. He asked us to recreate ourselves according to the pattern that He Himself lived.

Jesus possessed the Spirit of Joy. St. Paul taught us to imitate Jesus: **"Rejoice always, and in all circumstances give thanks to the Lord, for this is the will of God for you in Christ Jesus"** (1 Th 5:16).

Is this being realistic? How can you rejoice when someone you love has just died, or when your country is under attack from vicious terrorists? Is Joy really possible in extreme circumstances? Jesus answers, **"With men it is impossible, but not with God; for with God all things are possible"** (Mt 19:26).

Either you accept His teaching, or you do not. It is your choice. The idea of living joyfully may seem too good to be true, but it is true, and it is possible. Accept the Lord's words, and you will be on your way to experiencing the greatest Joy you will ever know.

I know that you have already begun your journey. You already know that Joy can improve your health, release your bitterness, reduce stress, soften your hard-heartedness, and even build up your immune system. Joy can fill you with a deep satisfaction, which will abide with you on good days and bad.

Eternal Bliss may be a distant goal, but you don't have to wait until you reach heaven to enjoy your precious life. You can begin right now.

I advise that you read this book one chapter at a time. Read it, and let the lesson sink in before you move on to the next chapter. I have been deliberately repetitious to hammer home the essential points involving faith, trust and will training. Most of the Scripture quotes are my own translation. Though I have always remained faithful to the meaning of the text, I have tried to use contemporary language when I thought it useful.

I want to express my heartfelt gratitude to those who have helped and encouraged me with this manuscript. I pray that God will shower abundant blessings upon them.

May the Lord be your strength and our Joy.

Father John Catoir
Easter 2002

Part One

UNDERSTANDING JOY

St. Augustine once wrote these intriguing words, "*Love God, and do what you please.*"

It means that if you love God, you will only strive to do what pleases Him. You won't become self-centered. You will lose yourself in the process of becoming a loving person.

It is precisely in the effort to please God that we find the fullness of Joy.

Faith brings us to an awareness of God's love, which in turn awakens our love for Him. Joy follows the supernatural relationship of love.

St. Augustine's most famous poem, *Late Have I Loved You*, from his *Confessions*, tells of the gradual development of his soul:

> *Late have I loved You,*
> *O beauty, ever ancient, ever new!*
> *Late have I loved You!*
> *And behold,*
> *You were within, and I without,*
> *And without I sought You....*
> *You were with me and I was not with You;*
> *Those things held me back from You,*
> *Things whose only being*
> *Was to be in You.*
> *You called. You cried.*
> *And You broke through my deafness.*
> *You shone,*
> *And You chased away my blindness.*
> *You became fragrant.*
> *And I inhaled and sighed for You.*
> *I tasted, and now hunger.*
> *I thirst for You.*
> *You touched me;*
> *And I burned for Your embrace.*

1

CHRIST CAME TO BRING JOY

"I have told you all these things... that your Joy may be full."
(Jn 15:11)

Joy is not a feeling; it is a way of life. By expanding your mental horizon to enter this way of life, you will find a higher level of Joy than you have ever known. As a child of God you have a right to experience supernatural Joy.

For many years I have given talks and days of recollection to priests, sisters and members of the laity. I often open with this question: "What is the keynote message of Christianity?" After the audience offers a variety of answers, they usually agree that "love" is the key idea.

Then I ask: "What is the recurring motif of the Gospels?" A motif refers to a central theme, which is repeated over and over in a literary work or a piece of music. They usually answer: love, sacrifice, the cross, salvation, grace, prayer, etc., etc. Surprisingly, the word Joy is almost never mentioned.

Then I read them this quote from the writings of Pope John Paul II:

"Christ came to bring joy; joy to children, joy to parents, joy to families and friends, joy to workers and scholars, joy to the sick and elderly, joy to all humanity. In a true sense joy is the keynote message of Christianity, and the recurring motif of the Gospels. Go therefore and be messengers of joy."

A look of surprise usually appears on all their faces. Why? Because they are learning something they didn't realize before. Joy is not usually at the top of one's consciousness when it comes to the saints.

G.K. Chesterton said that JOY is the gigantic secret of Christianity. He liked to quote this text: **"Do not be sad, for the Joy of the Lord is your stronghold"** (Ne 8:10). When I apply that text to myself, I put it this way: "The Joy of the Lord is my strength."

Why is this Joy such a secret? After all, the saints and mystics were for the most part joyful people. Why do Christians find it difficult to believe that Joy is central to the Christian message? Perhaps it's because they have forgotten the intimate connection between love and joy.

Love and joy go hand in hand. They are two sides of the same coin. When Christ challenges us to love one another, He is in fact inviting us to a life of Joy. He wants us to experience the joy of loving. Think about the arrival of a newborn baby. A lot of work will be entailed, but that idea is shoved aside, as the spirit of joy and love takes over.

A saint is one who loves much, and lives joyfully. The experience of love makes one joyful. So many biographers present the saints as individuals consumed by religious piety. Piety is fine, but Joy is the superior gift. Christ never said that He came to bring piety. He gives us Joy.

The servant is not greater than the Master. We too will suffer in our lives, but the cross is not an end in itself. Our goal is an eternity of Joy, and Joy begins today.

On the night before He died, Jesus talked about Joy as the very purpose of His mission. He suffered for us precisely so that our joy may be full. He gave His life so that we might live in His Joy, both here and in eternity.

JULIAN OF NORWICH

Blessed Julian of Norwich, a mystic who lived through the ravages of the Black Death in the second half of the 14th century and the beginning of the 15th, received a series of sixteen revelations on Divine Love in the year 1373. For twenty years she was still studying these revelations when she finally decided to write them down. Her main idea was that we should not waver or doubt about the fact that Divine Love is the solution to all the problems of life. Here is my favorite quote from her writings:

"The greatest honor we can give Almighty God, greater than all our sacrifices, is to live joyfully because of the knowledge of His love."

I used that quote as the basis of my book, *Enjoy the Lord* (Alba House), which I wrote in the late 1970's at the age of forty-six. Now I am in my seventy-first year, and I still find her words fascinating. I want to explore how we can live joyfully, in order to honor the Lord.

It seems to me that it all begins with a deep conviction that Christ came to bring Joy to all His followers. Those who understand this see that we have a duty to rise to the challenge. How can we deepen our awareness of God's love?

Julian pondered this question, and came up with this insight:

> *"He showed me a little thing, the size of a hazelnut in the palm of my hand.*
> *"I thought 'What might this be?' and was answered,*
> *"It is the whole of creation."*
> *"I wondered how it might last, and I was answered in my understanding,*
> *"It lasts and shall ever last because God loves it."*

Divine Love, according to all the saints and mystics, is the source of our Joy. (I use the capital "J" when I refer to that Joy which the world cannot give.) Julian spent her whole life meditating on how God communicates His Joy to us.

THE WORDS OF JESUS

"Be of good cheer. In this world you will have many problems but I have overcome the world. Take courage, have confidence and do not be afraid. When you get weary and feel heavily burdened come to me, and I will refresh you. I am telling you this that your joy may be complete.... Love one another, forgive one another. Let your light shine so that all your actions will give glory to your Father in heaven."

It's not enough simply to hear those words. You must also believe them, and act upon them. This takes the will to obey.

"Not everyone who says, 'Lord, Lord,' to me will enter the Kingdom of Heaven, but only the one who obeys the will of my Father" (Mt 7:21). The Kingdom of Heaven is a kingdom of Joy. To communicate His Joy, Jesus asks for our obedience. So when He says things like, **"Be of good cheer, take courage, have confidence, love one another, be a light in this world of darkness,"** He wants us to be willing to cheer up, to take courage, to trust in His love.

These are passive activities. Patience is a passive virtue, which requires enormous strength. Some people believe that the perfect Christian is one who engages in a flurry of activities, but Jesus railed against the Pharisees who were compulsive activists. They were legalists, and they placed heavy demands on others. The Pharisees often paraded themselves as virtuous men because they followed the law, but Jesus rebuked them because they missed the essential point. Orthodoxy without charity is not Christianity.

The Supreme Law commands us to love God and neighbor as we love ourselves. This was clearly spelled out in Deuteronomy 6. Those who are interested in obeying the law of love do not put needless burdens on the shoulders of the weak.

The Pharisees did this in much the same way the Taliban did it in Afghanistan. Before their fall from power they imposed severe beatings in the name of Allah. But religion without charity is a distortion of the Supreme Law. Love and joy go hand-in-hand. There was little joy in Afghanistan under the Taliban.

True Christians are those who are filled with the love and joy of the Holy Spirit. *"Joy is the infallible sign of the Holy Spirit,"* according to Leon Bloy. Self-righteousness on the other hand is usually the sign of a self-serving braggart.

Jesus commanded us to love one another. This was not a suggestion, it was a demand. He wanted us to love one another so that our joy may be full. In speaking about the connection between love and joy, Pope John Paul II had this to say, *"True happiness lies in giving ourselves in love to our brothers and sisters."*

True happiness of course includes spiritual Joy. Worldly happiness passes away quickly. The Joy Jesus offers is far above anything the world has to offer.

Joy is more than the feeling of wellness. Though good health certainly gives a glow to the face, it does not constitute joy itself. True Joy comes from an inner knowledge that God is living within you. You are a carrier of Divine Love. His Joy is His Love. Human life elevated by grace is indescribably precious.

The call to joy is not a call to warm feelings. It is an invitation to share in God's Love and Joy. Once you partake of God's love, you will experience a need to spread it to others.

"The religion that God our Father accepts as pure and faultless is this: to look after orphans and widows in their distress and to keep oneself from being polluted by a worldly spirit" (Jm 1:27).

The worldly spirit sees joy as the satisfaction of superficial appetites; however, pleasure for pleasure's sake can be self-defeating. Too much ice cream makes you sick. Once the appetite is satisfied, new appetites are waiting to be awakened. The cycle never ends.

Choosing the Way of Love

Jesus teaches us that love is the way to achieve a joyful life.

Joy can be an integral part of your life whether you are rich or poor, healthy or sick. Joy is not something you can muster at will. Rather it rests on the miracle of God's gift of Himself to you.

The pleasures of life are here today and gone tomorrow. Granted they can contribute to human happiness, but they do not last long enough to deeply satisfy the human spirit. To attain the higher level of Joy spoken of in the Gospels, we have to care for the soul, and the body. After all, grace builds on nature. We should strive first for natural joy, understanding that the fullness of Joy will only come from God. When the soul is properly disposed God sends this free gift, which can never be merited. You can never earn it or lobby for it. It simply comes to those who are disposed to listen to the words of the Lord, and obey them.

This is difficult to grasp at first. We must believe enough to ask for Joy, but Joy is not a reward for doing good deeds. It is God's gift, freely given. He wants you to live your precious life joyfully by traveling the right path.

Supernatural Joy can coexist with pain. Jesus was the Most Beloved Son of the Father, and He suffered. Joy is not necessarily the absence of pain. It is an inner quiet that makes pain more bearable.

The knowledge of God's love is not a feeling, but it eventually spills over into our feelings. Even though bad feelings can coexist with Joy, they can never cancel it. Grief, for instance, does not eliminate the knowledge of God's Love. We know that our deceased loved ones are in a better place, we miss them terribly, but we trust them to God's mercy.

There are many kinds of emotional and physical pain. The saints suffered, but they proclaimed their Joy openly. St. Catherine of Siena put it this way: *"All the way to heaven is heaven."*

Admittedly, in this world, no one can be completely free of grief, sickness, villainy, injustice or any combination of the above. Even the Lord suffered a terrible agony in the garden. The servant cannot be greater than the Master. Nevertheless, even though we may have to suffer for a little while during our sojourn on earth, the Lord will never abandon us. There is always grace.

CLAIMING JOY

Once you firmly believe that a higher Joy is possible, you can begin the process of learning how to claim it. You can claim it in times of turmoil and suffering. You can enjoy your precious life in a new and wonderful way. In all circumstances you can rejoice, and give thanks to the Lord. The will can claim Joy, no matter what.

Once you are ready to accept this premise you will advance in Wisdom, Peace and Joy. The door to this level of true happiness only opens from the inside. You must open that door.

Begin by testing your humble state of dependence on the power of the Holy Spirit.

Turn to the Holy Spirit, and ask for the grace to live in His happiness. This is a good beginning. Learn to be happy with Him. Enjoy the Lord.

Give yourself to God and He will do the rest. (I refer to God as "He" because our language does not contain the proper pronoun for God, who is neither masculine nor feminine. God is above gender. To avoid the convoluted reference to God as He/She, I feel more comfortable with the traditional usage.)

Living joyfully is possible in spite of the many sorrows that life brings. The deepest sorrow comes from the emptiness of the human soul, separated as it is from the Joys of heaven. The soul was made for God, and it cannot be filled with anything less than God Himself.

Is it difficult to find this Spiritual Joy? Must you be a brilliant person? No, it is not difficult, and you don't have to be a brilliant person. Many illiterate people down through the centuries have possessed a joyful spirit, while hordes of well-educated and highly sophisticated people lived joyless lives.

Worldly people do all the obvious things to satisfy their appetites, and gain the esteem of others, but most of them do not prosper spiritually. More often than not they end up feeling sad and empty. Some drink themselves into oblivion, avoiding the pain of life at all costs. They do not realize that alcohol is a depressant. Harmony with God is the only answer. In His will we find strength and Joy. Real happiness is as close as God Himself. He is the mother lode of Joy. If you open your heart to Him, He will communicate Himself to you, and invite you to a life of joyful service.

Losing Yourself in Love

For three years, I was the executive director of a poverty program called Eva's Village and Sheltering Programs, Inc., in Paterson, New Jersey. We began as a small soup kitchen, and today we feed over 700 meals a day to the poor and homeless. During my time there I made a conscious effort to see the face of God in all our clients.

Most of them, on the surface, were a motley crew to behold, and yet, I prayed for the gift to see their inner beauty and dignity. It wasn't difficult because they were almost always respectful, humble and very grateful. I would rather have worked among them than serve in the richest parish in our diocese. They had suffered much, and asked little in return. There were exceptions of course, but they were usually mentally sick.

In our drug and alcohol recovery program we had about 120 men and women living in long term treatment; resident for a year or more. As they tried to win back their lives, after years of abuse, I saw Christ in them. It was not the glorified Christ mind you, but the bruised and battered Christ; the Jesus who was taken down from the cross by His tender-hearted mother.

Seeing God in others brings you out of yourself. The Psalmist spoke of seeing the face of God everywhere. **"Lord, what great Joy your saving love gives me. You have granted me my heart's desire.... You gladden me with the Joy of your countenance"** (Ps 21:1-2, 6).

Joy is a constant theme in the Gospels. The Church's Liturgical calendar proclaimed Joy from the very beginning. For instance, the season of Advent brings with it a wonderful invitation to Joy.

The word *"Gaudete,"* meaning "Rejoice," appears in the Latin text of the entrance antiphon. It is taken from St. Paul's Letter to the Philippians (4:4-5): **"Rejoice! Delight yourself in the Lord. Yes, find your joy in Him at all times... never forget your nearness to Him."**

We are living in a time of terrorism and germ warfare, and we all need to be reminded of this call to Joy. **"Even the desert and the parched land will exult; the steppe will rejoice and blossom, they will soon see the glory of the Lord"** (Is 35:1).

Pope John Paul II wrote: *"It is the joy of Advent, which in the faithful, is accompanied by the humble and intense invocation to God: Come! Lord, come and save us."*

The Liturgy presents these eternal truths year after year, and we need to hear them now more than ever. If you have been away from Church, think about coming back, but come back with a new attitude. Look past the human faults and failings of the priests and bishops. Look to the Eucharist. Christ comes to bring you Joy. Take this gift, the Bread of Heaven, which He offers you, and cherish it. Receive Holy Communion as often as possible and draw strength from the Lord.

He comes to save you, and He wants you to experience His Joy. Once you firmly believe that Joy is possible, you can begin to claim it. You can enjoy your precious life at all times. Even in the worst of times, His light shines within you.

The great Rembrandt portraits contain both brilliant golds, and deep shadows. This light and darkness motif is a reflection of life itself. Pain is part of life, and so is Joy. Every moment is a precious gift. Painful moments have spiritual meaning, and eternal consequences. They teach us perseverance. Patient endurance purifies the soul, and makes us ready for the rapture in heaven.

JOY IS A VOCATION

Jesus offers us a way to deal with all aspects of life. He tells us how we can attain a wonderful way of being. He offers us Joy, not merely a state of mind, though we can certainly condition our thoughts to be more positive and upright. He offers us a way of life, a vocation. The Lord is calling you to Joy when He says, **"Seek first the Kingdom of God, and everything else will be given to you"** (Mt 6:33). "Everything else" is precisely the Joy that this world cannot give. This Joy is a gift of God.

St. Paul says: **"We are not competent to take credit for anything as coming from ourselves. Our competence comes from God"** (2 Cor 3:4-5). The Kingdom is freely given to those who seek after it. Jesus gives Himself immediately to those who ask. You only have to believe the gift has been given. At that point, whether you feel it or not, His Joy flows to you.

Just as you have to answer a calling, to cooperate with God's grace, so too you have to take responsibility for your own happiness. The Lord will supply all the supernatural help you need, but you must navigate intelligently.

If you want to be a safe driver, don't speed and then pray for protection from accidents. Drive safely, and expect God to protect you. God helps those who help themselves.

The only adequate response to the gift of Joy is gratitude. You can say, "Thank you Lord," even before you are conscious of having received His Joy. You can live joyfully because of the knowledge of His love, on the basis of blind faith. You believe before you begin to feel anything. Try not to get hung up on feelings.

"Feelings are not facts." These words of psychiatrist Abraham Low, M.D., were intended to help the emotionally disturbed to regain their mental health. This wisdom applies to spiritual health as well. Dr. Low was teaching the principles of mental health, and we can apply them in this context because spiritual health is related to mental health.

While psychiatry has nothing to do with religion, in a very real sense it has everything to do with spirituality. Low was talking about feelings in the sense that they cannot be taken as objective truth. Feelings can be quite upsetting, but they are not always truthful.

A person may feel like a worthless piece of garbage, but as a matter of fact, he or she, without realizing it, is a living tabernacle of the Holy Spirit. God's life is present in the least of the brethren. Do not believe all your feelings. Sometimes they deceive. Bad thoughts can produce bad feelings. Bad feelings in turn will produce bad actions.

If you falsely believe that someone is out to hurt you, you

can easily whip yourself up in anger. This in turn can lead to a fight, where you might harm an innocent person.

If you feel like a loser, you would be wise to reject that feeling as a bad interpretation of who you really are. Feelings of unworthiness, will lead to misery and discouragement. What is the remedy? Imagine the Lord saying, "I chose you in spite of your unworthiness because I love you."

To be is to be chosen. Pick yourself up and say, "Yes, I am far from perfect, but the Lord loves me, and He intends to help me to reach new heights."

Joy or sorrow follows from the vision you have of yourself. That's why it's so important to condition your thinking according to your Faith, not your feelings.

Of course you can't simply brush aside all the bad feelings you will experience in life, but you can discipline yourself to claim Joy nevertheless. Work on it. Suffering can come in a variety of forms. Emotional pain is never easy to bear, but the Lord offers comfort to those who believe in His love. Claim that comfort.

Certainly Jesus was not joyful during His passion and death. His Blessed Mother was not joyful when she stood beneath the cross. At that moment she must have lost all human joy, and yet she always had the Joy of the Holy Spirit within her.

In this valley of tears we may never experience the fullness of Joy, but we can stay in touch with the Lover within. We can find our wellspring of Joy. We can fight the good fight and awaken to Joy and Hope. We are called higher.

St. Paul challenged us to **"rejoice in the Lord"** (Ph 4:4). Jesus tells us not to be afraid. He gives us the ability to turn away from fear. Our faith comforts us. We do not have to wait for perfect justice in this world; we can find Joy long before all the broken fences are mended.

During slavery, the joyful singing of the slaves often put their masters to shame. We too can give ourselves permission to rejoice in all circumstances. To overcome the pain of life, Joy is the best remedy.

Never postpone Joy. Rise up and enjoy your precious life. Count your blessings, and insofar as it is possible, refuse to be overcome by sadness. If this is beyond your strength, then at least pray for the grace to claim Joy. Discover God's Joy within you. Pray as if everything depended on Him, and act as if everything depended on you.

Doing Your Part

Karl Barth once said that Christians should not become "melancholic owls." Many in today's society have become morbid couch potatoes, glued to the TV. The daily news reports can be toxic. Too much exposure to the woes of the world can be damaging to your mental health, as well as your joy. Limit your TV viewing.

Jesus died to bring us Joy, and it is up to us to protect our minds from sadness. Claim Joy. Cultivate a joyful spirit, in the same way you would train yourself to develop good character. If you want to project a joyful presence, you must will it. I do not mean to imply that you can be joyful by the sheer power of your will alone, but with the help of God you can turn your life around. You can see that the cup is half full, instead of being half empty.

If you want to be generous, you must will it. If you want to be joyful, you must will it. This is a form of self-discipline that is within your power. Jesus told us He wanted to give us His Joy. Why not accept it? The Joy we seek is essentially from the Holy Spirit. He empowers us to see the silver lining in every dark cloud. Ask Him to help you to be more joyful, and He will teach you how to enter His life of endless Joy.

Listen to the Lord: **"Come to me all you are burdened and I will refresh you"** (Mt 11:28).

Trust Him on this. Just as the body knows how to attain greater comfort, so too does the soul. In order to relieve your thirst, your body knows it must drink. To get warm your body knows enough to come in out of the cold.

The soul also knows how to attain relief. If you feel guilty about something your conscience will tell you that you need forgiveness. If your life is on the wrong track you will feel dissatisfied until you set things right. Don't proceed against your conscience, or you will end up holding your soul hostage. The soul needs purpose and direction in order to be comforted. It needs meaning, and all of this is rooted in its need for God.

Each person is a complex composite of gifts and talents. God made everyone for a unique purpose. The process of growing to maturity is one of gradually finding out who you are, and what your purpose in life will be. If you have already found meaning, good for you! But if not, if your personal talents are hidden from your eyes at this stage of your development, and you don't yet know who you really are, then be patient. The Spirit will lead you.

Many people do not find themselves until middle age, or later. Don't be surprised if you are not settled yet. Even though you may not see it, your gifts are there within you, waiting to get out. Finding yourself takes time. You must be patient. The frustration of not knowing what God wants of you is painful, but this pain is part of the process.

I lived in doubt about my vocation for many years, but when I found myself, I discovered that the key to my inner happiness was in my calling to be a priest. Then I discerned that I had a vocation, within my priestly vocation, to be a saint.

On Being a Saint

The Lord wants you to become a saint too. You have to find the venue in which you will work out your purpose. You are called to be a healer, not a critic. You are called to be a lifter, not a leaner. You are called to be one who smiles, not one who frows. You are called to be forgiving, not vindictive. You are called to be an actor on the stage of life, not a passive observer.

In brief you are called to live a life of love.

This world will not give you much of a tumble if you go around without a purpose. Joy comes from knowing that you are doing what God wants you to do. **"Do not merely listen to the word, and deceive yourself. Do what it says"** (Jm 1:22).

The pursuit of joy is not merely a matter of seeking job satisfaction, but common sense will tell you how important job satisfaction is. If you were born to be a musician, and you become an accountant, you'll never be truly happy. You may need your bookkeeping job to survive, but your soul needs music. Play a musical instrument. Use your musical talent in some way.

Wouldn't it be wonderful to make your living doing the things you love most? Many people opt to follow their dream. Whether they fail or not, just having the courage to try gives hope and joy to the soul.

At every step of the way we have to take care not to make serious mistakes. No matter how well you may organize your life, things can go badly if you are not prudent. A successful musician may have found his bliss in performing, but if he succumbs to drug use, he risks losing everything. Once he moves from experimentation to addiction, he hands his soul over to his addiction and it is held hostage for as long as he indulges in this dangerous folly.

Once this tendency to self-destruct takes over, there is no chance for true Joy. Some users begin selling drugs to pay for their habit. The music becomes secondary as the skills of the music-maker become sullied. It is only a short time before the victim goes to prison or dies.

However, there is always hope. When I was running the drug and alcohol rehabilitation center, we had four separate graduations a year. We saw the ravages of addiction reversed miraculously in the lives of hundreds of victims. By the grace of God, and lots of hard work by the addicts themselves, we came to know that recovery is possible. By praying and cooperating with God's grace, hundreds of burnt out addicts lifted up their heads and their hearts to regain their self-respect. It wasn't easy, but they did it.

With God all things are possible. Faith gives us the knowledge we need to break through the darkness, and find the hope. Faith enables us to be our own best friend. Faith in divine revelation gives us the knowledge we need to perfect the "street smarts" we already have. This higher form of knowledge, which we call Wisdom, comes from God directly.

The Joy Jesus wants you to have is from the Holy Spirit. This Joy is the by-product of a meaningful life. By accepting the truths of faith, and allowing them to guide your decisions and actions, you will be rewarded with a deep satisfaction, and an abiding sense of spiritual Joy.

Do not accept a counterfeit form of happiness. Look for the real thing.

Keep Your Hope Alive

You cannot have hope without an abiding knowledge of God's love. One cannot be at the peak of happiness every minute of the day, but we can be aware of God's union with our soul. Experiencing spiritual Joy and Peace in all circumstances, even in times of sorrow may elude you for a time, but never give up.

The unbeliever may scoff at the idea that healing is possible, but Jesus told us to trust Him, and He always tells the truth.

Granted, those who are living wretched lives of destitution, oppression and pain are not going to leap to a state of Joy in the wink of an eye, but they can begin one step at a time.

Perhaps some justice issues need to be addressed before the mind is free to rise to the heights of Joy, but we can always turn them over to the Lord's tribunal in heaven.

Perhaps the misery of physical pain is keeping you from Joy. No matter what, you can still have hope. You can look beyond the present moment, and carry on with courage until the pain passes, and it will. The main thing is to keep your spirit positive and hopeful.

With hope, everything changes. When there is light at the end of the tunnel it is possible to feel a surge of Joy. Joy is the reward of faith. Those who accept the vision supplied by faith are given the wonderful gift of hope. Hope stabilizes the human spirit. Getting to the next plateau is only a step away.

In his book, *Crossing the Threshold of Hope*, Pope John Paul II writes: *"To accept the Gospel's demands means to affirm all our humanity, to see in it the beauty desired by God, while at the same time recognizing our weaknesses.* **'What is impossible for men is possible for God'** *(Lk 18:27)."*

God's Kingdom is a place of Love and Joy. Faith leads us to the Hope and Trust we need to attain the fullness of Joy. Hope enables us to trust the Lord's promises.

The theological virtues of faith, hope, and love are gifts from God. Some people accept these gifts, some do not. They turn away. They are not willing to gamble on the promises of Christ. They want happiness on their own terms. They want a sure thing. They want empirical evidence before they will trust the Lord, but who knows, maybe if they had such proof, they might not choose to love God anyway. You can't prove God's existence scientifically. You can bring a person to the water, but you can't make him drink.

No matter how anyone tries to avoid it, the God problem won't go away. Where did we come from, and why are we here? Agnostics carry the burden of their own skepticism. Many of them are in denial about God. Some boast, saying that their skepticism protects them against sentimentality.

They know that we all need a little skepticism to avoid the religious fakers and charlatans who take advantage of the gullible. But absolute skepticism is a curse. Those who hide behind doubt their entire life are shortchanging themselves. They have gambled and lost.

The test of faith is in the ability to live with mystery. Accepting what we cannot yet understand takes courage. At first it seems foolish, but it soon pays off big-time, and leads to a new level of understanding. God's revelation may seem at first to narrow one's chances for happiness, but soon everything changes. The gift of wisdom comes, and the person sees changes that enhance life.

By relying on your natural instincts alone, you will fail to find the formula for true Joy; namely, that faith leads to Joy. Out of God's infinite bounty He offers each of us a share in His happiness.

Heaven is our supreme goal, and we will have to make some sacrifices to get there, but all along the way there is Joy. May you see that clearly, and may the Lord be your strength and your Joy.

Jesus spoke of Love as the supreme commandment. But Love and Joy are two sides of the same coin. A mother's love is arguably the highest form of human love, and where there is true Love there is true Joy. Kathy Neal of Little Rock, Arkansas proclaims her maternal Joy in this prayer she wrote for *The Arkansas Catholic.*

"Thank you God for my daughter. Thirty-two years ago she was placed in my arms for the first time. Her tiny fingers curled around mine. Her eyes opened and searched for me as she listened to her mother's young voice. Her skin so soft and supple held the fragrance of my firstborn baby.

"I loved her.

"I see now how she was created by you — not that I did not see it at her birth — but today I see her individuality. I praise her uniqueness.

"If I had created her, she would be completely different. I would have created her based on my needs and wants. Instead you created her in your image and likeness so that she would have the tools she needs to meet the demands of her life.

"How lovely she is!

"I pray for her today that she will continue to live in your almighty grace. Self-discipline is one of the best character assets I see in her. What a gift! She meets each day with determination and dedication to her role in life. She knows who she is — wife and mother. She cares for her family by loving them and nurturing their growth toward you.

"Her home is filled with gladness as she prepares meals for her family, mends broken hearts and corrects her children out of love.

"She loves me with unconditional love. She forgives the mistakes I made as her mother while she learns of them through her own experiences.

"Today she is a woman and not only a daughter but also a friend.

"I cherish her.... Send your great love to surround her and all she does on this her birthday. Thank you God for the daughter you chose for me."

2

JOY, FAITH, AND DOUBT

"Therefore everyone who listens to these words of mine
and acts on them, will be like a sensible man who built his house
on rock... but everyone who does not, is like the foolish
man who built his house on sand." (Mt 7:24, 26)

The predisposition to doubt will always weaken your spiritual
Joy. A doubter goes on searching endlessly, when the truth is
staring him in the face. Without trust in the Lord, he cannot
find spiritual Joy. Doubts and fears shape one's character and
thereby affect one's destiny.

In this Chapter we will examine the thinking of those who
do not accept the words of Jesus as being true. He is the
fulfillment of the messianic promises: **"For God so loved the
world that He gave his only begotten Son, that we may be saved"**
(Jn 3:16). Those who do not believe in Jesus, cut themselves
off from the spiritual blessings He promised to those who believe.

One of the great theologians of the 20th century, a Jesuit
priest-anthropologist named Pierre Teilhard de Chardin, held
that the great religious problem of modern times is the problem of the two faiths: faith in Jesus Risen, and faith in this world.
I have chosen Teilhard de Chardin and astronomer Carl Sagan
as the spokesmen of the two different faiths.

Teilhard insisted that the two faiths are neither incompat-

23

ible, nor mutually exclusive. He was both a scientist and a man of faith. Those who put their faith in science alone, trusting only unaided reason, find themselves with scores of unanswered questions, no matter how brilliant they may be. Teilhard de Chardin was a paleontologist, an anthropologist, and a theologian. He discovered the "Peking Man" during his digs in China. There he learned a great deal about man's origins. He integrated this new knowledge with the traditional teachings of the Church, and wrote this beautiful prayer:

"I thank you Lord my God, for having in a thousand ways led my eyes to discover the immense simplicity of things…. I can no longer see anything, nor any longer breathe outside that milieu in which all is made one."

He was a Catholic priest and a scientist who accepted both the theory of evolution, and the truth that God has a divine plan for our salvation. The reality of the supernatural basis of the revelations of Jesus Christ infused all his thinking. He worked strenuously to develop a synthesis between science and religion.

In his book, *The Future of Man* (NY: Harper and Row, 1964, p. 260), he acknowledged that scientific advancement causes many people to have suspicions about their faith tradition. He spoke of the 'upward' movement of the human race. He maintained that the problem of these two competing faiths causes a crisis of hope. Science is unable to offer hope about the future of the world, and this creates a crisis that can only be resolved successfully by placing one's full faith in the Risen Christ. In the evolutionary scheme of things, Teilhard de Chardin uses St. Paul's reference to Jesus as our future destiny. Jesus is the beginning and the end, the alpha and the omega. He is the one toward whom we are all ascending.

Dr. Carl Sagan, on the other hand, believed in science alone. The famous astronomer died in 1996 after a two-year battle with bone marrow disease. He was one of the high priests of science, maintaining all his life that there was not a shred of evidence in the entire universe for the existence of the super-natural.

He didn't deny the possibility of God's existence, as I found out in my correspondence with him, he simply side-stepped the issue. He said that he just didn't know enough to believe one way or the other. This is the classic position of the agnostic.

Webster defines an agnostic as one who holds the view that any ultimate reality, as God, is unknown and is probably unknowable. An atheist is one who denies the existence of God, a position which rules out the possibility of any knowledge coming to us from any source other than our senses. But we believe that our knowledge is not limited to what we can see, feel or touch. There is faith knowledge, which comes to us by way of Divine Revelation.

Since joy is the central topic of this book, I have a question for you: Can an agnostic like Carl Sagan experience joy? Yes, of course, he can experience human joy, which is available to every human being, but he could not have experienced supernatural Joy, unless God showered him with an extraordinary gift at the end of his life.

Those who do not believe in God do not ask for His grace. This doesn't mean that they are living in a state of perpetual sadness. I sense that Dr. Sagan had a highly developed appreciation for life. But he did not have access to that whole world of knowledge and happiness, which is available to the believer.

Human joy comes with the gift of life. Good men and women, even atheists, can experience human joy no matter what their religious beliefs may be. But the higher levels of Joy will elude them.

In this chapter I will share the correspondence I had with Carl Sagan. As a brilliant scientist, he understood much, but he missed the obvious fact that something doesn't come from nothing.

Dr. Sagan did not accept the reality of any supreme intelligence behind the universe, as Einstein did. He stayed with inductive reasoning, and rejected deduction. He was a good man, always faithful to his conscience, and a leader in the peace movement, but he could not make the leap of faith. He demanded that God prove Himself in some empirical way before he would deign to believe.

In the meantime, he had to live without any really satisfying answers to the big questions: Where did we come from? Where are we going? And what is the meaning of it all? His answers were puzzling even to himself. He said there never was a beginning, and since we are all going to turn to ashes, there is no meaning behind anything in the universe beyond what we see.

True believers answer the big questions very differently. They are more in harmony with common sense, and God's will. Science is important to them, but they know there is more knowledge in this world than science can provide. They know for sure that they need more than science can supply in order to live their lives fully and joyfully.

Science has given us in the world many material blessings, like air-conditioning and automobiles; but it has also given us the arms race with its nuclear stockpiles, its threat of germ warfare, its pollution and its chemical waste. What will become of this planet? Science doesn't know, but it has set the stage for disaster. We have greater knowledge, but we are also custodians of millions of weapons of mass destruction. The annihilation of nations is a real possibility.

Instead of being able to solve the big problems of life, science has created the weaponry, which has put us on the brink of extinction. This indeed brings us to a crisis of hope.

In spite of it all, Jesus tells us not to be afraid. He nourishes us with His Spirit of hope. We have faith in the Risen Lord, who gives meaning to our lives.

Carl Sagan put his faith in science. He refused to use deductive reasoning when it came to believing in God, but he cleverly used it when it suited him. For instance, there is not a shred of evidence to prove the existence of extraterrestrial life out there, but he believed it on the basis of the sheer abundance of galaxies and stars. There must be some other intelligent life forms in the universe. He argued that it was absurd to hold otherwise, and wanted to send signals to contact aliens in the universe.

I have no problem with the supposition, there probably are other forms of life in the universe, apart from angels, but I am one who believes that deductive reasoning makes sense. When it comes to believing that God exists, Sagan did not.

We exchanged letters on the topic for about a year, and I have permission to share them with you. I respected Dr. Sagan, and liked him very much. He wrote to me first, concerning a syndicated column I had written about him. The following exchange speaks for itself.

16 June 1988

Dear Fr. Catoir,

I've been sent a number of copies of your syndicated article printed around Christmas week, in which you claim my theological stand, and my stand on extraterrestrial intelligence together constitute, "a classic case of deliberate inadvertence, and inconsistency."

Here is my position. Please tell me if you think you see any inconsistency. Both for the existence of extraterrestrial intelligence and the existence of God, I would require compelling physical evidence. Both constitute important hypotheses well worth pursuing, but to believe, on so important a matter, in the absence of compelling evidence is foolish. The argument from first cause does not demonstrate the existence of God because modern cosmology is perfectly consistent with the universe that is infinitely old and therefore, never created.

I am in favor of spending small amounts of money to use radio telescopes to listen for possible signals from extraterrestrial intelligence. Such signals if discovered, would be taken seriously only if all other natural explanations of their source had failed. I would take exactly the same approach on "miracles" and other purported evidence for the existence of God. In both cases I advocate keeping an open mind until unambiguous evidence is in hand. Please tell me where the inconsistency lives.

With best wishes,
Cordially,
Carl Sagan

June 23, 1988

Dear Dr. Sagan,

I see your point, but I believe you miss an important fact: Something doesn't come from nothing. To say that the universe is infinitely old begs the question.

Granted, no one can offer empirical proof that God exists, but no one can disprove it either. The degree of probability for God's existence is at least as compelling as the probability that there is extraterrestrial life out there.

Neither idea can be proved scientifically, but you give no weight to the former.

Sincerely,
John Catoir

15 July 1988

Dear Father Catoir,

Just to sharpen the focus a little more: You say something doesn't come from nothing. But that, of course assumes that it came. If the universe was always here, then there is no reason for it to come from anywhere, and therefore no reason for a creator. If we do not know that the universe came from nowhere, then we cannot use what you call the "principle of causality" (and even if we did know that it came from "nowhere" there is a respectable body of scientific opinion that says it could have been a quantum mechanical vacuum fluctuation). The conclusion, I claim is clear: We are too ignorant to draw reliable conclusions on this matter. Since it is a question of great importance, do we not have an obligation to withhold judgment until better evidence is available? I do not ask you to accept it as fact. I only ask for a greater tolerance for ambiguity.

With best wishes,
Cordially,
Carl Sagan

August 12, 1988

Dear Dr. Sagan,

I agree with your final point. We are quite ignorant of these mysteries. However the statement, "If the universe was always here," is a big "IF." How did it get here in the first place? "A quantum mechanical vacuum fluctuation" is not very helpful in explaining something as tiny as the human brain, much less the universe.

We may not be able to prove God's existence scientifically, but what about the "clouds of witnesses." The Bible uses that phrase to refer to the billions who have attested to God's reality down through the ages. In literature and anthropology we see evidence of it written in the hearts of people everywhere. An immense longing for the invisible reality of God is part of the human condition. Billions of people of all faiths and no particular faith find in God an ever-flowing source of refreshment and hope. Can this be lightly dismissed?

There may be no data to prove the existence of God, according to your standards, but His reality is written in the hearts of people, in the petals of a rose, in a pebble, and in any star.

> With kind personal regards, I am sincerely yours,
> John Catoir

September 9, 1988

Dear Father Catoir,

Many thanks for your letter of August 12, which I think permits us to make another step toward common ground. Yes, an infinitely old universe is a big "if." I hope you will acknowledge that a universe created from nothing is also a big "if."

I don't know which "if" is bigger. But I think it is clear that both are well beyond human experience.

You talk about witnesses. Yes, religion is common to every human culture, but the Judeo-Christian-Islamic God is not. I agree that people have a great need to be taken care of by a supreme, all-knowing, all-powerful and benign God. In effect, a wish to recreate the circumstances of infancy and childhood, but that does not prove the existence of such a God, merely the human passion to know one.

Yes, there is something written, in your lovely phrase, "in the hearts of people, in the petals of a rose, in a pebble and in any star." But the question remains, What is it? What is written there? And do we believe it because the evidence is secure or because, frail creatures that we are, we have a need to believe?

> With best wishes,
> Cordially,
> Carl

October 5, 1988

Dear Carl,

We differ on the meaning of the word evidence. If you wish to withhold judgment on the existence of God until compelling physical evidence is found, I respect your conscience.

However, I think we can know things about the supernatural order through other means than the scientific method. The leap from Newtonian Physics to Quantum Physics taught us a whole new way of looking at the universe. Perhaps you owe it to yourself to be more open to another way of knowing.

After all, you already use deductive reasoning when it suits you to advance your beliefs. You say you would be astonished if there were not some form of intelligent life in the universe, given the billions of galaxies. You even ask the government to finance your efforts to contact this alien life.

Why are you not more open to the possibility of God's existence? Carrying this unanswered question must be something of a burden, I would imagine.

> Sincerely yours,
> John

October 28, 1988

Dear Father Catoir,

I believe I derive some strength from my skepticism — although doubtless it would be more reassuring to believe that an omnipotent, omniscient and benevolent God is watching over me and mine. Knowing how much I would like to believe this makes me aware of how vulnerable I am to fraud and fuzzy reasoning, and in this small way protects me. But I am passionate to know the truth as best I am able, even if it is not fully to my liking.

Of course I cannot prove that God doesn't exist. There could always be a sufficiently subtle and remote God who does not manifest himself in everyday human affairs and is still the creator of the universe. If he wishes to hide himself that is his business, but he cannot justly reproach me for not believing in him.

On the comparison between the search for extraterrestrial life and the search for God, there is one difference that I see. I have a clear and coherent method of looking for extraterrestrial life.

In the remote contingency that after death I will stand in judgment before my maker, I do not think I will be too severely reprimanded for attempting to make consistent use of the tools he gave me.

With best wishes,
Cordially,
Carl

November 15, 1988

Dear Carl,

I, too, would be astonished if there were no other intelligent life in the universe, but I would be more astonished if God did not exist. You seem to show no inclination to admit God's existence, and yet you try to vindicate your belief in alien life, raising money to set up a permanent radio receiving station. Aren't you showing a bias for one set of beliefs over another? Is this not inconsistent?

All I ask is that you open your mind more. You will not need a radio receiver to reach God. All you need is a desire to make contact. Do you ever pray? I am not trying to win an argument here. I am really hoping that you will make the leap of faith toward God, as you have toward the existence of intelligent aliens. It's been fun. The last word is yours if you care to write again.

Respectfully,
John

December 14, 1988

Dear John,

I also have enjoyed our recent exchange of letters and am warmed by the deep feelings it has evoked. I thank you for offering me one last crack.

On an issue of this importance we must demand the most rigorous standards of evidence. The purported "proofs" of the existence of God do not even approach such standards.

I appreciate your words of support and your prayers, and hope that you continue to help bring love, compassion and mercy into the world.

Cordially,
Carl

It was a fascinating exchange, but as you can see, nothing I said would budge him. He was a confirmed skeptic; a good man, and a believer in human progress, but science was his religion. He wanted to know more about the universe. Perhaps implicit in his quest was an unconscious hunger for God. I'm sure a merciful God will see that quality in him.

Dr. Sagan remained an agnostic all his life, as far as I know. By limiting his knowledge to that which comes from unaided reason, he cut himself off from a vast body of wisdom. The truths found in revelation were not available to him. He wanted to make the act of faith, an act of reason: "I will believe, but only if I first understand." Unfortunately, it is just the other way around. One believes in order to understand the mysteries of faith. Faith is above reason. Faith is indispensable if you are to gain access to the world beyond. One must make the leap of faith in order to experience Supernatural Joy.

He wanted to protect our planet from global warming. He was a peacemaker, and he respected other peacemakers. He collaborated with religious leaders around the world in an effort to bring science and religion closer together. And yet, sadly, he could not bring himself to accept the fundamental premise of religion, namely that there is a mysterious intelligence behind the universe. His willingness to correspond with me showed me that he was of good will, and open to dialogue. I found it interesting that he thanked me for keeping him in my prayers. Perhaps in a tiny corner of his soul, there was the feeling that a little prayer from a priest couldn't hurt.

This quote from one of the characters in his book *Contact* may reflect something of his ambiguity on these topics: *"I had an experience I can't prove. I can't even explain it, but everything that I know as a human being, everything that I am tells me that it was real. I was part of something wonderful, something that changed me forever; a vision of the Unknown that tells undeniably how tiny, and insignificant, and how rare and precious we all are. A vision that tells us we belong to something that is greater than ourselves. That we are not, that none of us is, alone."*

I think in the heart of every skeptic there is similar ambiguity, but without the leap of faith, he or she cannot experience the Joy of the Lord. Why is that? Because by closing the mind to the supernatural one cannot draw from it. If you don't turn the spigot on, the water will not flow.

DEALING WITH SKEPTICS

Don't be down on yourself if you are unable to persuade a close relative or friend to believe as you do. Trust them to God's mercy, and be at peace.

Be at peace about your own skepticism as well. The Apostles had a doubting Thomas among them. It is a time-honored custom. When doubts come to mind, just laugh at them. After all we believe in mysteries, so it is natural that we question how this or that can be true.

I have often prayed, "Lord, I believe; help me in my unbelief," because there are imponderable mysteries out there, far beyond my understanding. It takes a decision to accept them, and here is the interesting moment of faith.

Whether to accept Jesus as the Divine Son of God, or not, is a decision you must make before you understand how it is true. Understanding follows faith, not the other way around. We begin to comprehend the mystery better when we say, "Yes, Lord, I will follow you." John the Baptist once sent his disciples to Jesus to question Him: **"Are you He who is to come, or are we to look for another?"** Jesus replied, **"...the blind see, cripples walk, the deaf hear, dead men are raised to life, and the poor have the good news preached to them. Blest is the man who finds no stumbling block in me"** (Mt 11:4-6).

Linda Nero of Cranston, Rhode Island tells how her faith helped her to weather the storms of her life.

I have truly been blessed with a wonderful life. It didn't start out that way. I had an abusive childhood. My mother was an alcoholic and died when I was 12 years old. My father remarried soon thereafter. From that point on my life went downhill. I was sent to live with an older sister who also had a drinking problem. By the time I was 15 I was pretty much on my own. I had a Catholic upbringing, but by this time God was not in my life. By age 17 I got pregnant, and married (not by the Church). I stayed married in an abusive relationship for 9 years. I finally divorced with custody of my child. I went back to school and started a profession of dental assisting. This is where I met my present husband, Peter. He adopted my daughter.

For 15 years Peter and I tried to get pregnant. During this time, we both went back to Church and rediscovered Our Lord. I never once stopped praying that we would have a child.

In 1992 after not having any contact with my father for 18 years, he called and asked me to come help his wife take care of him. I didn't hesitate. I was with him when he died.

The next month I conceived my son, Michael. God blessed us with a wonderful child. We discovered, 4 years later, that little Michael had Cystic Fibrosis, a fatal genetic disease. Not once did I ever ask God "why?" God gave us this wonderful child, and I will always be thankful. Michael has touched many people in many ways. He has brought us closer to God. Because of him we met so many wonderful people at our parish of Our Lady of Good Counsel. I have become a religious education teacher. We have this wonderful parish family that I'm sure we would never have been part of it if it weren't for our son. God has blessed me in many ways. I believe once I truly found God, I never lost faith. Michael is 7 years old, and still battles his illness everyday. He never questions why he has this disease. He is God's gift to us.

I have truly been blessed with a wonderful life.

Joy can prevail over sorrow if you have faith. When you listen to the words of Jesus and act on them, you will put yourself into the position to receive a Joy this world cannot give.

3

JOY AND SANCTIFYING GRACE

"I want my Joy to be in you, so that your Joy may be complete."
(Jn 15:11)

Sanctifying grace is a participation in God's life. This grace, this sharing is a pure gift. To receive it, all you need to do is open your heart to God.

The art of opening your heart to God is so simple, it cannot be taught in a book.

"There are so many self-help books on the market, so many gurus trying to make people feel better, enjoy living, become more confident and successful, but the Gospels cannot be reduced to the category of self-help literature. The Holy Scriptures can surely bring comfort to the weary, but the Bible is essentially an invitation to share in God's life" (Catherine de Vinck).

If you are not in harmony with God's will, you cannot share in His life. He is the Source of all Love and Joy. Turn away from Him and you deprive yourself of the best that life can offer.

You may try to find temporary happiness in this world. You may succeed in drowning your sorrows in chemical substances for a while, but the soul's yearning for Ultimate Joy will not be satisfied.

Your Joy will be proportionate to the degree to which you open yourself to God's sanctifying grace. When you sense Him living within you, you will be able to smile more. You will know how great a gift you have received.

HUMAN JOY AND SPIRITUAL JOY

There are two kinds of Joy: human and divine. Human joy is the kind that comes to mind when you have a really good time. We all love a party, a picnic, a playful diversion from the humdrum business of life.

Life is filled with many forms of human joy. In spite of all the woes and worries of the world, we can come alive when we hear the laughter of children. Acts of unexpected generosity can awaken feelings of joy in us. These feelings are the normal human reaction to love.

The word "joy" comes from the Latin, meaning, "to be glad." When the spirit of gladness permeates a person's entire being, they are said to be joyful. Human joy can take many forms, like the sheer delight one experiences in being aware of the wonderful gift of life. Joy is the self-respect that comes from a clean conscience. It is the satisfaction of relaxing after completing a difficult job. Perhaps the best kind of human joy comes from knowing that someone loves you. If that Someone is God, you have all the more reason to rejoice.

We enter a higher level of Joy when we experience gratitude because of the knowledge of God's love. This Joy becomes even richer when you realize that God has empowered you to help Him deliver others from their misery. This is more than joy, this is spiritual Joy. It not only makes you feel good; it makes the people you help happy.

I find it a Joy to write a book with the Holy Spirit as my Muse. There is the human joy that every writer feels during the process of creating a new piece of literature, and then there is the supernatural Joy which comes from the knowledge that I am co-writing this book with the Holy Spirit.

The grammatical errors, and the awkward sentences are all mine, but the inspiration is all His. I sometimes wake up in the middle of the night with the specific awareness that I have to make a correction on a particular page when I return to the computer. I thank God for this interaction.

Divine Joy is constantly being communicated to my soul. This spiritual Joy comes from the knowledge of God's love. I enjoy the Presence of God, and respond to the Lover within. This is a supernatural gift. It is a grace beyond all human understanding. One accepts it in faith, or one misses the whole point.

The Holy Spirit is always loving you with an infinite love. Not only that, but He delights in loving you. He forgives you everything whenever you ask, and He never leaves your side. He is closer to you than your own heartbeat.

St. Paul instructed us about the immanence of God: **"In Him we live and move and have our being"** (Ac 17:28). We live in Him, so we don't have to do anything to get His attention. We always have His undivided attention. Our holiness is God's life within us. *Our holiness has always depended more on His love for us, than on our love for Him.* Our inner Joy will find a way to express itself in our words and in our appearance.

"A glad heart makes a cheerful face" (Pr 15:13).

A glad heart is a soul glowing with Joy.

Mother Teresa of Calcutta said a smiling face is an integral part of Christian love.

St. Francis of Assisi and his friars were known for their laughter and Joy. They always tried to find a reason to smile rather than brood. Joy is the noblest way of living the Christian life.

St. Thomas Aquinas once wrote: *"If you want to be a saint, will it."* The same is true for Joy. If you want to be a joyful person, you must will it. You should never force feelings of any kind, but practice your smile, never forcing it.

Joy is the heart's gladness. It is found in the harmony of body, soul and spirit. Joy wells up from within. If you have any Joy in you, please notify your face. Accepting yourself as a joyful child of God is the key to experiencing spiritual Joy.

It is said that, after forty, we are all responsible for our own face. Joy or sorrow in the soul has a way of coming to the surface. If you choose to be joyful, it will permeate your whole body, soul and spirit.

THE THREE LEVELS OF JOY

There are three levels of joy, and all three are part of one personality. There is joy of the body, soul, and spirit.

The body has it own delights, which we experience through the senses. The soul is made up of intellect and will. Joy comes to the soul on the natural level when you find purpose and direction in life. A person who has not found meaning is like a cork bobbing around in the ocean. The soul also receives Joy from the Holy Spirit.

Think of the soul as a water pitcher. You can fill the pitcher with clean or dirty water. The will decides what you will do. If the soul is filled with the Holy Spirit, the graces of Peace, Love, and Joy flow into it. But if you fill it with the spirit of evil, hatred will poison the water. The Holy Spirit is God living in us. The evil one brings death. You must decide what thoughts you will think, for as you think so will you act. The choice is yours.

Some people disown God because He is too mysterious, and they fear the demands He might make on them. He is inscrutable, and they need to control their lives. Acknowledging God's existence interferes with their autonomy.

Deliberate inadvertence is the sin by which the angels fell. Lucifer was brilliant, a true light, but, as the Bible story goes, he chose to turn away from God: "I will not serve." Those who blind themselves to God's Sovereignty, through the folly of human pride, end in hell.

Humility opens the soul to the source of all Joy. Pride is self-sabotage. Many people compare themselves to others: "She's better looking, I'm smarter, he's stronger, she's more devious, he's more generous." This is not wise. St. Teresa of Avila once said, "Comparisons are odious." It is better to compare yourself to God rather than other human beings. That way you will see yourself as you really are, a tiny creature, unworthy in every way, but made worthy by God's love. This understanding of who you are is at the heart of the virtue of humility.

Let's review all that I have said above, but now in more detail.

JOY OF THE BODY

Our five senses connect us to the world around us. They can give pleasure, and enable us to experience our "noble emotions." These are human feelings, which give glory to God. By working to increase our human joys, we can worship God more beautifully.

Natural joy is highly desirable, but it is not the fullness of Joy.

"As people, we are meant to have human joys, the joy of living, the joy of love and friendship, the joy of work well done. As Christians, we have cause for further Joy: like Jesus, we know that we are loved by God our Father" (Pope John Paul II).

Human joy and Supernatural Joy complement one another. It is our duty to rejoice because of the knowledge of God's love. The noble emotions bring us human happiness. The grace of God brings us Joy at high tide.

Natural joy is God's gift to all His children. In a true sense it is a prelude to the greater gifts of the Kingdom. Enjoying a good meal is a delight worthy of the children of God. When we give thanks to God for our sustenance, the meals we eat can be seen as natural pleasures, and the occasions of spiritual gratitude. They give both pleasure to the body and Joy to the spirit.

If you overeat, you tarnish the joy, and experience needless physical discomfort. Stuffing yourself leads to obesity, guilt, and eventually poor health. These maladies can weigh down the spirit in more ways than one.

On the other hand, all five senses: sight, smell, sound, taste, and touch can elevate you to higher levels of joy. There are always the richer Joys of the soul waiting to be discovered. Watching a golden sunset can lift your spirit, and enable your soul to give glory to God. The same is true for the fragrance of a rose, or the magnificent sound of a symphony orchestra. Your senses can give you an appreciation of God's beauty residing just beneath the surface of creation. Your senses can lift your soul to new heights.

The sense of touch deserves special mention because it involves your sexuality. Since all the pleasures of the body are good, **"God saw all that He had made, and indeed it was very good"** (Gn 1:31), it follows that sexual pleasure is a good gift from God. Only when sex is used in a way that violates the Golden Rule does it become sinful.

Sexual pleasure is God's creation and it is good. Illicit sex outside of marriage, or sex which abuses another person, is sinful. The selfish use of sex degrades. Treating another person as a sex object is a sin. Moral theology teaches us that the malice is not in the pleasure, which is natural and God-made, but in the unbridled lust.

Sex related heresies have abounded down through the centuries. There were those who taught that every kind of sexual pleasure is degrading. These were the Jansenists who claimed that the body is evil, and the soul is good. This idea goes back to the Manicheans, and later to the Albigensians who carried this belief to Europe and beyond.

Jesus did not come to earth to turn us against our own bodies. When the Bible says that the spirit and the flesh are at odds, you must not interpret this in a heretical way. It does not mean that the soul and the body are adversaries. The word "flesh" refers to the anti-Christian spirit, which wars against the good of the soul.

In Scripture, the correct interpretation of the word "flesh" does not refer to the body per se, but to all the vices that tear the human soul away from God. If you fill the soul with pride, gluttony, greed, lust, anger, envy and sloth you will poison your spirit. All seven vices together make up the sins of the "flesh." It is incomplete to think of the "flesh" as referring to lust alone.

These seven vices war against the spirit. Only in this sense should you understand the idea of the body warring against the spirit. Unbridled sexual desire and activity is lustful. Good sex, practiced artfully within marriage is holy.

Lust is a sin, but human sexuality within marriage is holy, because Matrimony is a sacrament. By definition, sexual intimacy is the outward sign of the love commitment. This gift was instituted by Christ to convey grace.

That means that human sexual desires are not wrong in themselves, unless they lead to illicit sexual activity. Those who are not in a marriage sanctioned by the Church are not necessarily sinning however. Some relationships fall into the category of "good conscience marriages," where pure love is practiced, and where the commitment is one of mutual respect. Confer my Chapter on "Joy and Tough Love," Case #5 for more on annulments in the Church.

The joys of the body are precious. The sexual intimacy connected with true love is both graceful, and grace giving. The thrill of human love elevates the spirit as well as the body. It becomes clear therefore that we are responsible for our happiness in more ways than one.

The senses can be used in a noble way, to expand our Joy.

Joy is magnified when we see the deeper meaning of reality. The soul is capable of growing in wisdom through the gift of faith.

A group of Georgia students studied the Seven Wonders of the World. At the end of the session they were asked to list their own seven wonders. Most of the votes went to Egypt's Great Pyramids, the Taj Mahal, the Grand Canyon, Niagara Falls, the Panama Canal, the Empire State Building, St. Peter's Basilica, and China's Great Wall.

One student however, took a long time before writing anything. When she was finished the teacher asked her to read her choices. The girl hesitated, then read, "I think the Seven Wonders of the world are these:

1. to touch
2. to taste
3. to see
4. to hear.

She hesitated a little and then said,

5. to run
6. to laugh
7. and to love.

This is wisdom.

Too many of us miss this insight. We overlook the great "wonders" of the human body. Seeing, touching, feeling, laughing, playing, loving: these are the greatest wonders. We should never take them for granted.

The saints do not take little things for granted. They see God in the face of every stranger. They look at the sky, with its billowing clouds, and see God's beauty in it. They pray without words. They see Divine Beauty hidden behind every part of creation. They see with the eyes of faith. Faith can detect Him.

JOY OF THE SOUL

The soul is made up of intellect and will. The will decides what thoughts the mind will be allowed to think, for as you think, so will you behave. The will controls the decisions we make in life. The mind does the fact gathering, and the will has only one function: to say yes or no.

With the eyes of faith to help, the will says yes to this good inspiration, and no to that occasion of sin.

Faith knowledge is part of the information we use to live our lives joyfully. It is the knowledge we receive from Divine revelation. God exists. God is Love. Eternal life is a reality. We will be rewarded or punished according to our deeds.

Acting on this knowledge, which is provided by the Bible, is crucial to achieving supernatural Peace and Joy. Taking good care of your soul means doing what is necessary to become your own best friend. Make the wrong decisions, and you will become your own worst enemy.

St. Irenaeus once wrote: *"The glory of God is found in a man (or woman) fully alive."* To be fully alive is to be physically, emotionally and spiritually healthy. It is so important to decide to be joyful early in the game of life. Discover the path to true happiness, and follow it.

The will says yes, and moves the whole personality in the right direction. Your yes supplies the power to change.

Let me give you an example of how this works. If you think that there are some people you can never get along with, some people you have a right to detest, you will be going against the Gospel of Jesus Christ. He said, **"What good is it to love those who love you? Even the pagans do as much. You must love your enemy and do good to those who hurt you"** (Mt 5:46).

If you say that this is impossible, you are not yet a true Christian. Is it because you don't want to obey the Lord? I don't think so, but then again, maybe it is. You will have to stop and think about it. The best thing to do is make an over-reaching decision. Decide that God will give you the grace to get along with everyone you meet in your personal life. You may not have the skills to deal with the worst of them, but you can learn. God has asked you to love your enemy. Ask for His help and He will give it.

The key issue is in your will to say yes; with God, all things are possible. As you believe so will you act. Faith gives the knowledge you need to make all those corrections you need to make. Changes for the better produce good fruit.

The intellect starts the process as you learn what Jesus wants, but the will makes the final decision. The will commands the body to choose righteousness. Decide to do what the Lord asks, and let Him be your strength and your Joy.

Let's review this again. I know you understand it, but repetition helps. We can easily lose our grip on the basics. We can't skim over the truths of our faith.

Whereas the five senses help you to relate to the world around you, thus enabling you to experience normal human joy, the soul helps you to relate to your inner world by enabling you to love God and the things of God, to love your neighbor and yourself. Once you decide to do what you now know to be in your own best interest, you can stop sabotaging yourself, and increase your chances for happiness.

If you decide to fill your soul with love, you will reject all "stinkin'-thinkin'." If you behold the goodness all around you, you will keep out the negativity. This is what we mean when we say the eyes are the windows of the soul. If you look at the world with bitterness for past hurts, you will feel surrounded by darkness and hostility. Those who are angry and bitter interpret everything that happens to them through the prism of hostility and fear. This approach can only bring you misery.

Everyone gets angry from time to time, and justifiably so. But thankfully, those who are able to forgive manage to hold on to their Joy. It may take a long time to get over your bad feelings, but once you say yes, "I will forgive" all those negative feelings will begin to fade away. It may take a year, but patience will always win out.

Ask the Lord to teach you how to forgive and forget. Get on with your life.

"There are three things in which I delight says the Lord, and they are also delightful in the sight of human beings. Here they are: concord among brothers and sisters; friendship among neighbors; and married couples who live together in perfect harmony" (Si 25:1). Harmony requires the will to forgive, even when you don't feel like it.

Husbands and wives need two things to keep their marriage alive: a forgiving heart, and a sense of humor. Forgiveness releases a person from the dead weight of anger. It is better to let go and let God, better to become bright and optimistic, better to find opportunities for new joy, than to wallow in the misery of anger and resentment.

The joy of forgiving is the reward of choosing love over hatred. The will says yes or no to Joy every day. Some see the cup as half full; others see it as half empty. You have to be predisposed to find joy, and you have to be in the Lord to be filled with His Joy.

Thomas Edison excelled in this. When his assistant became downhearted after another failed experiment in their efforts to invent the electric light bulb, Edison said, "Don't be discouraged, we now know one more thing that doesn't work. Soon we'll find exactly the right filament that does work." He saw that each of the 2000 failed experiments in his quest to light up the world, was not a sign of failure at all, but a way of gaining deeper understanding of the problem at hand.

Taking an optimistic view of reality is a choice, and choices are the work of the will.

For instance, in order to be steadfast in love, you need to

put on the will to bear discomfort. Patience requires a strong will. To be still when you want to run away, takes will power.

A strong character is necessary for real charity to flourish. That means you have to decide to endure discomfort. If you want to make progress in the spiritual life, and achieve great heights of sanctity, you will have to grin and bear it.

Think about how this works in other areas of life. For instance if you want to get a good job, you know you will have to be educated. Going to school for years is not easy. Without study, you will never be a college graduate. The will says yes or no to all those boring classes. The will acts to secure the greater good by ignoring all feelings to the contrary. You don't give up. This is putting your faith in delayed gratification. Pay now, enjoy later.

The same is true for attaining Joy. Unless you control your thoughts, they will control you. God is the giver of all good gifts. Thinking positively is the best formula for successful living. It takes will-training and perseverance to work it all out, but it can be done.

Once again, the soul consists of the intellect and the will. St. Thomas Aquinas taught that the will has only one function: to say yes or no. Your intellect offers a variety of thoughts and directions for you to consider, and your will decides what to accept or reject.

Therefore you are ultimately in control of your own character, and your own destiny. The will is ultimately in control of the thoughts you allow yourself to think. These thoughts will influence the way you feel. Feelings follow thoughts like thunder follows lightning.

If you fill your soul with negative, destructive thinking, you are poisoning your emotional life. Dark thoughts will destroy your peace, and dark actions will follow.

If your mind is allowed to think thoughts like these: "I'm no good, I'm a loser, I'll never make anything of myself," these thoughts will be a self-fulfilling prophecy. You'll soon become depressed. Then it is only a short time before sick actions take over.

But if you place your thoughts under the control of your will, resolving to be positive and constructive in what you allow yourself to think, your emotions will eventually become brighter, and more positive: "I am a good person trying to be better. I am a winner. I will succeed. God is my strength and my Joy." Whether you believe these thoughts or not at the moment, you must claim them as your mantra. They constitute the direction you want to travel. Such thoughts will lead to healthy emotions, which in turn will lead to good and noble actions. Fake it until you make it.

You can't put out a fire with dry wood, and you can't snuff out the fires of negativity with self-defeating thoughts. If you fill your mind with anger, jealousy, greed, lust, pride, and self-reproach, you will reap a harvest of misery. Why lose any chance you might have for a joyful life? Feed the soul with Jesus. He is the Way, the Truth and the Life.

JOY OF THE SPIRIT

The body relates you to the world around you, and the soul shapes your inner life. The human spirit connects you to God. The soul shapes your decisions and your character, but your spirit is either open to the Holy Spirit, or not.

The will decides whether you will live in Joy or misery. The Joy of the Spirit is God's Joy, alive within you. When you seek first the Kingdom of God you will think as God would have you think. You will need to develop a firm discipline over your thoughts to accomplish this.

Jesus gave us the Scriptures to guide us. He also gave us the Church, which is an extension of His life on earth. We can all gain an advantage by listening to the Church as it interprets Scripture. For instance, the Apostles Creed contains the essential teachings of the Lord, as they were transmitted to the Church.

The influence of Jesus did not end two thousand years ago, He is still acting in the modern world, through the Church and the Sacraments. With all its faults the Church is the custodian of the treasures handed down by Christ. We have access to His wisdom at every stage of life. Down through the ages we see the hand of God behind all the human sinfulness. It began with St. Peter and Judas denying Christ. Peter begged for forgiveness, but Judas despaired. The Church survived the trauma of the crucifixion, and lived on, immersed in the family of man.

Consider the opening paragraph of Vatican II's *Pastoral Constitution on the Church in the Modern World*: *"The joys and hopes, the grief and anguish of the people of our time, are the joys and hopes, the grief and anguish of the followers of Christ. Nothing that is genuinely human fails to find an echo in their hearts."*

We are more fully in harmony with the mind of Christ when we carry out His mission on earth. He wants each one of us to come to a knowledge of the truth and be saved. He wants us to help make this a better world, each in our own unique way. He wants us to help others, and enjoy our own lives in the process. By finding your purpose and direction in the greater scheme of things, you also find your greatest fulfillment.

You may not be a perfect human being, but if you turn yourself over to the Lord, He will bless your efforts, and give you victory over selfishness and sin. Here are a few ideas to help you on your journey:

Don't soil your own back yard. Take care of the environment. You have to live in it.

Love your neighbor, you will need your neighbor's help one day.

Every day take out five minutes to sit in silence, and be happy with God.

Live simply. Do not acquire more things than you really need.

Take care of your health. Eat properly and get sufficient exercise.

By tending to your overall health you will live longer, and enjoy life more.

TRUE JOY, A REVIEW

True Joy is found in one's awareness of God's abiding Presence. This Joy isn't a feeling. The Joy of which I speak is a way of being, and a way of sharing in the Lord's eternal Joy. It begins with a decision to be a joyful person. You must first notify your face, and project Joy to the world.

This may all sound a bit too simple. However, Joy is rooted in God's love, so you won't have to worry about your mood swings because God's love never changes. The cause of your Joy is constant, it is present on good days and bad, whether you feel it or not.

Therefore, Joy is not the absence of turmoil. Your inner Joy will not change the craziness of the world around you, but it will help you to keep that craziness from entering your soul. God will help you to cope every time you come to Him.

Most of the saints have gone through hell during their time on earth, but somehow, like St. Paul, they accepted the challenge to remain joyful. Remember Paul's words, **"Rejoice always! In all circumstances give thanks to the Lord"** (1 Th 5:15).

How could he ask such a thing? Because he knew there was always enough grace to make it possible. Joy is a grace, and as such it is infinitely more wonderful than mere pleasure. Pleasure fades, while Joy abides. Pleasure is fleeting. Spiritual Joy endures.

Spiritual Joy is not a feeling but it can spill over into the emotions at times. The body, soul and spirit are integrated into one marvelous whole. The invisible part of each personality is what we call the human spirit, and the spirit outlasts the moods of the moment.

Just as true love can endure, long after romantic emotions fade, so can Joy pervade one's whole being long after one's health begins to fail. Joy transcends dark moods.

Grace is a permanent, abiding gift, which conveys true Joy to the soul. It stays alive in all circumstances. Therefore you can claim Joy any moment of the day. You can give thanks to the Lord in all circumstances and in any situation.

Once you know this you must cling to it. You must will this state of awareness over and over again. To be aware of the Joy of the Holy Spirit living in the center of your soul, you must be alert at all times so that you do not sink back into sadness or discouragement.

In a way your Joy is like the deepest part of the ocean. While the surface may be boiling with turbulence, the waters beneath are relatively still. Being aware of your true happiness, the Lord's love abiding deep in your soul, is a matter of faith, perseverance, and will-training. Feelings can help you at times in this discipline, but it is faith that will carry you through the storms when good feelings fail.

This Joy of the spirit dwells within the heart of every child of God by means of sanctifying grace. Once you say that, your life will become more endurable and more splendid because of God's grace. You will become more aware of God's Joy within you, and enjoy your precious life more.

The indwelling Trinity is your Spiritual Joy. Awareness of the triune God living in you can become a conscious part of your life as soon as you put on the will to believe. Accept His Love with gladness.

God is Love. Joy and Love are two facets of the same diamond. You live and breathe, and have your being in God's Joy. Come home to Joy. Accept God's invitation to share in His Joy.

Realistically, it may not be possible to be on an emotional high all the time, but you can always decide to count your blessings. This is a matter of the will saying yes or no. The formula is easy: *cling to God, think of others, and stop putting yourself down.*

If you put yourself down all the time you are engaging in self-sabotage. This is the sure path to sadness and despair. Lift yourself up. Be patient, God is not finished with your maturing process just yet. Love yourself. St. Paul gives us his definition of love:

"**Love is patient, and kind. It does not envy; it is not pretentious, or puffed up. It is not ambitious or self-seeking. It is not provoked. Love thinks no evil, does not rejoice over wickedness but rejoices with the truth; it bears all things, believes all things, hopes all things, endures all things**" (1 Cor 13:4-7).

Apply this definition to yourself, where it seems appropriate. (Insert your own name here _____) is patient, kind, humble, etc., etc. Learn to be kind and patient with yourself.

A true love relationship with God will always make you feel more joyful. Since God is Love, and He is the source of true Joy, His presence will always bring the assurance of Joy.

You can summon God's Joy whenever you need it just by remembering to ask for it. "**Ask and you will receive**" (Mt 7:7).

A sad person may seem to lack joy, but it is possible to be sad and still have Joy. One can be sad about the death of a friend, and still be deeply joyful that he or she is in a better place. It is much better, in fact, knowing that the deceased is no longer in pain.

Joy is not the absence of pain. There can be pain on the surface while the underground stream of God's unchanging Joy pervades your entire being. Granted, severe pain will overpower anyone, but the knowledge of God's love can never be wiped away. One who has true faith falls back on this knowledge in times of trouble.

The truths of Faith add immeasurably to our capacity for

happiness. Those who want more than half a loaf in this world can make the leap of faith, and secure it. By doing that they will not only have their capacity for natural joy enhanced, but also their Joy from the Holy Spirit will increase. God's gift of Himself is the supreme grace, and His Joy comes with it.

Listen to the words of Jesus: **"Stop worrying about tomorrow. God will take care of your tomorrow. Live one day at a time"** (Mt 6:34). It takes will power to discipline your mind to obey this command.

Jesus has an abundance of Joy to give, but you must claim it. Purify your thinking by removing as much negativity from your mind as you can. Become a more positive, optimistic person. The spiritual happiness that God will put in your soul will upgrade the natural joys of life. Life will become a happy adventure instead of a doleful burden that you must accept.

Joy is like a room full of jewels, closed off by an immense door. The door is always there, but it can only be opened from the inside. Jesus said, **"Knock and it will be opened"** (Mt 7:7). But He might also have said, "Knock, and turn the latch; the door is open."

Mother Teresa of Calcutta was once asked what criteria she used in accepting applicants to her community. She put it very simply: *"If they are joyful I admit them; if not, I send them home."* Joy is visible. You can see it in a person. Develop the art of projecting a joyful presence. Be glad you're alive. *"The fullness of Joy is to behold God in everything"* (Julian of Norwich).

Being joyful is the sweetest way to give glory to God. The Lord, who inspires acts of love, is pleased when we carry them out for His glory.

This Joy will make you happier than any intellectual pleasure you may imagine. On the human level, it is a great celebration of life. I think the angels must be a little jealous when one of us becomes fully alive. They do not have a body to shout out their Joy.

The exuberance of a young mother snuggling her newborn infant is among the highest forms of human joy. If she has Faith, spiritual Joy is added to her happiness. The awareness that God has sent her a beautiful child is overwhelming. God loves her, and she knows it. He puts His love for the baby in her.

The Joy of wholehearted gratitude after receiving such a gift is indescribable. Wherever people give thanks to God for His goodness, they are living in the Spirit of Joy, the Holy Spirit. This is the life of Peace, Love, and Holiness.

One day may we all experience the Joys of heaven. We have accepted Jesus as Lord, and the Joys of heaven have already begun here and now.

St. Paul said, **"Eye has not seen nor ear heard what is in store for us in heaven"** (1 Cor 2:9). We know we have not attained the fullness of our potential, but the anticipation of heaven adds an inner peace that this world cannot give. In times of trouble, our Joy sustains us.

The Lord is preparing an eternal resting-place for all those who come to Him.

Pope John Paul II wrote: *"The essential joy of creation is completed by the joy of salvation, and the joy of redemption.... Therefore, Jesus is the real cause of our joy. He gives us the strength we need to defeat evil and to become the Children of God. This is essentially the Good News of the Gospels"* (*Crossing the Threshold of Hope*, NY: Knopf, 1994).

Accept God's Love. When the soul is rightly directed Joy bubbles up to the surface from the depths of your soul. Joy will come to you, not because you have attained perfection, but because you are God's child. He wants to give you His Joy.

"Blessed are those who not only hear the word, but keep it" (Lk 11:28).

Enjoy the Lord, and enjoy your precious life.

There are many things in Scripture that are difficult to understand. One of them is this quote: **"With God all things are possible"** (Mt 19:26). Jesus implied that the one who trusts Him will be given a share in His happiness.

A New Yorker named Bill struggled with this idea. He had just enough faith to pray for help. He gradually learned to control his negative thinking, and found his way. Bill shares his story.

I was once plagued with impure thoughts and repeated acts of self-abuse. In the beginning, the hardest part of overcoming it was getting rid of the thoughts which had become such a major part of my life. To do this I said a Hail Mary whenever such thoughts occurred. Which came to many rosaries each day for the first year. But eventually the thoughts diminished dramatically as did the occasions of self-abuse. With time I applied different forms of prayer and was eventually able to overcome a pattern of self-abuse, which I thought was impossible since my teen years.

Of course temptations still come; it's only natural. But now they're less frequent and definitely less intense, so that I am able to deal with them. Plus Our Lord never lets any effort go without its reward. I wouldn't even compare what once gave me only a few seconds of gratification with the pure satisfaction, which I get from knowing that I am living my life on a higher plane.

Whereas before my thinking was always clouded and confused. Now there's a new sense of confidence and accomplishment. I feel good about myself. I never could say that before.

The rewards of faith and prayer are remarkable.

"If you are willing to obey, you will eat the best food the land has to offer" (Is 1:19).

4

JOY, FEAR, AND GUILT

"Fear is useless, what you need is trust." (Mk 5:36)

Fear kills joy. Our fears are either subjective and therefore useless, or real and normal. If you fill your mind with fears that have no basis in reality, and allow them to go unchecked, you will become mentally sick. The remedy is to trust in God's power to protect you.

Guilt is a form of fear: the fear of being caught and punished, or the fear of failure. Guilt can arise in your mind if you do not forgive yourself for some past sin. Some people stew over non-sins. They sabotage their own chances for happiness by failing to trust God's unchanging love. No matter what kind of fear you are dealing with, "what you need is trust."

Objective fear is the normal response to real danger.

Dorothy Day tells of a time when she and a friend were coming home from Mass. They were walking down Mulberry Street in New York City when suddenly white objects came whizzing past their heads. At first Dorothy thought they were snowballs, but as another one flew past she saw it crash against the wall. Her friend Judith Gregory said, "That was meant for us!"

They saw the broken bits of a hard-boiled egg where it had landed. Afraid to turn back for fear that someone would hit them in the face, they walked away at a faster clip.

Later Dorothy wrote about her fear that day. *"I should have been delighted, as Charles de Foucauld was when he was pelted in the streets of Nazareth, but my feeling was one of fear. I'm glad I have it because it helps me to understand the fear that is eating at the hearts of people in the world today. No one is safe. We are no longer protected by the oceans separating us from the rest of the world."* (This was written before World War II, but it still rings true.)

In case you have never heard of the Venerable Charles de Foucauld, he was the desert hermit who died in 1916, who was the inspiration for the community known as the Little Brothers of Jesus. Here is my favorite quote from his writings:

"O God, tell me about hope! How can hopeful thoughts originate in this poor world? Are they not bound to come from heaven? Everything we see, all we experience, all we are, proves our nothingness to us. How can we realize we were created to be Jesus' brothers and sisters and co-heirs, and your children, unless you tell us so? Mother of beautiful love and sacred hope, pray to your son Jesus for me and inspire in me the thoughts I should have.

"The hope of being one day in heaven, at your feet my Lord, in the company of the Holy virgin and the saints, gazing on you, loving you, possessing you for all eternity... what a vision of true peace.... It is a hope far above our dreams, and raises us far above our normal selves.... O God how good you are!"

Dorothy was wise enough to think of Charles in analyzing her state before God. She prayed to be delivered from fear. She prayed specifically for the love that casts out fear. *"I pray to grow in the love of God and man, and to live by this charity we must love our enemy... not because we fear him, but because God loves him."*

People accused Dorothy of being mad, but most of us agree that she was a saint. What makes a woman like her so effective in handling objective danger? She was able to spot her fear and pray. Once she realized that she was afraid, she immediately turned to prayer. She prayed for protection, and later for the grace to forgive her assailant. She showed us how to act in a crisis.

The fear experienced by those poor victims of the terrorist attack on the Twin Towers was real, objective fear. We still suffer the aftershock of that event. The lurking fear we all feel over a possible future terrorist attack is definitely objective, but how far we let it disorient us is a matter of self-control. We know we have to prepare for the worst, but we can't let our imagination run away with us. We can't let the terrorists keep us from going about our normal day to day routines, including some travel and recreation when we get the opportunity.

The fear caused by a fire in a crowded theater is certainly objective. It will surely create fear, but you will have a better chance of surviving if you stay calm. Otherwise, you may panic and be trampled to death.

Whether it is objective fear or subjective fear, stay calm. Jesus urged you to trust Him. To do this you have to prepare your mind in advance by turning all your fears over to God, even your future fears. At the same time trust Him enough to hope for the best in all circumstances. Protect yourself as best you can when there is objective danger; pray, stay calm, get yourself out of harm's way, and trust God.

You can save yourself a lot of trouble if you immediately discern that your fear is merely subjective.

SUBJECTIVE FEAR

Subjective fear is a feeling and feelings are not facts. You may feel that you are in danger, even when there is no objective threat. If the threat is purely imaginary, and you react fearfully, you are accepting false feelings as real. If you do this frequently you will become a neurotic. Neurotic fear is all in the mind.

Trust is the answer. Trust God blindly. Get real. Be objective. Understand that feelings can delude you. You are not in danger when you imagine that a ghost is in the closet. Trust the Lord. When irrational subjective fears come, cancel them. When you know your fear is merely a figment of your imagination, talk sense to yourself. Your internal dialogue should be an emphatic call to courage and trust. Command yourself to cancel negative thinking. You are not in danger. Repeat that phrase over and over again: "I am safe in the Lord. I am not in danger."

Dealing with your inner demons is a skill you can develop through will-training. Train yourself to control your thoughts. Soon your hope for Christian Joy will be realized. Subjective fears if unchecked will poison your soul. Subjective emotional turmoil is often more distressing than objective threats. The inner voices that warn you of false danger can be your worst nightmare.

In psychological terms this battering from within is called the tyranny of the super-ego. It is the memory of a thousand voices from your youth, correcting you, scolding you, condemning you, and punishing you. Words like these plague the mind of the victim: "You're no good, you're stupid, you'll never amount to anything." These voices must be canceled, or they will damage your personality and create inner chaos. Trust the Lord to save you. Turn all these thoughts over to Him immediately.

The people in AA call these inner voices "the committee." It's comical to think of a committee inside your own head, but that is exactly what is happening. If untreated the condition can only get worse. Unchecked negative thinking will kill your joy.

Once "the committee" starts taking over your thinking, you have to find a way to cancel all communications with them. Once you know that the negativity is all inside your own head, you must say, "No, I will not listen!"

Your inner demons are not really devils, they are just feelings of fear gone awry. The voices might tell you that you're ugly, or too fat; or that you'll never amount to anything. Learn to laugh at them. Do not believe them; do not engage them; and do not be afraid of them. Once you spot the demon, you can cast it out by turning to the Lord and trusting Him to purge you of them.

Repeat the maxim that Dr. Abraham Low tells his clients, *"Feelings are not facts. Nervous symptoms are distressing but not dangerous."* Tell yourself, "This is only a feeling. I am not in danger. It will pass. With God I am safe. In Him I find my strength and my Joy." Repeat these ideas over and over again until the panic subsides.

Oprah had a woman on her TV show who felt that she had a little demon on her shoulder whispering bad things to her: "You look awful. Your hair is a mess." She asked the guest author a good question: "Can you kill this demon?" The answer came, "No, but you can learn to ignore it." You can't kill "the committee" either, but you can learn to laugh at it. You can choose to disregard it when it pesters you.

Did you see the movie, *A Beautiful Mind?* In it, the lead character John Nash manages to regain his psychological balance by ignoring his committee, the trio that had once controlled his life. He just turned away from them, and went on with his life. They showed up from time to time, but he ignored them and regained control over his life.

Like him, you too can refuse to listen. You can reject the committee's lies. You can move on. This will take will-training. To live gladly you will have to put on the will to cancel the tyranny of the super-ego. Put a stop to self-sabotage today and trust God.

USING FEAR TO YOUR ADVANTAGE

Dark thoughts can spur you on to find solutions. The Holy Spirit often uses the dark night of the soul to help us find a new path through our worries. Sometimes God allows certain fears to torment us, to test our level of trust, and to bring us closer to Him.

He uses our negative feelings and subjective fears to make us aware of how much we need Him. Discovering your spiritual poverty can be helpful. Knowing that you are powerless, and that God has all the power is crucial to recovery. At that point you must begin to turn your life and your will over to the God of your understanding.

At the root of the *Twelve Step Program* is the simple idea that: *God can do for you what you cannot do for yourself. He can make you strong. He can free you from danger.*

Darkness can be overcome by moving into the Light.

If you have a panic attack, you know you are in need of help. Any fear can be turned over to the Lord. Fear is an invitation to pray. Cry out for help, and trust that the Lord will send you His grace. The fear may last for awhile, but it will ebb away in time, as you trust Him more.

The spiritual masters teach us that fear can help to restore balance. For instance, feelings of unworthiness can be highly exaggerated, and become an inferiority complex. Such fears have a modicum of truth to them. We are all unworthy. The saints all had a holy dissatisfaction with themselves. It was a sign of their humility. Feelings of inferiority can be used to draw us closer to God.

However, when this feeling is allowed to run wild, we find a person with an inferiority complex. Such a person needs to know that God chooses unworthy people because He loves them. A person who says "I am a sinner, I am unworthy of God's love," needs to understand God's response, "Yes, you are unworthy, but I choose you in spite of your unworthiness, and you have been made worthy by my grace."

God is the hunter; we are the prey. He seeks after the lost sheep. We only need to wait to be captured (or "rescued" might be a better word). The Lord may allow some fears to haunt you for a little while to let you find your way home to Him.

You can surmount these fears by gradually putting your full trust in His love.

GUILT UNDERMINES JOY

Guilt disorients us the same way that fear does. Guilt about something you did or failed to do, can make you sick. Over 75% of the people who go to psychiatrists do so to work out their upset feelings of guilt about one thing or another. The remedy is simple: Trust the Lord to forgive you, and then forgive yourself. Don't torture yourself endlessly.

Easier said than done, I know, but you have to realize that there comes a time when all things wrong can be made right. People do bad things and get caught. Then they spend years punishing themselves. They go on and on calling themselves stupid, foolish, unworthy, and bad.

This kind of mental dialogue if unchecked will addle your brain. You have to ignore "the committee." If a mistake was made, it was made. Admit that you made a bad choice, and it cost you. But also admit that you can only make it worse by carrying it around with you for years. You can't undo what you've done, but you can "let go and let God." Choose a new path for yourself.

OBJECTIVE GUILT

Some guilt is objective, and some is artificially manufactured by a false sense of sin. God wants you to be objective in these matters. Objective guilt is healthy. For instance, if you have really hurt another human being in the past, you should feel guilty, and you should apologize. But if you suffer tormenting guilt over an unintentional breach of etiquette, you are clearly overdoing it.

Making a mountain out of a molehill is not Christian humility. This is a malady called scrupulosity. Those who suffer from this exaggerated form of guilt are in need of help. Their feelings are not proportionate to their faults. Needless guilt and anxiety can be a plague. Self-inflicted misery is not from God.

Some people do a bad thing in a fit of anger. Some cause accidents by taking their eyes off the road to search for something in the glove compartment. The accident is a bad result, but there was no deliberate intent to do harm. When the circumstances of a bad action are mitigating, you are dealing with a sin of weakness, not a sin of malice. Do not make sins of weakness into an opera.

If you have scrupulous tendencies you must seek professional help. Stop indulging your worrisome nature. Stinking thinking is the enemy of Joy.

False guilt is merely your mind playing tricks on you. God loves you. He does not want to punish you, and He does not want you to punish yourself. He sent His only beloved Son so that you might become a more joyful, happy person. Why not start loving yourself now? Why not claim your new life? Why not be spiritually alive?

Did you know that Mother Teresa of Calcutta was once a victim of scrupulosity? She used to drive herself relentlessly. In her early days she always felt guilty for not doing enough. She had some counseling, and eventually found the correct balance.

She then led a heroic life of charity, always striving for perfection, but avoiding the pitfall of perfectionism.

Mother Teresa was an Albanian woman who first became a teacher. She entered the convent and followed all the rules, but she felt she had to move on and work more directly with the poorest of the poor. Her superiors were against her leaving. They told her she was misguided. She struggled for a long time trying to be obedient, but she knew she had to go. Eventually she did get the permission she needed, and off she went, risking everything to follow her grace.

It was a decision that led her to the dying people of Calcutta. These heroic choices made her the woman we have come to know as Mother Teresa. These choices also made her the most famous saint of the 20th century.

This quote from Mother Teresa may help those who are trying to follow their own conscience:

"If you do good, people may accuse you of selfish motives.
   Do good anyway.
"The good you do today may be forgotten tomorrow.
   Do good anyway.
"Give the world the best you have, and you may get hurt.
   Give the world your best anyway."

Whatever your vocation may be, you have to find your own voice. You have to ask yourself: Who am I? What kind of a person do I want to be? These are haunting questions, but if you want to find Joy you must try to become the person God wants you to be. God wants you to bloom where you are planted. Once you find your place, you will experience a Joy that this world cannot give.

Stop looking back. Focus on the present moment. Planning for the future is necessary, but do not allow fear of the future to dominate your thoughts. Make it a happy future, which is free of the burden of worries about the past. If you do lament some tragedy, like the loss of a spouse, you have a right to grieve, but don't make it any worse by indulging your guilt feelings. No one is perfect. If mistakes were made you have to forgive yourself and move on with your life.

You'll become depressed if you overdo your sense of regret. Don't spend time thinking about the "What ifs" of life. There is no future in it. Break out of the cycle. If you have faith, repent. Believe that you are forgiven, and begin again. If the feelings persist, keep on forgiving yourself. Forgive, forgive, forgive, forgive, forgive, forgive, forgive, not seven times but seventy times seven, and then begin again.

Embrace your weaknesses, and boast of them as St. Paul did. **"I am glad of my weaknesses, insults, constraints, persecutions and distress for Christ's sake. For it is when I am weak that I am strong"** (2 Cor 12:10). He boasted of his weakness because it taught him to depend more on God's strength than his own.

The mistakes you make give you a graduate degree in the school of life. You graduate to where you can begin helping others to keep from making the same mistakes you made.

Sometimes people are hurt so badly that they say they can never get over it. This is pure nonsense! Every day is a new beginning. Once you realize that forgiveness is in the will, and not in the feelings, you are free. In spite of bad feelings you can forgive yourself and others. Forgetting takes more time, but you have time.

If only to get the monkey off your own back, you must forgive. You will please the Lord when your will says, "Yes I forgive." Let the feelings take care of themselves. You are in control, not your feelings.

If you did something wrong, summon the courage to admit it. You made a mistake, but you don't have to carry this heavy burden forever. Get to confession, repent, receive absolution from Christ through the ministry of the priest, and breathe a sigh of relief.

SUBJECTIVE GUILT

Guilty feelings are not always objective. A distinction must be made between what is real and what is coming from inside your own twisted thinking. Needless fretting over counterfeit sins is pointless. See yourself from God's point of view, see yourself as an object of His love.

If you once did something terribly wrong, and have asked for His forgiveness, presume that He forgives and forgets. This is a matter of faith and trust. Make amends if possible, but realize that you can't undo what has been done. Once forgiven God wants you to get on with your life.

Decide to be happy. Suppose you have the nagging feeling that someone you respect is disappointed in you. Cancel that thought. You were not put on earth to meet the expectations of anyone but God. Decide to deal with Him directly. He wants you to be happy. Make a new plan for your life. Do not let yourself stay in the same old rut.

What is it that you really want right now? Decide that you're going to live your life joyfully because of the knowledge of His love. Don't blame your problems on someone else. Don't wait for the world to validate you. Don't spend time sinking deeper into the pit of self-pity. The outside world is not coming to your rescue. You must rescue yourself. The door to happiness opens from the inside.

You've got to stand up for yourself. Pick up the pieces, and begin again.

Getting out of a rut is a choice you can make. Trust the Lord's strength. It is easier to trust when you habitually live in the Spirit of Joy. Once you decide to take back your life everything will change for the better.

Admit your mistakes, forgive others, and get back in the game of life. Be confident. Tell yourself you are strong and ca-

pable. Talk yourself out of sadness. Program your mind to be
positive and happy.

"I am happy, I am strong. God loves me. I will succeed."

Choosing Joy

A friend of mine named Frank always seems to be happy.
One day I asked him how he did it. "Well, Father," he explained,
"I look at it this way. It takes about as much energy to be joyful
as it does to be sad. So I just made up my mind to invest my
energy in being joyful."

Some might say that his approach is an oversimplification,
but I don't think so. There is a childlike spirit in his attitude. I
think it pleases the Lord very much when we just decide to be
happy in spite of everything that has happened to us.

The four Gospels may not be self-help books, but they do
teach a lot about positive thinking. They are sacred books, which
urge us to accept Jesus as Lord. They invite us to live in Him,
with Him, and through Him. They challenge us to a life of love
in the Lord.

Love can be very demanding. It almost always involves service and sacrifice. Nevertheless love is the only certain path to
Joy, and it is the foundation of true happiness. Read the sixth
chapter of Matthew where Jesus invites us to study nature.
**"Look at the birds of the sky. They do not plant seeds, gather a
harvest, or put it in barns, and yet your Father in heaven takes
care of them. Aren't you worth more than birds?"** (Mt 6:26).

We are often beset by worry. But what can anyone do
about the future? How can you protect yourself against a terrorist attack? Actually you can't. There is so much objective
danger out there, you would go mad stewing about it all the
time. It is damaging to your mental health, as well as your physical well-being.

Jesus rebuked those who are caught up in fear. He wants us to trust Him.

THE MEANING OF TRUE SUCCESS

People torture themselves with fear of failure. They worry over whether their life has any meaning. This is needless worry according to Ralph Waldo Emerson. He answered that problem with this simple passage:

> *"Whether by a healthy child, a garden patch, or a redeemed social condition,*
> *"To know that even one life has breathed easier because you lived:*
> *"This is to have succeeded."*

Some people seem to be caught up in worry all the time. They feel doomed to a life of sadness. The Lord tells them to snap out of it. He wants them to break free of needless worry. Think joyfully. The best defense is an offense.

Trusting Him can make you look silly at times. Those with no faith often scoff at people who believe. They consider them naïve. But it is the believer who has a tremendous advantage. Unbelievers are the ones to be pitied.

Let's take a moment to examine the words of Jesus on this important topic. He doesn't tell us how to do it, He just commands us to stop being afraid.

"Do not be so worrisome.... Oh you of little faith. There is no need to add to the troubles each day brings.... It is the unbeliever who worries about such things" (Mt 6).

Remember the song: "Don't worry, be happy"? It became a hit because it had a ring of truth to it. Didn't Jesus say basically the same thing? Didn't He tell us not to worry?

The issue, as far as He is concerned, is one of trust. Are

you able to trust Him? Can you turn yourself over to the Holy Spirit? Divine Life is within you. When you catch yourself out of sync with the peace God wants to give you, calm yourself down. Call on the name of Jesus right away. Remember the words of Julian of Norwich, *"All will be well. All manner of things shall be made well."*

Granted, you're human, and it's normal to worry. The fact is you will never be entirely free of worry. But needless worry and sustained anxiety are damaging to your health. Learn to control your fears. You do that by first controlling your thoughts.

Don't waste time reproaching yourself for being a worrier; in fact don't even judge yourself at all. Treat yourself kindly when you are afraid, the way you would try to comfort an upset child. Become your own best friend, and cancel your negative thinking.

Turn off the worry spigot because it only leads to sorrow. Turn it off, go to a quiet place, and rest in the Lord. Rest in His Peace, Love, and Joy. Remember how little you are, and how loving He is.

"Let the little children come to me" (Lk 18:16). Become like a child, and cry if necessary. It may do you good.

In the process try to keep up your spirit of optimism. Cancel the first sign of panic. Say no to fear, and say yes to Jesus. You are not in danger when He is there. Brighten up. Repeat the phrase "I am not in danger, I am safe in the Lord's love, I will succeed."

I wrote a little piece for myself when I was in a tense situation a few years ago. I then repeated it to myself over and over again.

I am not alone, for God is always within me.
I am not afraid, for God is my shield and my fortress.
I am forgiven everything, for God loves me.
I am bearing good fruit, for God is giving me power.

I am persevering, for God wants me to succeed.
I am going home to heaven, for God is saving me.

When you rely on faith you can deal with your nervous symptoms more easily. There will be crosses in your life, but you don't have to make them any worse than they are by dwelling on them. Laugh at yourself for believing your worst fears. Trust the Lord.

Learn to be your own best friend. Control your thoughts. Believe you are protected by His love. Tell yourself there is no danger; there is no problem that you and the Lord cannot solve together.

There are times when you may feel sad. When such feelings come, you will undoubtedly tend to get down on yourself. A vicious cycle begins. You might be tempted to believe things that are not true. Doubts arise: "What's wrong with me? I must be losing my faith.... The Lord doesn't really care about me.... I can't go on."

Stop it immediately. These feelings are not facts. When they come over you, especially in times of sickness, summon up your faith. *"I am not alone, I will get well, the Lord is with me."* Make up your own mantra. **"Rejoice always"** (1 Th 5:16).

Turn to the Holy Spirit. He is always closer to you than your own heartbeat. The fact that dark thoughts and feelings might come over you does not mean that you are in danger. Quite the opposite, the Holy Spirit is closest when you need Him the most.

Negative thoughts played over and over can turn you into a neurotic. Counter them. Do not label yourself: "I'm neurotic, I'm bulimic, I'm handicapped, I'm divorced." These are merely labels, but you are so much more. You are precious to Almighty God. Don't use these phrases as an excuse for self-pity.

If the label with which you identify yourself is positive, that's great. If not, it is a lie. One woman I know who was the victim of childhood abuse always says, "I am not a victim, I am a survivor." God loves you, and He wants to build you up. Don't undo God's plan for your happiness. He wants you to believe in Him, not in your own misleading labels.

Negative labels do not make you who you are. The truth will make you free. What you decide to be is who you are. You can be a person of faith and courage if you choose, or you can be an angry, discouraged victim. You are what you think you are.

You may need some outside counseling or spiritual guidance if you persist in beating yourself up, so don't be afraid to ask for help. It can be part of your recovery.

All the saints were imperfect human beings. They all had fears of one kind or another, and they all trusted God. As they developed into the holy men and women they eventually became, they nevertheless remained imperfect human beings. They grew beyond their earlier limitations, but they still remained human. Like them we are always going to be human too, and like them we can claim the gift of Joy in spite of our weaknesses. One has to cultivate the gift of Joy. We grow, not only in wisdom, age, grace, but in Joy as well.

Eventually Joy can become the dominant virtue of your life. It will overpower fear if you let it. Persevere in your intention to be joyful, and you will surmount your fears quickly and decisively.

You may never be entirely free of objective fear in this life, but the Holy Spirit will continually teach you how to be brave. As you work to rid yourself of useless, subjective fear, you will become more trusting of the Holy Spirit, and more joyful.

JOY PREVAILS OVER SADNESS

Joy and sadness can coexist in the same person at the same time. This is a subtle point that deserves comment.

"Don't let anything so fill you with sorrow that you forget the Joy of Christ Risen" (Mother Teresa of Calcutta). Joy is the result of remembering the Joy of the Risen Lord. It is the by-product of the knowledge of God's love. Joy, however, can coexist with sorrow. If you are grief-stricken, of course you will feel sorrow, but you will also know a quiet Joy. Your loved one is out of pain, and home at last in the arms of God.

If you settle for a life that is less spectacular than what you hoped for, don't let the disappointment drown out your Joy. If you try to please others all the time, hoping to win their approval, decide to take care of yourself first. Follow your own grace, and be happy. Sadness is not your vocation. Joy is. You will not be true to yourself unless you keep your hope alive. Choose Joy and in time your sadness will dissolve.

You have choices to make, which will either lift you up or pull you down. Choose to live the way God calls you, and your life will have meaning.

In the Book of Sirach 15:15, we read, **"When God created man, he made man subject to his own free choice.... There are set before you... life and death, whichever you choose shall be given you. Choose life."**

In the Book of Deuteronomy 30:15, **"Moses said to the people, 'Today I have set before you life and prosperity, death and doom. If you walk in the ways of the Lord, keeping His commandments you will live... if you do not listen, and are led astray, you will perish. Choose life then, that you and your descendants may live, by loving the Lord, heeding His voice and holding fast to Him'."**

There is Joy in fighting the good fight. Even though the battle itself will bring you pain and frustration at times, it is still the best that life can offer. Every day you stay on course you will grow in self-respect, and gain the respect of others. They may give it grudgingly at first, but in time it will grow.

So what if you are not yet a saint! You don't have to get bent out of shape over it. Do not get down on yourself. Laugh at your weaknesses. St. Paul boasted of his. The saints knew they were unprofitable servants, and this made them even greater saints. Knowing how much they needed God helped them to be better human beings. They kept doing the best they could, and when they fell, they just got up and started all over again.

All the saints went to confession. They all had good days and bad, just like you. They all knew it was only by God's grace that they were capable of doing any of the good that they did.

It should be a comfort to you to realize that your dissatisfaction with yourself is partly an inspiration from the Holy Spirit. When your conscience gently tells you to make changes for the better, you know you are receiving God's encouragement, not His rebuke.

Never think of yourself as a failure. There will be little failures or big ones along the way, but it only takes a little bit of faith to awaken a new spirit of confidence. God's Love is always present. If you ask Him for a greater openness to the Holy Spirit, He will give it. Be patient, and Joy will come. In fact, if you think about it, you will come to the realization that you already possess Joy in your heart.

Be at peace then, and enjoy the Lord. Then you will be better able to enjoy your precious life.

Sandi Matts, of Erie, Pennsylvania shares her faith story with us.

As I sit here on the eve of my return to work, I thank God for the life he has given me. As I reflect back on the last two months, I am reminded of how precious life really is.

On the morning I was to be admitted into the hospital, I read my devotional reading and Scriptures for the day. The message was that we must depend on the spirit of God to guide us, and in our weakness he is strong. I was then referred to Isaiah 6 and read the following: "Then I heard the voice of the Lord saying, 'Whom shall I send?' Then I said, 'Here I am, send me.' And he said, 'Go and tell my people; Lest they see with their eyes, hear with their ears, understand with their hearts; and repent and be healed.'"

The tears flowed at the realization that God was talking directly to me. I prayed, "Here I am, Lord," and rededicated my life to him. Relying on God's word I claimed the healing he had promised, as my own. I was instantly filled with an overwhelming sense of peace and love. In my weakness, he was strong!

The next morning the doctor came to deliver the news. The tests revealed a growth, conceivably a tumor. The blood tests indicated the probability of cancer. Surgery would be necessary.

Later that day, a special priest friend came to pray with me. We prayed for God's total healing. When we finished, he whispered to me that the cancer would take a miracle, but with God all things are possible. Then, not knowing what I had read the previous day he said, "You know when God heals you, you need to give your life to him." Tears of joy again, this was confirmation that not only would I be healed, but also that God needed me and was counting on me to bring others to him. I awoke from surgery three days later, my family all around to share the good news. No cancer! There was a red mark, evidence that something had been there, but it was gone. No tumor! No cancer! This was the miracle we had prayed for! The gift of new life! God is awesome. In our weakness, he is strong.

5

JOY AND THEOLOGY

"Come to me, all you who labor and are heavily laden, and I will give you rest." (Mt 11:28)

The Church has a theology of Joy which is grounded in God's infinite love for each one of us. The opening words of the official *Catechism of the Catholic Church* (I, 1) reflect the truth that God wants to give us His Joy.

"God, infinitely perfect and blessed in himself, in a plan of sheer goodness, freely created man to make him share in his own blessed life. God draws close to man. He calls man to seek him, to know him, to love him with all his strength.... He sent his Son as Redeemer and Savior... and through him invites all to become his adopted children, and thus heirs of his blessed life."

To be an heir of His blessed life is to share in His bliss both here and in the hereafter.

"God made me to know Him, to love Him, to serve Him in this world, and to be happy with Him forever in the next" (*Baltimore Catechism*). When I was growing up this quote from the penny catechism was all the theology I needed. It contained a synopsis of the theology of Joy, which has sustained me ever since.

The theological foundation of our Joy is in God's purpose in creating us. He created us to be happy with Him forever. God wants us to be happy with Him not only in the next world, but in this one as well.

Joy is the foundation of Christian revelation. As a community, we are living in the spiritual climate of joyful expectation. Jesus told us all that He did, so that our Joy may be full.

ADVENT

The season of Advent gives us a foretaste of what is to come: **"The Lord is near"** (Ph 4:5). In fact, the Lord is in your midst. It was announced to Mary, **"Hail full of grace the Lord is with you"** (Lk 1:28). The first words addressed to Mary are full of hope. She receives an invitation to exult and rejoice! The coming of the Savior was a Joy for one and all. It was announced first to Mary, and then proclaimed to the entire world.

The angel appeared to the shepherds after the birth of Jesus and said, **"I bring you good news of great Joy, which shall be to all the people"** (Lk 2:10). Our Christmas hymns sing it out, "Joy to the world, a savior is born."

Pope John Paul II sees Mary as a model for all Christians: *"In her, the joy of ancient Israel is concentrated and reaches its fullness, and the happiness of the messianic times bursts forth unrestrainedly. The Virgin's joy is particularly the joy of the 'remnant' of Israel, the poor who await God's salvation, and experience His fidelity. To share in this feast it is necessary to await the Savior with humility and to welcome Him with confidence.... The faithful are invited to take the Virgin Mother as a model, and to prepare themselves to meet the savior who is to come. They must be vigilant in prayer and joyful in praise."* (*Marialis Cultus*, 44).

The theology of Joy finds its basis in the Divinity of Jesus.

Agnostics and atheists may require empirical evidence before they will believe any of it, but that is their loss. Exaggerated individualism is one expression of the sin of pride. Those who cast themselves adrift from God end up very much alone. Jesus wants to bring them back to the Father.

Many find in Christ a stumbling block. There have been a variety of errors about Him that deserve attention. These Christological heresies have circulated from the beginning, undermining the faith of millions. Those who have faith, manage to transcend them. They don't need scientific proof to accept the truth that Jesus is the Lord of history.

WHO IS JESUS CHRIST?

Who is this Son of Mary? How does He come to speak with such authority? Let's take a moment to examine these questions.

Believing that Jesus came to bring us Joy, is the *sine qua non* of all spiritual progress. You had better be clear about who Jesus actually was and is. That He has the power and the authority to challenge those in authority is a matter of faith. It is certain that Jesus can transform the darkness into light. He can produce life out of death.

The Church has always taught that Jesus is a Divine Person who assumed a human nature. **"I am the vine, you are the branches"** (Jn 15:5). His followers are called to be carriers of His Divine Life. As a Christian, you have God living in you. You are a carrier of Divine Love and Joy. The Blessed Trinity is dwelling in your soul. When you look in the mirror you see a tabernacle of God's Love and Joy.

These truths are not self-evident. Only the leap of faith can make you a believer. You must decide if you want to make that leap. In today's world it is not easy. There are so many different and conflicting teachings about Jesus depicted on TV and in the movies. Most contain what the Catholic Church calls "Christological heresies," errors dating back to the fourth century. Let me tell you about some of them.

ARIANISM

The mother of all Christological heresies was started by a priest-theologian named Arius (A.D. 256-336). He came from the city of Alexandria, an Egyptian seaport. In denying the divinity of Christ, he argued that *"God must be unbegotten, and since Jesus was begotten of the Father, he could not be God. There cannot be two Gods."*

The Church declared him a heretic. He was not a bad man, quite the contrary. He wanted to defend monotheism, the idea that there is only one God. However, he ended up diminishing God's glory, rather than enhancing it, by claiming that God was too powerful, and too aloof, to play a role in human affairs. He insisted that God was unapproachably majestic; consequently, Jesus could not possibly be of the same nature as God.

As Arius attracted more and more followers, the bishops became more and more furious with him. They knew that the divinity of Jesus was central to the Faith. Nearly all of them had lived through the horrors of the Diocletian persecutions (A.D. 304). They had seen their own family members tortured and killed for believing in Christ's divinity.

The martyrs were all commanded to worship the Roman gods, which also involved the public denial of Christ's divinity. The price of refusal was a cruel death.

By the year was A.D. 325, the Arian movement had spread far and wide. In reaction, the bishops assembled in the city of Nicea for the first Ecumenical Council. They opposed Arianism by writing a Profession of Faith called the Nicene Creed. Christians have been reciting it at worship services ever since.

Jesus the Christ is true God and true man. The Council Fathers condemned Arius, and explained the meaning of all the Scripture texts in question. They said Jesus is not merely "begotten," He is "...the *only* begotten Son of God." The word

"Son," was chosen not merely as a metaphor, but as a spiritual reality. Jesus is not merely one of many sons; He is unique. He is of the same divine substance as the Father. The Eternal Son proceeds from the Father in a procession that is not in our time-space continuum, but rather in an eternal relationship.

Jesus once alluded to His unique relationship with the Father: **"No one knows the Son except the Father, nor does anyone know the Father except the Son, and anyone to whom the Son chooses to reveal Him"** (Mt 11:27).

The Council Fathers wanted to be absolutely faithful to the teachings of Jesus. They taught that *"Jesus is God of God, Light from Light, true God from true God, begotten not made,"* using the phrase, *"begotten not made,"* in order to attack the Arian heresy at its core. For them, Jesus was begotten, but not created. By saying that the Son is of the same substance as the Father, they taught that He and the Father are co-eternal, and of equal nature.

For 1700 years this doctrine of the Incarnation, which attests to the divinity of Jesus, has been a settled Church teaching. Arius missed the whole point of the New Testament. When he insisted that God is aloof and unapproachable, he did not calculate for the possibility that God entered human history. God took the initiative, by sending His only begotten Son to bring us eternal Joy. God is definitely not aloof, and certainly not disinterested.

Other Christological heresies have come along, and the Church has repudiated all of them. For instance, the Docetists didn't believe that a Divine Person could really suffer. They thought that Jesus only seemed to suffer on the cross. Like Arius they had trouble with the distinction between the human and the divine nature of Jesus. They could not understand that His human nature was real, in spite of the fact that He was a Divine Person. It wasn't until the Council of Chalcedon in A.D.

451 that the two natures of Jesus, the human and the divine were defined as distinct natures, coexisting in one Divine personality.

This is called the Hypostatic Union. His human nature was taken from Mary. He was truly bone of her bone, flesh of her flesh, and therefore truly human. However, He was the Second Person of the Blessed Trinity before His human birth. As the Second Person of the Blessed Trinity, He enjoyed eternal life. He assumed a human nature, while always remaining a Divine Person.

New Age Heresies

The mysteries of our Faith are obviously difficult to comprehend. If we could comprehend them they wouldn't be mysteries. Faith is basically living with mystery. It is the surrender of the intellect to truths that are beyond human understanding.

Do not let any heretical theories about Jesus undermine your faith in His Incarnation.

Do not be drawn into the confusion of New Age thinking. They reduce Jesus to the merely human level, and like the Gnostics of old make the claim that it was by means of a special knowledge that Jesus became a God. And since we have that special knowledge, we can become gods too. In claiming to be equal to Jesus, they are in effect denying His divinity.

Jesus is true God and true man. Accept this mystery. Accept it as it is has been explained and taught by the Church for nearly two thousand years.

We believe that God is Love and Mercy. He sent His only begotten Son, Jesus, the Christ, to tell us of the Father's Unchanging Love, and to bring us the fullness of His Joy.

Once you accept Jesus as your sole authority in these matters, He will send you the Holy Spirit of Joy, Peace and Love. The same Holy Spirit that raised Jesus from the dead will come to live in you. He will enable you to share in the Joy of the Spirit. You will in fact become a messenger of Joy.

There are millions of believers out there who sense that the entire universe is throbbing with signs of God. Most scientists believe this as well, even though they may not believe it in the way God is portrayed in the Bible.

They deduce that there must be a Supreme Intelligence behind this well-ordered universe. Most philosophers believe it too. On the basis of unaided reason, they know there is a Supreme Being.

Theologians believe in God on the basis of reason and revelation. God has revealed Himself to us in the Bible. Theologians make a study of Divine revelation. A theologian like Teilhard de Chardin spoke of the two faiths: faith in Jesus, and faith in the world, insisting that they may seem to be in opposition, but they, in fact, complement one another.

Faith in Jesus embraces the whole world because Jesus is the Lord of all creation. He will come again at the end of time to reconcile the world to Himself. Those who put their faith in this world, without any consideration of the existence of the supernatural are wrong. They may be in good faith, but they are ignorant of the truth.

Many of the leading intellectuals of modern times, like Marx and Engels in the 19th century, came up with false answers to the problems of society. Communism promised heaven on earth, but failed miserably in delivering it. In the process the communists destroyed millions of lives. Nations were reduced to abject poverty. The communist system was a disaster. Those who followed Marx were monumentally deceived.

This doesn't mean that all modern thinkers were in error. Teilhard de Chardin accepted Darwin's theory of evolution as a fact of life. He called evolution the horizontal movement of mankind through history. This approach implies a kind of faith in human progress.

The vertical movement of man touches faith issues, like belief in the afterlife. Science helps us to prolong life, but not indefinitely. The reality of death is inescapable. It frightens people to think that they will one day turn to ashes.

The possibility of heaven intrigues even the unbeliever.

After the Twin Towers disaster in New York City on Sept. 11, 2001, many who had lost their faith returned to their religious origins. Many skeptics found themselves praying. Our churches were overflowing for weeks. People didn't want to be isolated. Their skepticism did not sustain them in a crisis. They felt frightened and empty. How long this return to the faith will last remains to be seen.

A priest friend of mine told me about a man who resisted the Church his entire life. After the terrorist attack, he attended the funeral Mass of a friend who had died in the disaster. At the end of the service he went up to the priest who celebrated the Mass, and said emotionally, "Father, we need you guys."

Where did his cynicism go? Was his response based on his fear of death or was there a glimmer of faith coming alive? The fact that anyone of us can die in the blink of an eye sobers the imagination. Did the shock of death hit home, and make him a believer? Who knows? I hope it did for more than a minute.

In the 20th century, we fought two world wars; endured the holocaust; and fought the Korean and Vietnam wars. We have lived for decades under the threat of nuclear destruction, a threat that is by no means over. All of this turmoil suggests that we need God in our lives.

The miserable condition of the world is the legacy of our failure to love one another. Both religion and science have made a lot of mistakes, but we can begin to work together to make this a better world.

We all hope for the best, and we feel let down when we don't achieve it. Many have searched for new answers to the age-old questions. Many turn to New Age religions, feeling that the traditional religions are outdated. They are searching for spiritual answers, and yet most of them seem to keep coming up feeling empty.

The world has truly been thrown into a crisis. We all want something to believe in that is more than can be found in this life. Modern people who opt to remain agnostics, by definition do not know how to satisfy their spiritual hunger.

DOUBT AND SKEPTICISM ARE THE ENEMIES OF JOY

So many are frightened by the industrialization of modern warfare. Living on the brink of disaster, as we have been for decades, leaves little room for joy.

One response to this anxiety is to look for an escape. The drug sub-culture supplies society's need to escape. Addicts band together because misery likes company. Fear motivates them to shut off the pain of life.

For the first time in history we are scientifically capable of destroying every living thing on our planet. Large numbers of people turn to drugs, which is a more subtle form of self-destruction, because they like being bombed out of their mind. They soon find out however that they have to wake up each time to the same reality. The difficulties of life do not go away when people numb their minds with drugs.

Doubt, skepticism and fear haunt the lives of most escapists. There are some who repress their conscience, and feel nothing. Some put their trust in science.

There are times when faith and science are on a collision course; for instance when it comes to the morality of cloning.

Science can do things that can have profound, unforeseen consequences. For the most part however science and religion are seeking after the same truth.

One can believe in the theory of evolution and still be a person of faith. God created the world by means of an evolutionary process. We don't fully understand how the world developed, but we do know that the human race has progressed. We have solved one problem after another.

We are becoming better as we grow and develop. In spite of the condition of the world today, there are positive signs concerning human progress.

They said there would never be an end to colonialism, but it has ended. They said there would never be an end to slavery, but it has ended, except in a few remote areas of the world.

Over the centuries human progress has produced higher states of awareness, intelligence and organization. As mankind evolves, we become smarter. Unfortunately, in some ways, we show an extraordinary lack of wisdom. Science helps us to make airplanes, computers, and all kinds of gadgets, which enhance our lives, but science cannot tell us how to enjoy life itself.

Scientific advances give rise to the hope that human progress is limitless, but wisdom tells us there is more to human progress than economic prosperity.

"Henceforth, my pursuit of happiness has ended.
Now I know that happiness hides not in that new house,
*   that new career, that new friend. And it is never for sale.*
Whenever I depend on things outside of myself to supply me
*   with Joy*
I am doomed to disappointment.
Happiness, I see now, has nothing to do with getting.
It consists of being satisfied with what I've got, and what I
*   haven't got.*

*So long as I have something to do, something to hope for
I shall be happy."*

Og Mandino, *The Choice*

If we neglect the inner spirit, all the toys in the world won't bring us happiness. Only the Holy Spirit can bring us true Joy.

The crisis of hope begins when we start to believe that science can save us. The younger generations going back to the 1960's have rejected this idea. Do you remember Jerry Rubin? He coined the motto of the 60's generation: "Don't trust anyone over thirty."

Who can blame young people for being skeptical? The world they inherited has been filled with turmoil and danger for decades. What we need to teach them is that skepticism, pessimism and fear are not the answers.

Everyone has to trust someone. We cannot discard the wisdom of the prophets. We need our internal compass to guide us along the way. We need God to help us to find the meaning of it all. What good is human progress if it leaves us vulnerable and afraid?

Today nuclear weapons are not properly controlled. We have huge stockpiles of radioactive waste. Industrial chemicals continually pollute the air, giving rise to cancer. Terrorists plan new threats every day. Where will it all end? The crisis of hope is distressing, but with God hope is possible.

Modern progress has been so rapid that we haven't had time to assess it all. However, we cannot allow ourselves to be downhearted.

If you want to live a joyful life, avoid being a skeptic, and embrace the Lord. Trust Him. Christ is your Lord. He will soothe your troubled heart.

We know that even greater scientific developments will take place in the future. They may not be able to bring us any closer to the Joy, Peace and Love we so desperately need, but they can make life more comfortable. Air-conditioning in the summer, and a good heating system in the winter are the products of science. We need them. But we also need a healthy spirituality

In Teilhard's theology of Christ, he identifies the Risen Jesus as the "Omega" point of all creation. Everything in the evolutionary process seems to point to a future, which Teilhard identifies as Jesus. The Lord will come again at the end of human history; He is center of the world, and the very meaning of the entire life process. Jesus is not only the Lord of every individual person, but also the Lord of history.

We eagerly listen to His message, and accept the truths He reveals. Our future rests in Him. It takes faith to see beyond the limitations of science. We can cancel our fears if we understand that we are in the hands of the living God. We can trust Him and follow Him. It takes courage to drop our hatreds. It takes courage to discard our fears.

Christ asks us to be carriers of His Divine Love. He even asks us to pray for evil doers. Those who disrupt our peaceful world need prayers. Conversion is possible. Human beings are perfectible.

God wants us to remain calm in the midst of the storms that surround us. It is important to remain serene, if we are to find Joy. With God all things are possible, including a peaceful soul and a joyful heart. Return good for evil. Think of God as being nearer to you than your own heartbeat. Find a way to allow love to rule your life. Dress the wounds of those in need. Do not lose a single opportunity to pray for them.

Here is a little prayer I wrote for myself to maintain my spiritual balance in a world filled with terror.

Help me Lord not to demonize our enemies the way they have demonized us.

*I pray for them Lord, because You ask me to return good for
evil.*

I also pray that You will protect me from them.

*I pray that we will all come to a knowledge of the truth and
be saved.*

*I accept Your will in all things, and I bow before Your
majesty.*

Accepting the pain of life, and living peacefully is a gift the Lord wants to give us. He wants our Joy to be full. We may not understand how it all works, but we can still benefit by our faith in the mystery.

A priest told me this story about one of his parishioners who had a serious case of arthritis for many years. When asked how she coped with the constant pain and confusion, she said,

For many years now I have been offering my pain up to God.

When I offer up my pain to God, I show Him that I am going along with His plan for my life. You see, when I was a little girl I always dreamed of one day becoming a mother. So when I had my children, I got into the habit of offering God all the pain connected with my role as a mother.

I offered it all for His greater glory: the pain of childbirth, the raising of the children, the sacrifices I had to make along the way. I offered everything as a prayer.

I asked to be a mother, so I knew that all the pain that went with it was part of God's plan for me. I accepted both the Joys and the sorrows, and everything in between. I got into the habit of doing that. Now I am doing the same thing in my old age with my arthritic pain.

Do you see how simple it can be? This woman is very close to the heart of Jesus.

On the night before He was crucified Jesus said, **"Now the Son of Man is glorified, and in Him God is glorified"** (Jn 13:31). He knew His pain would give glory to God. This enabled Him to accept it. Pain is the coin that purchased our redemption.

When unavoidable pain comes into your life, offer it to the Father. Even if you don't understand what you are going through or why, do not give in to despair. Trust that He will not give you more than you can bear, and trust that what He does permit you to suffer will be for the greater glory of God, and for the salvation of souls.

6

JOY AND THE CROSS

"If you wish to come after me, you must deny yourself
and take up your cross every day. For if you wish to save your
life, you will lose it, but if you wish to lose your life
for my sake you will save it." (Lk 9:23, 24)

Obviously, the cross is central to our faith. But the cross does
not exclude the notion of human joy, and it certainly doesn't
mitigate spiritual Joy. There are many ways to view the crosses
that come to you in life. St. James gives us his perspective:

**"Consider it pure Joy… whenever you face many trials,
because you know that your faith is being tested, and this develops perseverance"** (Jm 1:2, 3).

The cross is not an end in itself, it is a prelude to Easter
Sunday. Faith leads to love, love leads to service, and service
leads to the cross. We do not become holier because of the pain
we suffer, but because of the love and sacrifice given in His
Name. Jesus suffered and died that we might live. His purpose
was not to call us to suffering. He died that we might live. He
actually said, **"I have told you all these things that your Joy may
be full"** (Jn 15:11).

The cross of Christ reconciled us to the Father. The cross
is the key to understanding the redemptive act of Jesus. The
Lord's suffering and death have two redemptive aspects. One
is the negative aspect of expiation for sin, and the other is the
positive aspect of true reconciliation. Teilhard de Chardin places

a stronger emphasis on the reconciliation aspect, and so do I.

In this view, the cross reconciles us to our destiny in Christ. Jesus becomes central to the future of the human race. The Pauline idea of inclusion comes into play: **"In Him we live and move and have our being"** (Ac 17:28). Human progress is future oriented, moving steadily toward the Omega point, Jesus Christ.

Too much emphasis on the negative effects of sin in the past has muted the significance of the Joy of Easter. The Joy that Christ came to bring is revealed in God's love, which goes to the point of death on a cross. This is the gift of reconciliation. God plans an eternity of love for us. His Joy is our destiny. Joy and the cross are not in opposition. *"Everything I have ever done, I have done to make God happy. And this has made me happy. I am happy to suffer for Him"* (St. Thérèse of Lisieux).

This attitude is from the Holy Spirit, and it embodies the Good News of the Gospel.

St. Paul reminds us that **"we are God's work of art created in Christ Jesus to live the good life as He meant us to live it from the beginning"** (Eph 2:10).

Father Walter Ciszek, S.J., picked up on this image of the human person: *"You are like a precious but rough diamond, which needs to be purified. The diamond cutter must chisel and smooth, rub and buff the diamond in order to show its light, its radiant beauty."*

Suffering in this light becomes the refining process of love. Each of us is a diamond in the rough. Our purification cannot be achieved alone. The Divine Artist polishes us until we are just the way He wants us, the finished product of His genius. It takes spiritual insight to see that every moment of life is precious, no matter what we are undergoing at any given moment.

Father Ciszek, who is being considered for canonization, added this additional perspective: *"Every moment of our life has a purpose... every action of ours, no matter how dull, or routine,*

or trivial has a dignity and worth beyond human understanding"
(*He Leadeth Me*, p. 201).

The cross of Christ, and the cross we carry, not only purifies
us, but also has the purpose of reconciling us to God. It is an
instrument of expiation, and it also represents all the hard-
earned progress made throughout the entire history of the world.
All the suffering of human history has contributed to human
progress, but the suffering of Christ has sanctified it.

The cross therefore is not merely a symbol of expiation,
but also a symbol of the Joy of our evolutionary progress. It
speaks of the painful growth of the human race, and includes
all the suffering of the human family, which has brought us to
this present moment.

We have come this far because of the sacrifices and labors
of our forefathers. We owe our ancestors an enormous debt, and
we must not stumble into retrogression.

We must labor for those who come after us, by protecting
our planet and one another from violence and hatred. Jesus had
a plan for this. He called us to serve one another. St. Paul put it
well, **"Help carry one another's burdens; in this way you will
fulfill the laws of Jesus Christ"** (Ph 2:6-11).

By easing the burdens of others, we let them know that
they are loved. At the same time we increase our own self-respect. This provides a quiet Joy that pervades the soul. *"We are
an Easter people, and Alleluia is our song"* (St. Augustine). In the
midst of trials we sing our "alleluias." We hold on to our Joy.

Pope John Paul II commented on this plan: *"Wherever there
is a heart that overcomes selfishness, violence, and hatred — wherever there is a heart that reaches out to someone in need — Christ
is risen from the dead, risen today, and may the whole world rise
in Him."*

The traditional belief, namely, that the cross stands for
one's own death in Christ, is the spiritual way of interpreting
the meaning of the cross for each individual. In that sense, the

cross is a doorway to our final union with God. Unless you die
to self, you cannot live. The essence of Joy will be found in losing yourself in Love. The cross therefore reconciles us to the
Risen Jesus. (cf. Teilhard de Chardin's *The Divine Milieu*, NY:
Harper and Row, pp. 101-104, "The Meaning of the Cross.")

Theologically speaking, the cross has always symbolized the
entire paschal mystery. It is the symbol of the life, death and
passion of Jesus. The open tomb symbolizes His resurrection,
but the cross is often depicted artistically with the corpus soar-
ing, or slightly lifted, from the wood.

Jesus' resurrection gave glory to the Father, but so did His
passion and death. The cross is therefore a prelude to full reconciliation of the world to God the Father.

Living in Christ includes the idea of living in His passion,
death and resurrection. The act of faith therefore is not merely
the mental act of accepting Jesus as the Lord who atones for
our sins, it is also an act which incorporates us into the Mystical Body of Christ.

Through Baptism we become the branches of the Divine
Vine, we carry Life, Love, and Joy to everyone we meet. That
is why it is so important for us to claim Joy as our baptismal
right, for unless you claim it, you cannot give it away.

G.K. Chesterton said that joy is the gigantic secret of Christianity, and we must try to let the secret out of the bag. Joy
comes to those who love well. Since love and sacrifice go together, joy is the by-product of sacrifice and self-denial.

A man once asked Mother Macrina, a 4th-century mystic,
how he could acquire joy.

> *"You cannot acquire joy,"* she answered, *"you must find it."*
> *"But how do I find it?"* he asked.
> *"Oh that is simple,"* she replied.
> *"There is only one way.*
> *"To find joy you must lose yourself."*
> (Irma Zaleski, *Stories of Mother Macrina*)

Losing yourself is not exactly the same as being unselfish. It is more an act of self-giving. The ego gets lost in the process.

Unselfishness Is Not the Same as Love

Losing yourself is much more than being unselfish. The distinction between love and unselfishness is huge. Joy is not a reward for being unselfish. Unselfishness is too limited a term.

Being "unselfish" is seen by some as the highest Christian goal; however, the word is too ambiguous. Love often involves unselfishness, but true love gives without counting the cost, and is primarily interested in the well-being of the beloved, not in the unselfish deeds themselves.

There can be a kind of unselfishness that is self-serving. A priest who gives up marriage and children only to steal from the collection basket to pay his gambling debts and live an entirely selfish life, is a loveless soul. He may appear to many as unselfish, because he chose a vocation which demands altruism, but he is a hypocrite. He has chosen his vocation as a cover for sinfulness.

The word "unselfish" admits of too many nuances, none of which rise to the level of true love. The highest Christian goal is positive not negative. The highest goal is true love. Love always seeks the good of another, while unselfishness can be embraced as an end in itself. You might say that this is a selfish kind of unselfishness.

The best way to explain this is to think about Buddhism. There are no doubt many loving Buddhists. They are known for their compassion. However, we Christians are not Buddhists. Buddhists monks work diligently on the discipline of extinguishing all selfish desire. However, they are doing it to attain nirvana. This is a self-centered goal. Nirvana is the so-called subjective state of self-realization. It is perfectly moral to seek after it, but the ascetic practices they perform are in no way directed either to the worship of God, or to the good of their neighbor. It's all about transformation to a higher state.

This is not a bad thing; indeed it is noble to strive to be unselfish, but unselfishness is not the Christian ideal of love. Love will involve self-sacrifice, and it may hope for the reward of heaven, but it aims at the good of the beloved.

Though the Buddhists stress compassion, they do not to my knowledge promote social action. We would say that compassion is helping others, but for the Buddhist it is more a state of awareness. The four noble truths of Buddha never mention the love of God or neighbor. Love is not on their radar screen. Their asceticism aims at self-realization, which is the primary objective of Buddhist spirituality.

I use Buddhism as an example to show that being unselfish is not the same as being a loving person. The pursuit of Christian perfection, which is love, goes beyond self.

What about our Catholic monks? Are they not burying themselves away in prayer and self-discipline like the Buddhist monks? It is not the same. If a Christian chooses a life of prayer, and the self-imposed sacrifice of living in a monastery, it is done for the love of God, for the good of one's neighbor, and for the salvation of souls. If not, it is not Christian. Asceticism without charity is not Christianity. To give one's life for any other reason than love would be a distortion of the Gospel message.

Christian love has the good of the beloved in mind when any sacrifices are made. Sacrifices might very well involve discomfort, but when done in the name of love, they bring Joy to the soul.

Religious communities may train their novices to bear discomfort in order to prepare them for future service to the poor, the sick or those in need, but the goal is love, not self-imposed pain as an end in itself.

Ours is an asceticism of joyful love, not joyless self-abnegation. The good of neighbor, and the Joy of pleasing God are the goals of Christian asceticism.

The problem is that most of us have been taught to believe that the highest virtue is to be unselfish. Not so! To love is the highest virtue. Taking care of yourself is not a selfish activity. You are commanded to love your neighbor, as you love yourself.

Lent is about giving up things as a way of building spiritual muscles. We make sacrifices to become more loving. Lent is also about mourning the death of Jesus. This is good. To deny ourselves for these reasons is meritorious. As long as your real motive is love you are on safe ground. What you do for the love of Jesus, under the guidance of a superior or a spiritual director to keep you from going to extremes, is good. Offering up your sacrifices to please God can be a beautiful gesture of love, but Jesus warned against doing things to be seen and admired by others. He said those who do such things, **"have already had their reward"** (Mt 6:2).

Christian sacrifice is giving up a legitimate good for a noble purpose. Unselfishness is very different.

C.S. Lewis explains the difference in these words: *"You see what has happened? A negative term (unselfishness) carries with it the suggestion not primarily of securing good things for others, but of going without them ourselves, as if our abstinence and not their happiness was the important point.... I do not think this is the Christian virtue of love. The New Testament has much to say about self-denial, but not about self-denial as an end in itself.... I submit that this (negative) notion has crept in from Kant and the Stoics, and is no part of the Christian faith"* (The Weight of Glory, Macmillan, 1975, p. 1).

Lewis is saying that when we are told to take up the cross, it does not mean that the cross is an end in itself. The cross is a means to an end. Jesus told us to love so that our Joy may be full. Joy is not the enemy of Christian sacrifice. In fact true sacrifice will always result in Joy.

Joy is a legitimate goal of Christian asceticism. Joy and love go hand in hand. In order to be a better follower of Christ, you should understand that the challenge to love includes the challenge to love yourself. You need your health. Diet, exercise, and recreation help you to promote a state of well-being. Persevere in your good intentions. Without good health you run the risk of burning out before your time.

The Importance of Loving Yourself

There seems to be a false impression that God doesn't want you to desire your own happiness, as though such an idea would be selfish. Quite the contrary. God wants you to enjoy your precious life both here and in the hereafter. We were created for joy. We are destined for an eternity of happiness. Why would He want you to measure your fidelity to Him by the degree of your misery?

Be joyful. **"Your Joy has been bought at a great price"** (1 Cor 6:20). Why are there so many sad Christians? Why are they suspicious of Joy as a legitimate goal in Christian asceticism? Jesus assured us that He wants us to be joyful: **"I have told you all these things that your Joy may be full"** (Jn 15:11).

Julian of Norwich said it best, *"The greatest honor you can give to Almighty God... is to live gladly because of the knowledge of His love."*

Can there be any doubt that God wants you to love others in order to increase your own chance for happiness. To help them find purpose and meaning in their lives is one way to do that. Your good example will have eternal consequences.

Being happy doesn't necessarily mean indulging one's baser

appetites. Gluttony is not going to make you happy. "Eat, drink, and be merry for tomorrow we die," is a proverb that extols self-indulgence. But our time on earth is precious. We should eat properly, drink sensibly, and be merry. Joy is a Christian duty.

We need nourishment and laughter if we are to carry our crosses with courage. If we are to persevere in the name of love, we need to take care of our own needs.

We are the lucky recipients of a gracious God who wants us to enjoy our precious lives.

C.S. Lewis saw how easy it is to engage in self-sabotage: *"When infinite Joy is offered us, we are like an ignorant child who wants to go on making mud pies in a slum because he cannot imagine what is meant by the offer of a holiday at the sea."*

God made us for happiness not only in the hereafter, but also here on earth. He calls us to the highest virtue of love precisely to give us the experience of Joy. Jesus is the exemplar of true love. He laid down His life to save us.

The Cross of Christ Is Central to Our Faith

"If you wish to come after me, you must deny yourself, and take up your cross every day. For if you wish to save your life, you will lose it, but if you wish to lose your life for my sake you will save it" (Lk 9:23-24).

The cross is central to our faith, but it is not an end in itself. It must be understood properly. Jesus calls us to a form of denial that puts others first.

What Christ did for us on His cross was to free us from our slavery to ignorance, fear and sin. The more we are in harmony with His will, the more liberated we will become.

The superficial person may see the words, **"Take up your cross, and follow Me"** (Mt 16:24) as an invitation to gloom and doom. The cross seems to cancel happiness at every turn. Not so! But on deeper reflection we come to see that just the opposite is true.

Those who pursue their own happiness exclusively, avoiding the cross, seeking fame, fortune, power and pleasure, without any real concern for others, more often than not end in confusion and misery. Some get caught up in the use of mind-altering chemicals. For them relief is only a few pills away. And when the pills run out, they are no longer in possession of themselves; their souls are in bondage to their habit.

This kind of misery is legendary. How the Lord must lament the behavior of those who are bent on self-destruction. Love and Joy, on the other hand, lead us to the full possession of our faculties. Service always involves a certain amount of discipline. Putting others first can appear to be a cross, but it is a self-surrender that brings with it a measure of gladness. Everything done in the name of love can one day turn to Joy.

The pain of childbirth is a good example. The excruciating pain all but disappears from memory when the newborn babe arrives.

The Mystical Experience of Joy

The path from a self-centered life to one of self-giving is often gradual. Everyone who has ever followed a calling from God knows that the process of answering the call takes time. A vocation is a unique gift. It develops slowly because it is a mystical experience. God's voice speaks to the heart. God's calling takes time to discern.

No two vocations are exactly alike. I return to Dorothy Day, of *Catholic Worker* fame, for an example of the uniqueness of a vocation. She was one of the most God-haunted women I have ever known. She longed for a contemplative life, and yet she spent most of her adult years running a soup kitchen, feeding the hungry on the Lower East Side of New York City.

She had no money, but she felt the urge (she experienced a mystical calling) to open a soup kitchen anyway. Trusting in God's Providence she followed her grace, depending entirely on God for the food she would need day after day. Somehow, the supply of donated food never ended. She received all she needed. She fed the hungry and sheltered the homeless, one day at a time, for over thirty years.

When you trust the Lord, even the ordinary experiences of everyday life can have a mystical dimension. For instance, the desire for greater union with God, which the followers of Christ have, is in itself a mystical gift. So too is the desire to serve the poor, the sick, or the elderly. A person may have no extraordinary qualifications accompanying such holy desires, but they know intuitively that it doesn't matter. God will provide.

When all is said and done, a mystical experience is a direct communication from the Holy Spirit. It may take the form of a holy desire to do some good work. As we gradually become conscious of the fact that we are the carriers of Divine Love, we then begin to recognize how we are to release this love. In spite of our imperfections and unworthiness, God draws us closer to Him, filling us with His Presence.

He always respects our freedom. No one is forced to obey the urges they feel. But as they proceed in their transformation in Christ, they gradually move joyfully in directions, which they would not have chosen for themselves. God mysteriously brings them through their own doubts and fears, and leads them to a life of altruism.

In the end, each of them is able to say with St. Paul, "**I live, now not I, but Christ lives in me**" (Gal 2:20).

The cross is the price we pay for being fully responsive to the will of God. You do not have to look for a cross. It will find you. Once you accept the burdens and obligations of love, your surrender to the Father will have been complete.

The cross is good. It is a pathway to freedom. Catholics give things up for Lent, to become free of them. Sacrificing something to please God is a beautiful act of love. This positive aspect of self-denial is not only meritorious, but it is character building. When you turn away from the negative aspects of your personality to get in touch with your soul's desire for holiness, you are surely going to increase your level of Joy, and grow closer to God. During Lent, and all through the year:

> Give up resentment; decide to forgive.
> Give up hatred; decide to return good for evil.
> Give up complaining; decide to be grateful.
> Give up pessimism; decide to be optimistic.
> Give up worry; decide to be trusting.
> Give up sadness; decide to be hopeful.
> Give up anger; decide to be patient.
> Give up pettiness; decide to be noble.
> Give up gloom; decide to be joyful.

It takes discipline to control your thoughts and think positively. When you are sick, you know enough to follow your doctor's orders: drink lots of water, and get plenty of bed rest. So too when you are well, you have to follow your spiritual leader's orders. Turn to Jesus and ask Him to help you be more self-controlled. Shed all those negative thoughts and emotions: resentment, hatred, complaint, pessimism, worry, sadness, anger, pettiness, and gloom.

Sickness can be an ordeal, but it can also help you to focus on your real purpose in life.

Jesus prayed to be released from the agony He was about to face, and yet He commanded Himself to say, **"Not My will but Thine be done"** (Mt 26:39). He knew His purpose was to surrender to the Father's will. That was the supreme test.

Accepting the things you cannot change, but doing every-thing in your power to change the things you can, will liberate you. Surrendering to your Father's will may seem to be beyond your strength but St. Augustine had some simple advice: *"Do what you can do, and pray for what you cannot yet do."*

We have to pray for the grace to say, "Thy will be done." The Supreme Law is the goal of Christian perfection. It calls us to the love of God, the love of neighbor and the love of self. The degree of suffering we endure in the process of loving is not the issue. *"It is not* what *we do, but how much love we put into the doing,"* according to Mother Teresa of Calcutta.

ACCEPTING PAIN

Only grace can help you in your hour of need. If you can't pray, or even think straight because you are in acute pain, then of course increase the painkillers. I remember being somewhat scandalized as a young seminarian when I learned that Pope John XXIII had asked for painkillers during his final illness. How naïve of me, or is stupid a better word? Even popes need to reduce their level of pain.

I often think of Our Blessed Mother standing beneath the cross. What suffering she must have endured looking up at her son, feeling so helpless. She can teach us so much. Turn to her for help.

Catherine de Vinck, the well-known poet and spiritual writer, honors Mary's courage in the following poem.

LADY OF THE CROSS

When the tongue fails
    When words crack open
    Like frozen meatless fruits

When terror travels in the blood
Screams and spills
Through all the pores of the skin,
Come in haste
To the heaving, hilly country of our need.
Come with hands cupped
To the shape of our pain
With feet like silver leaves
On the path of our weeping.
Come with linen and oil
With the dazzle of all that is forged in fire
And burns toward morning.
Drive us out of our midnight cell
Where we fast
On tepid water
Hard crust.
Drive us into the open
Where the sun will sew our wounds
With golden threads
COME MARY
LEAD US HOME.

The poet understands both the sorrow of Mary, and the Joy. Catherine de Vinck reflected, *"Every day for many years I have prayed the* Magnificat, *which is Latin for, 'I rejoice in God my Savior.' In French the words,* mon espirit tressaille de joie en Dieu mon Sauveur, *are translated literally to mean: 'my spirit thrills with Joy in God my Savior.' This Joy is not an ordinary worldly joy; it is the thrilling of God's Joy. The same Joy that filled the Apostles at Pentecost, filled the soul of Mary when she became pregnant with Jesus."*

It is the Joy of the Holy Spirit, filling us with His Presence on good days and bad. Sorrow can coexist with Joy. The Lord did not come into our world to take away pain. He came to bring

Joy into our sorrow by uniting Himself to us in our suffering. Mary knew this and accepted it. She knew that God was not absent when she was in distress. She knew that it is in the dark moments of life that God's Love is most powerful and most hidden.

In the joyful moments of life God is palpably present. In the sorrowful moments God is mystically present in silence.

Ask Mary for the wisdom to understand that God's love enfolds you, both in joy and in sorrow. Jesus said, **"Ask and you will receive"** (Mt 7:7).

FEELING ABANDONED

The feeling of being abandoned can be emotionally distressing. People ask, "Where was God when I needed Him?" Believing their feelings, which are not facts, they wrongly conclude that God was absent. They mistook the silence of God for the absence of God. They failed to realize that God's silence was broken once and for all by Jesus.

He came into our world to tell us that God is with us in all circumstances. **"Do not be afraid… do not let your hearts be troubled"** (Jn 6:20; 14:1).

His message gives us hope, and helps us to say with St. Augustine, *"We are an Easter people, and Alleluia is our song,"* even when painful feelings torment us.

You may ask, how does all this faith help a person to cope with the actuality of searing pain? It does, that's all there is to it. We do our best to relieve our pain through medication, or anything else that is moral and that works.

However unavoidable pain must eventually be endured. Once you've done everything possible to get rid of it, you have to put on the will to bear it. What you cannot change you must pray for the grace to accept with courage. Offer your tears up to God in a spirit of loving surrender.

At certain times in life you just have to bear it; you never have to grin. Accept the pain if only to offer something beautiful to God. Very often it isn't so much what you are going through that is the worst part of it, rather it is the way you react to your plight. I do not want to give instructions here because I am the world's greatest coward when it comes to severe pain.

I'd like to think I would use pain as a love gift to Jesus for the salvation of souls, like the love gift He gave to His Father. But I'm realistic enough to see myself screaming for the nurse to give me more painkillers.

Jesus doesn't ask us to become Stoics, He simply asks us to turn to Him. To be intimate with the Lord, is to allow Him to suffer with you and in you. Someone once said that pain is God's way of getting closer to you.

I don't want to mystify suffering too much, but it does have a mystical dimension. It is part of every human life, and yet, Jesus used it as an instrument of redemption. Pain is not sacred in itself, but it becomes sacred when it is accepted and turned over to the Lord as a gift of love.

Whatever works best to relieve your pain is worth trying. Avoid becoming addicted to drugs, if possible, but do what you have to when pain becomes unbearable.

Follow your conscience. Pope John accepted his pain as far as he could, then he cried out for relief. Jesus cried out to His Father, too, when He was in His agony.

When you're in severe pain, you can't think straight. Your agony can become your noblest prayer, even if you don't understand what that means.

DEATH AND DYING

Those on their deathbed should be made as comfortable as possible. Needless to say, euthanasia, which is the direct taking of a life, is not morally permissible. However, the removal of life-support for a comatose patient for whom there is no hope of recovery, is an option that must be weighed carefully.

With the help of your doctor, your pastor and your family you should carefully weigh your options. What would the patient want in this circumstance? What is the financial burden to the family in sustaining a life that can never be normal again?

The final decision rests with the head of the family. Having consulted widely, he or she must make the fateful decision to let the person die with dignity, rather than to perpetuate an artificially maintained semi-dead patient. It is essentially a decision not to continue extraordinary means to support a life that is fading away.

Faith gives us the confidence to trust God in all circumstances. It's not an easy thing to deal with these heavy responsibilities, but deal with them we must.

The serenity prayer may be of help:

> *Lord give me the serenity to accept the things I cannot change, the courage to change the things I can, and the wisdom to know the difference.*

A friend of mine, who is recovering from cancer, sent me the business card of his oncologist, Doctor Marshall Lynch Leary. On the reverse side of the card there is this message:

Cancer is so limited,
It cannot cripple love, shatter hope, or corrode truth.
It cannot eat away at peace.
It cannot kill friendship.

It cannot shut out memories, or silence courage.
It cannot invade the soul.
Cancer cannot reduce eternal life. It cannot quench
    the Holy Spirit.
Cancer cannot lessen the power of the resurrection.
Can cancer conquer you?
I doubt it.
For the strengths I see in you have nothing to do with cells,
blood and muscle.

Our strength and our Joy is in Jesus. Joy is possible even in the midst of pain, but this level of Joy comes only from God. In order to find this Joy, we must claim it. If you allow self-pity to take over, you will become sadder and more miserable. Remind yourself that you were not put on this earth by chance. Your suffering is part of a larger purpose that may be hidden from your eyes. Pain is redemptive. It can purify the soul. You may need a purification from time to time.

God put you on earth for a reason. He knows all about you, and what you are going through. He wants you to have Joy to help you through the trials that come your way. Try to live each day, gratefully accepting the many blessings He sends you. You will become stronger by focusing on Joy. You will become sadder if you coddle yourself in the spirit of self-pity.

Joy is not merely a gift to pray for, it is a Christian duty. A smile on your face is possible even in the midst of sorrow. This smile can be a sign of the Holy Spirit living in you.

St. Paul had his crosses, and yet he fought the good fight. He said: **"Nothing can separate me from the love of Christ, neither hunger, nor prison, nor death"** (Rm 8:35).

> *"No heaven can come to us*
> *unless our hearts find rest in today.*
>   *Take heaven.*

No peace lies in the future that is not hidden
in this precious instance.
    Take peace.
The gloom of the world is but a shadow.
Behind it, yet within our reach is Joy.
    Take Joy.
Courage then, claim it, that is all."

Fra Angelico (15th century monk)

HOLINESS

Holiness is not something that comes from doing good.
    We do good because we are holy.
Holiness is not something we acquire by avoiding evil.
    We avoid evil because we are holy.
Holiness is not something that follows from prayer.
    We pray because we are holy.
Holiness is not the result of kindness.
    We are kind because we are holy.
Holiness is not something that blossoms when we are
    courageous.
    We are courageous because we are holy.
Holiness is not the result of character building.
    We build character because we are holy.
Holiness is not a gift we obtain after a lifetime of service.
    We give a lifetime of service because we are holy.
Our holiness is God living in us, Emmanuel,
    and while it is true that holiness carries with it,
    both the cross and the Resurrection,
    it is more a gift than a reward.

7

JOY AND HOLINESS

"Do not be afraid, I bring you good tidings of great Joy."
(Lk 2:10)

In this chapter I would like to change pace and engage in a dialogue about holiness. Try to imagine that you are asking the questions.

Q: You imply that joy, love and holiness go together. What exactly is holiness? When do you know you're holy?

JC: You don't feel it, you know it. You know that God is the vine and you are one of the branches. His holiness flows through you. It is not a matter of having pious feelings. They may be comforting, but holiness is much more than piety. Believe that God is living in you; you will know that He is your holiness.

Mother Teresa was on her way to an airport once when a reporter called out to her, "Mother, some people say you're a living saint. What do you say about that?"

Without missing a beat she replied, *"You, sir, have to be holy in your position, just as you are, and I have to be holy in the position God has put me. So it is nothing extraordinary to be holy. Holiness is not the luxury of the pure. Holiness is a simple duty for you and me. We have been created for that."*

Her marvelous answer deflected the question without appearing to be boastful. She stated a simple fact. We are all called to be holy, and by virtue of the Holy Spirit living in us, we are indeed holy. This is what is meant by the term "the common holiness of the faithful."

The reporter asked a good question, but Mother refused to be drawn into self-analysis. He might have asked, "What is your definition of holiness, Mother?"

Her answer to this question would be just as simple. Holiness is God in us. Holiness is allowing God to use us as instruments of His love.

Of course, you and I know that some people, by the grace of God, are better instruments than others. The essential ingredient of holiness is the Holy Spirit.

Q: Where does the word holiness come from?

JC: It is derived from the Anglo-Saxon word "halig" or "hal" meaning whole and healthy. The English word "hale" (hale and hardy) comes from this root. Over the years it has acquired a religious significance coming to mean, "one who is spiritually healthy, whole, well-integrated." A person who is holy is aware of God's presence, in an unselfconscious way.

Consequently, there are more holy people than you might imagine. Since all those who are baptized have received the Holy Spirit, there are multitudes of holy people out there. Those who believe that Jesus is the Lord of their life, are holier than those who were merely baptized, but have no relationship with Jesus. Among those who do connect in an intimate way with the Lord, there are saints, and there are saints in training.

Jesus is the perfect model of holiness. Compared to Him we are all in training.

Q: That's the thing. I feel so inferior to any saint, not to mention Jesus Himself. How do I improve myself to become more holy?

JC: I know you really want to be holy just by the questions you ask. That thirst for knowledge is in itself a grace from God. Be happy. Your name is written in the Book of Heaven. It really is. Every baptized soul receives an indelible mark of the Holy Spirit. Accept Jesus as Lord, and stop worrying about it. Don't judge yourself harshly.

Q. Am I doing that?
JC: Yes, to some extent you are. Stop judging yourself that way. You have a spiritual inferiority complex. It's a common problem. Many of the saints had the same thing. To feel meek and humble of heart is a good thing, as long as you trust in the power of God residing in you.

St. Thérèse of Lisieux (1873-1897) dealt with her inferiority problem in a most creative way. She knew that compared to Jesus she was nothing and could do nothing, but she always had the good sense to rely on His power. She prayed with humility, but she had difficulty feeling love for one of the sisters in her community. She was ashamed of herself for this failure.

One day she got an inspiration in answer to prayer. It was a wonderful insight. She realized that she had to turn her problem over to the Lord. And so she began praying this way: *"Dear Lord, I will never be able to love her as you love her, but you Lord, living in me, can love her for me."* She just delegated the task to Jesus, and decided not to fret about it. Her weakness became her strength. She trusted the Lord and gave him the job of loving this sister for her, knowing He would make up for her lack.

God works with any raw material we care to offer Him. So stop trying to be holy and let Him do that for you.

Q: It seems too simple. You just can't go on doing what you've always done and delegate all your obligations. What if I did that with prayer? Could I just delegate prayer to Jesus? Prayer bores me.

JC: Everyone gets bored with prayer from time to time. However, we all need to pray every day. As far as always doing what you've always done, you will need to be honest with yourself. Change is part of growth. The maturing process takes time. A teenager may be a good person, but he or she is not fully mature. When it comes to prayer there is also a growth process.

I find that I have a natural desire to pray, but not on any precise schedule. I don't always feel like praying. I don't force myself to pray. I don't force feelings of any kind, but I do trust the Holy Spirit to pray within me. I open myself to the inspirations of the Spirit. I ask for guidance.

Writing this book is a prayer for me. I feel the Holy Spirit guiding me. I know I am in the presence of God as I write. I am happy to be a messenger of Joy.

There was a period in my life when I gave up meditating because I couldn't stand the boredom. I would doze off a lot. We all yearn for some response from God. During the dry spells, I simply felt that I was a failure at prayer. I believed in God, but I couldn't feel the spiritual consolations I wanted to feel.

When God is silent, as He always is, you are tempted to think that it's all in your imagination. Love presumes an object, a person to love, but when God is silent it seems like no one is listening. Once I learned that feelings are not facts in matters of faith, I began to make progress. Feelings had nothing to do with it. If I became bored, I just smiled at my blindness. God was with me in spite of feelings. I began to realize that I was praying all the time.

Without the benefit of an alarm clock, I was waking up in God's loving embrace. I turned to the teachings of Abbot John Chapman for help. I will tell you more about him in the next section on prayer. His simple definition of prayer made a big difference in my ability to understand this mystery of communicating with God.

"Pure prayer," he wrote, "is in the will to give yourself to

God." Each one of us can say yes or no to this proposition. Dull feelings and wild distractions are not an issue if you are of a mind to give yourself to God. You just give your bored self to God and relax. If crazy distractions come, you just laugh at them.

Gradually I came to see that my boredom was not a sign of failure at all. I learned that I didn't have to force feelings of any kind. It was normal to be bored. I learned to laugh at my boredom. I just gave it to God along with my distractions, and my feelings of dryness.

Now I find peace in the knowledge that I am praying, whether I have warm, cozy feelings or not.

Q: That's interesting. I'm going to try it. By the way, finish the story about St. Thérèse. Did she get any feedback from that sister on how it worked out?

JC: Strangely enough, after Thérèse died at age 24, that sister made this amazing statement, "I will miss her terribly. She always had a special affection for me, and I for her."

Q: That's awesome. St. Thérèse depended on God totally and He came through. She was canonized a saint in a relatively short amount of time, I'm told. Tell me, would you call a saint like her a sacred person once she is canonized? What is the difference between holy and sacred?

JC: The word "sacred" usually applies to things. The word "holy" applies to persons. Churches are sacred places. Church vestments are sometimes called sacred, but never holy. Only people are holy because they are filled with the Holy Spirit. The Scriptures are also called the sacred texts of the Bible. They contain the word of God, and they can transmit the fruits of the Holy Spirit to those who read them.

You can have holy thoughts. Your thoughts are important because they influence your moods and your actions. However, holiness is not merely a matter of the thoughts you think, though there is a direct connection. Holiness is God living in you, and your response to Him. Being happy with Him is the sign of a true saint.

Holiness is everyone's vocation.

Q: St. Paul suffered tremendously and was a great saint. Do you think he practiced everything he preached? Like rejoicing always, did he do that?

JC: Yes, of course. I think he was thoroughly committed to controlling his thoughts. He kept a virtual diary in the Acts of the Apostles where he tells us about the beatings he endured. We don't have a comprehensive record of his day-to-day inner struggles, but we see him encouraging the Churches every chance he gets to rejoice. In spite of persecutions, he wanted his followers to pick up their drooping spirits.

In spite of all he went through, he insisted on Joy: **"Rejoice always, and be grateful no matter what!"** That attitude became habitual. I think it was like a mantra for him. He recited it over and over again. Especially when he was down, he would say to himself: **"Rejoice always"** (1 Th 5:16). Those two words were like a battle cry for him, a way of reminding himself not to give in to self-pity.

It must have taken great courage to fight back the tears many times, and maybe he couldn't do it all the time, but he commanded himself to keep his sights high. If he fell down, he got right back up. His heavenly goal was always before him. He taught us how to put on the will to bear discomfort, and to rejoice in spite of feelings to the contrary.

Q: Is it really just a matter of will power?

JC: No, it's a matter of grace, which strengthens the will. The saints were all uniquely different, but they had one thing in common. They all prayed for the grace to do God's will, and to deal with life courageously. You get what you pray for. They put on the will to serve and love, and bear discomfort without complaint because they prayed for it. As a result they all experienced God's Joy. No one is 100% optimistic by nature, but they trusted the Lord, and they became optimists.

Q: I like that idea. I'm not too optimistic, but I want to be. Tell me again how prayer works. I have a brother who got into heavy debt. He went into a depression, and no one was able to reach him. He tells me all the time that God has abandoned him. Is there any way I can help him? What would you say to him?

JC: Sometimes those closest to you are the ones you are least able to help. When you're too close to people they tend to discount your wisdom. Pray that God will send someone to help your brother. If you can't help him yourself, don't think that your prayers are of no value. Trust me on this. Just pray for him, and somehow your prayers will be answered. If he shows any willingness at all, maybe you can even ask him to pray with you.

Q: I don't think anyone really gets that close to him. When he is depressed he's in another world. Do you know anything about depression?

JC: Not as much as I'd like to know. I do know this however. When a person is in a depression he or she should go for medical help. People in depression are often suffering from a chemical imbalance, and the right medicine can ease the emotional burden. The cause of the imbalance is part of the mystery of depression.

Actually there is chemical imbalance, which is no one's fault, and then there is a kind of depression a person doesn't have to have. Sometimes people bring on their own depression without realizing it. For instance, alcohol is a depressant. If your brother is a heavy drinker, he may be creating his own problem. No advice from anyone can change what he is doing to himself. The chemistry of his body is upside down if he drinks excessively.

Q: I don't think that's the problem. He is a social drinker, but I think it's more than that.

JC: OK, but you should know that any mind-altering substance taken into the body can be harmful and can lead to depression.

There are things people can do for themselves apart from taking medication. I dislike relying on any drugs. Obviously at times they may be necessary, and everyone should follow their doctor's orders, but it's better to stay drug free, as long as possible.

Having said that, it might be useful to take a look at the problem of repressed anger. People often deny that they are angry. They con themselves into thinking that it happened years ago, and they're over it. This type of thinking can be a form of denial. The person may never have gotten over the hurt. Repressed anger can cause a depression because it's like driving a car in neutral. As you rev the motor it heats up and begins to burn. When the gas is used up there is no power to move. In human terms the sheer energy taken to repress the anger is a loss of energy, which exhausts the person. They feel depleted and become miserable.

Praying for the grace to shed the anger can really help. It gives you perspective and makes you feel protected. Give your anger over to God. Walk away from the hurt, and eventually the power it holds over you will evaporate.

As for helping your brother, you should know that unless he asks for your help you won't be able to help him. All you can do is pray.

A depression will sometimes go as mysteriously as it came.

Maybe the person is trying to resolve some inner conflict, and hasn't yet figured out what to do. He or she may not want your help, so just be patient, and pray.

Depression is something like grief. Grief is terrible, but for most people it is relatively temporary. Some people make their grief last for thirty years. That is their deliberate choice. I do not recommend it. Depression sometimes goes away as mysteriously as it came.

Q: How can someone escape from depression?

JC: First, as I said, get medical attention. Many times the chemical imbalance can be corrected, but it also helps to understand that the will is at the core of the human personality. Your will may not be able to control the depression and make it go away. It's not the fault of the person who is depressed that they are in this state. However, there is a way of dealing with depression.

Emotions follow thoughts like thunder follows lightning. Positive thoughts produce positive emotions; negative thoughts produce bad feelings, which can lead to depression.

If a person feels trapped in a dangerous situation, and there is no apparent escape, the sheer frustration builds up and causes depression. The temptation to commit suicide can begin to haunt the victim. This is where medical help is critical. If your brother ever gets into that state call for help, and pray. Help will come.

On a less serious level, those who allow themselves to be filled with self-pity, are doing harm to themselves. It may not lead to a severe depression, but it can destroy their Joy. They tend to blame everything that happened to them on others. Every one of us has to take responsibility for our own thoughts and actions.

Self-pity is detrimental to your health. It's a kind of cancer of the soul. If you exaggerate your feelings of helplessness, and give in to the false belief that God doesn't care about you, things will go from bad to worse.

God is there for everyone who comes to Him for help, which means that feelings of helplessness should not lead to hopelessness. We can learn to cope with our distressed feelings. Emotions, in and of themselves, are not dangerous. A depression can be exceedingly distressing, but it will pass. It is only dangerous if you allow yourself to think you are in danger.

When the sun comes out the snow melts. You can find a way out of the darkness. You can pray for guidance. Remember that God knows all things. He is in total control over the entire universe. He loves you, and will guide you into the light.

Q: How do you think God brings about change in a person who is mentally or emotionally sick?

JC: All I know is that miracles do happen. God can draw good from evil. He knows exactly what you need before you ask, but you shouldn't make false assumptions about God when you pray. Give God credit for having a plan for you, and those whom you love. His plan is infinitely better than anything you might have had in mind. You may not see that right away, but in time it will become clear. With God all things are possible.

For instance, God may have an important task for your brother to perform in the future. It may be essential that he is alive to do some good that nobody else can do. The same is true for everyone of us. We cannot allow thoughts of suicide to enter our minds because each of us has to be ready to answer God's call when it comes.

There are so many heroes in human history who, at one point in their lives, were tempted to take their own lives. The world is better because they refused to give in to that temptation. They got through that dark night of the soul, and went on to glory.

In the present moment, when things get rough, we just have to tough it out. Keep the big picture in mind, and try to rely on God's grace.

Remember that feelings are not facts. Faith supplies you with knowledge that gives you supernatural facts. Here are a few: There is an all-powerful God; He loves you and He wants you to trust Him; He wants to give you Joy; He will work with you. Be patient when dark feelings come over you, or when you feel lost. In times of sickness remember that the Holy Spirit is closer to you than your own heartbeat. The fact that you have dark thoughts and feelings does not mean you are unprotected. The Holy Spirit wants you to rely on Him.

The Spirit awakens in us all kinds of feelings designed to bring us closer to Him. He even uses our negative vibes for good purpose, namely, to make us aware of our spiritual poverty.

Q: I know there is in me a longing for a better life. Is that something that comes from the Spirit?

JC: Yes. St. Augustine said, *"Our hearts are restless, Lord, until they rest in You."* Examine your own thoughts. A voice within may be speaking to you. I remember once being deeply upset about some opposition I was getting for trying to correct a situation. I suddenly heard a voice within me, telling me that I was upset because I was afraid of failing. I sat silently and thought about the truth of it. Then I heard, "But Jesus failed didn't He? He died like a common criminal."

Whether it was my own imagination or a voice from heaven I do not know, but it stopped me in my tracks. I learned to accept the fact that being unpopular or failing was the price one has to pay for virtue. Rejection often comes to those who do the right thing. When most people want you to shut up, and you keep protesting, they will get back at you. That's the price you may have to pay for following your conscience.

Jesus went through something far worse than any of us can

imagine. It eased my mind considerably to think of Him in that time of emotional upheaval.

Once I accepted failure as a good thing in this context, I was relieved of my fears, and Joy began to stir in my heart. The knowledge of God's love began to fill me. I was happy again.

It also comforted me to realize that the saints were confused and mixed up at times, just like the rest of us. At one time or another in their lives some of them were great sinners. They were all certainly human, and had their bad days, but eventually the stirrings of Joy came back to overpower their fear. Maybe they went through hell to get to that point, but they all found their Joy in the Lord. The important thing is that they did not let their doubts and fears sweep them away.

The Lord said, **"Fear is useless, what is needed is trust"** (Mk 5:36). We may never be entirely free of fear in this life, so the Holy Spirit continues to teach us to be brave. Even as we work to rid ourselves of needless fear and anxiety, we are loved. Trust the Lover within to guide you. It is in giving that we receive. Follow your own Inner Light in the way in which you will give of yourself. Your vocation is rooted in the desires of your heart. Once you find it, you will be able to open the doorway to happiness. God wants you to live in His Joy.

Part Two

PRAYING FOR JOY

Holiness is found in those who are struggling to regain their lives. They may have gone through hell. But once they decide to enter a recovery program, they submit to the God of their understanding and their lives turn around.

Since the members of Alcoholics Anonymous prefer to be left anonymous, I will not mention the name of the next writer. She is a grateful woman from Missouri who learned that God supplies power to the powerless, as soon as they turn their lives over to Him.

I was born a "Cradle Catholic" but my husband was not. He joined the Church a week before we were married which was June 15, 1946. We enjoyed a happy marriage with the exception of losing three children at birth. We were finally blessed with a healthy daughter on July 12, 1950. She has brought a lot of Joy into our lives.

In 1954 alcoholism entered our lives. My husband drank to excess often. I prayed over and over for God to help us. It seemed that my prayers would never be answered, until February 16, 1964 when my husband finally asked for help.

I called Alcoholics Anonymous. A very kind man named Bill invited us over to his home and told us all about the "Program." My husband started going to meetings, and still is a member today after 37 years.

I also joined a family program called Al-Anon. I am so very grateful that God saw fit to steer us in the direction of these two God-given programs. Our life is very full today going to meetings and conventions. My husband has had three heart attacks but is still able to carry the message of AA.

One of the ways AA is successful in changing lives is in giving the members a whole set of positive and constructive ideas to replace their negative thinking. Instead of sabotaging themselves, saying things like: "I'll never make it. I can't do it," they are trained to say, "With God's help I CAN do it. All I have to do is stay sober one day at a time."

With God all things are possible.

8

THE JOY OF FORGIVENESS

"So then, if you are bringing your offering to the altar,
and there you remember that your brother has something
against you, leave your offering before the altar, go and be
reconciled with your brother first, and then come
back and present your gift." (Mt 5:23)

Jesus proclaimed the coming of the Kingdom in His Sermon on the Mount. He took pains to set certain priorities. Before you begin praying make sure your heart is free from resentment. Hold no grudges. Get rid of your vindictiveness, and forgive your neighbor. Then come and offer your gift to God.

Jesus taught His disciples to adore, to obey, to seek, to forgive, and to ask for protection.

1. Adoration: **Our Father who art in heaven hallowed be Thy name;**
2. Obedience: **Thy Kingdom come, Thy will be done...**
3. Petition: **Give us this day our daily bread,**
4. Forgiveness: **Forgive us our trespasses as we forgive those who trespass against us.**
5. Protection: **Lead us not into temptation, but deliver us from evil.**

The importance of forgiveness cannot be overstated. God forgives us, and He made it clear that no one is excluded from

His mercy. So we must be ready to forgive one another. The liberating effect of forgiveness is enormous. Joy and relief follow immediately. The soul and spirit are released from the heavy weight of anger and resentment.

All of us need God's mercy and forgiveness, and all of us should be ready to give that gift to others. If you feel resentment so deeply that you can't forgive, then you must pray for the grace to forgive. The important thing is to ask for what you need to do God's will.

Jesus wants us to be reconciled with anyone toward whom we feel hostility. Before we offer our gift of self, He wants us to be purified and made joyful.

Therefore, if you want forgiveness from God, do not fail to forgive anyone who has offended you. The sheer logic of it is irrefutable.

If someone has offended you repeatedly, you will feel like striking back. How can you stop resenting that person? How many times must you forgive? Seven times? Jesus said, **"Forgive that person not seven, but seventy times seven times"** (Mt 18:22).

The number seven is one of those code words in the Scriptures. It means there is no limit to the number of times you must try to find in your heart a way to forgive. *"Forgiveness demonstrates to the world that love is more powerful than sin"* (John Paul II, *Rich in Mercy*, Vatican City, 1980).

The other side of the coin is to seek forgiveness when you are the one who has offended someone. You must repent if you want to restore Joy to your soul. *"To cut oneself off from Penance is to cut oneself off from an irreplaceable form of encounter with Christ"* (John Paul II, Address to U.S. Bishops, Vatican City, 1998).

The Parable of the Prodigal Son

No one should be afraid of asking for forgiveness. If you compare the love of God to the father's love for his son, in the parable of the Prodigal Son, you can see how easily God's mercy flows.

Then compare yourself to the prodigal son, who squandered his inheritance on loose living. His actions caused him misery to the point of starvation. When he returned to beg for mercy, his father saw him coming from afar, and ran to embrace him. The father then instructed his servants to prepare a feast to celebrate his son's return. So great was the father's love that he saw only the son, and not the folly of his son's sinfulness. We could easily call this the parable of the Merciful Father. It is a story which teaches many lessons.

We can learn that God will always forgive us if we repent. We can learn that God's mercy is limitless. The greater the sin, the happier is the Father upon our conversion.

There is another lesson in this parable. The older brother who had never gone astray resented the fact that his father was celebrating instead of being outraged at the return of his sinful brother. Having worked so faithfully, and for so long without a reward, he chafed at the spectacle of such a reunion. The idea of rewarding this brother, who had squandered his inheritance, disgusted him, so he stubbornly refused to attend the feast, expressing his resentment loud and clear.

His unforgiving spirit was certainly understandable, but he was terribly wrong. God expected better of him, and He expects better of us. All we can do to allay our confused emotions when we are not in harmony with God's will, is pray: **"Not my will but Yours be done, O Lord"** (Mt 26:39). God's ways are not our ways.

Pope John Paul II explains the obvious lesson succinctly: *"Let no one behave like the elder brother... forgive, and may the joy of forgiveness be stronger and greater than any resentment."*

"The joy of forgiveness" is what God wants for you. It will be better for your health, and for your family than anything your obstinate pride might conjure. There is an unspeakable joy connected to the act of forgiving. Letting go, and letting God handle the justice issue, releases you from the frustration, anger and resentment; the very emotions that will rise up to destroy you. Repressed anger is one of the most common causes of depression. Why not opt for joy?

In order to be free of the sadness of resentment, you have to forgive. If you are the one who has sinned you have to ask for forgiveness. If you have any responsibility for hurting another, you should have the courage to make amends by apologizing for your behavior. When you do, you can feel free to move on to a brighter future.

John Paul II surprised a number of people when he asked the whole Church, *"to make an examination of conscience for all those times in history when we departed from the spirit of Christ and His Gospel."* He did this in 1999 when he exhorted Catholics to prepare for the coming Jubilee year. The call to penance was an action that marked a clear shift away from the arrogance of the past, which so often characterized the attitude of Church leaders.

The Pope did not mention any specific failures, but he did refer indirectly to religious wars, and the execution of heretics. These were his exact words: *"Another painful chapter of history to which the sons and daughters of the Church must return with a spirit of repentance is that of the acquiescence given, especially in certain centuries, to intolerance and even the use of violence in the service of truth."*

He continued, *"The consideration of mitigating factors does not exonerate the Church from the obligation to express profound regret for the weaknesses of so many of her sons and daughters who sullied her face."* Such powerful words deserve our full attention.

In an earlier document entitled, "Message for Peace" (1997), the Pope insisted that offering and accepting forgiveness are essential conditions for authentic peace and joy. He admitted that forgiveness goes against human instincts, *"...but forgiveness,"* he insists, *"is inspired by the logic of love, that love which God has for people of every nation and for the whole human family."*

Forgiveness is an invitation to joy. Even though many may see it as sheer folly, the Church tries to be faithful to Jesus, proclaiming forgiveness to all people. The Gospels require us to ask for forgiveness as a way of showing confidence in God's infinite mercy and love.

From time to time throughout the year, and especially on Good Friday, the Pope spends time hearing confessions. Pilgrims come in droves to St. Peter's Basilica in Rome to confess their sins in a spirit of repentance. Those hearing confessions are ready and willing to forgive all those who are truly repentant, as a sign of Christ's mercy and power over sin.

"Whatever you bind on earth will be bound in heaven, whatever you loose on earth will be loosed in heaven" (Mt 16:19).

John Paul's most dramatic gesture of forgiveness took place when, in 1983, he publicly forgave, and asked for prayers for, his would-be assassin Ali Agca. The Pope's words on that occasion were: *"Pray for the brother who shot me, and whom I have sincerely forgiven."*

The attempted assassination had taken place in St. Peter's Square two years earlier. Ali was arrested and put in prison. Pope John Paul II went to visit him for the sole purpose of forgiving and being reconciled with him. Ali asked for his forgiveness, and the Holy Father gave it without hesitation.

CONFESSION

Telling God you are sorry for your sins, is one sure path to receiving His Divine Mercy. Why do we need to confess? Because there are times when the Lord wants us to. *"Confession is an act of honesty and courage; an act of entrusting ourselves to the mercy of a loving and forgiving God. It is an act of the prodigal son who returns to his father and is welcomed by him with the kiss of peace"* (John Paul II, San Antonio, Texas, 1987).

The distinctively Catholic understanding of Christian faith and forgiveness places an emphasis on the role of the Church, and the Sacrament of Penance in mediating salvation. Other Christian traditions insist that there is no absolute need to enter a confessional to obtain forgiveness from God, since His mercy is there for everyone who asks.

True, it is not absolutely necessary, but Jesus gave us a great gift when He spoke the words that established the Sacrament of Reconciliation: **"You are Peter, and on this rock I will build my Church.... Whose sins you shall forgive they are forgiven, and whose sins you shall retain they are retained"** (Mt 16:16).

This choice to forgive or retain implies that Peter would be in a position to know the difference. He would have to hear the sins to know who was genuinely sincere and who was not. The Apostles heard confessions from the beginning. The outdoor confessional goes back to the very first century.

Actually the only sin that is beyond forgiveness is the sin of an unrepentant sinner. For instance, if a person came to you and said, "I am truly sorry for murdering my oldest brother, but I am nevertheless planning to murder my youngest brother next month. I am doing this to secure my father's inheritance." Obviously he would have to be scolded, and denied absolution. There is no sincerity in him; no firm purpose of amendment. His confession is a fraud.

Jesus wanted us to be confronted by one appointed to this

task by the Church. The practice of going directly to God for forgiveness is commonplace, but it puts the entire burden of discernment on the sinner. Since so many sinners are in denial about what they do or fail to do, they exonerate themselves too quickly, and kill their own conscience in the process. This kind of self-delusion is abhorrent to the Lord.

Another example is the one about the thief who prays to God for protection, so that he won't be caught the next time he steals. He is living a lie, and is in a form of denial that dishonors him, and perpetuates the problem. The practice of going to confession on a regular basis makes you deal with reality. Your sins are an offense against God and neighbor. You must deal with them. Christ provided the confessional as a ministry of mercy for sinners, not to give men powers over others.

For two thousand years the Church has obeyed the words of Jesus calling us to confess our sins to the priests. They are specially trained for the task, and bound to secrecy. You don't have to be a Catholic to ask for the help of a priest. Find one whom you feel comfortable with and go to him. Confess your sins to the Lord. The confession can take place face to face, or in the privacy of a screened-off confessional. Either way it is designed to be a tribunal of mercy.

The secrecy of the confessional assures the penitent that no one will ever know what was discussed. Priests hear so many confessions that they are never shocked. They also have a knack of forgetting what they heard very quickly.

When they pray the words of absolution over the penitent, they know that Christ is acting through them. One formulary goes as follows: "May Our Lord Jesus Christ absolve you, and by His authority, I absolve you in the name of the Father, and of the Son and of the Holy Spirit. Amen." At the sound of these words, the penitent is assured that his or her sorrow for sin has been formally accepted.

The priest is acting as an instrument of God's forgiveness.

Before absolution is given, the priest assigns a penance, usually some prayers to be said. Once the penitent accepts the penance, he or she makes an act of contrition either from memory or from a prepared prayer card. As long as there is a firm purpose of amendment, a sincere desire to sin no more, the graces flow.

When the priest recites the prayer of absolution, he usually concludes the Sacrament of Reconciliation with the words, "Go in peace."

I want to stress that the "absolution" is Christ praying through the priest. In this way the Church mediates the power of Christ's forgiveness. Jesus alone has the authority to forgive, but He has delegated it for the good of souls. The priest conveys Divine Mercy in a way that is psychologically healing for all who take advantage of this sacrament.

Many polls have shown that over 75% of all those who visit psychiatrists or psychologists for reasons of emotional health, do so because of their deep, unresolved, feelings of guilt. Apparently it is not enough for them to pray to God alone. The privatization of forgiveness does not work for a lot of God's people. They are forgiven, but they don't seem to feel forgiven.

Recognizing this problem, there have been many ministers from the Episcopalian and Lutheran denominations who have erected confessionals in their churches.

They have come to see the confessional as a healing ministry. People have a need for some kind of ritual in these matters. Jesus knew this, and provided for it.

Pope John Paul II explains: *"It must be emphasized that the most precious result of the forgiveness obtained in the sacrament of Penance consists in reconciliation with God, which takes place in the inmost heart of the son who was lost and found again, which every penitent is. But it has to be added that this reconciliation with God leads to others, repairing the breaches caused by sin"* ("Reconciliation and Penance in the Mission of the Church Today," Vatican City, 1984).

To experience the joy that the Lord wants to give you, you must not only pray, but also forgive and seek forgiveness. That means you have to work through the issues of resentment and anger that plague your life. No one expects you to do this completely in an afternoon, or in a month, but if you want your joy to be full, you must begin the process.

Remember, the thoughts you think will affect your emotional life. Thoughts determine the way you feel. Depressing thoughts produce discouragement, whereas positive thoughts produce happy, optimistic feelings. Feelings in turn produce action. Your joy will depend in large part on the thoughts you allow yourself to think. Shed guilt at all costs.

If you dwell on angry, resentful and vindictive thoughts, your emotional life will be highly agitated and joyless. Joy will not return until you cleanse your mind of hostility. Even if you are in the right, and the other party is totally in the wrong, you must find a way to get beyond the emotional roadblock. Forgive if you hope to gain any level of peace and joy.

Forgive others, and confess your own sins. Do it quickly, and secure your own mental health.

How Do I Forgive When I Am Still Angry?

In order to forgive someone from the heart, you do not need to have good feelings toward that person. Forgiveness is not a feeling. If you are angry, and the other person doesn't give you the satisfaction of asking for forgiveness, it may seem impossible to forgive. Don't believe your feelings. With God all things are possible.

You don't wait until you feel like forgiving. You may never feel like it. That doesn't matter, God asks for forgiveness anyway. Do it for Him, and for yourself. The Lord asks you to forgive for good reason. He wants you to be healed, He wants you to have the fullness of Joy. How can you not forgive?

To forgive you just will it!

True forgiveness is in the will. Do not wait for warm cozy feelings to begin the process. Your feelings will catch up in time. Do it now. Be patient about the results. You give "forgiveness" before you feel like it. You "fore- give" the gift of forgiveness, before you feel good about it. Do it anyway.

In this way you show the Lord that you will not cling to your resentment like a dog with a bone. You drop it, and walk away. When bad feelings come back toward that person, say a short prayer for him or her. "My Jesus mercy. Have mercy on him, and mercy on me." You need help, and God will give it. Repeat your prayer over and over until the feelings subside, and they will.

In time you will actually forget why you were so angry in the first place. Forgiveness heals the soul. Let go, and let God.

Love Your Enemies

If you think you can't forgive your friends and relatives, how will you ever forgive your enemies? Obeying the Lord can challenge you to do things you would never think possible. There is one passage in Scripture that flies in the face of right reason. Jesus actually asks you to, **"Love your enemies, and do good to those who hate you"** (Mt 6:27).

Why would the Lord say such a thing? It doesn't make sense.

We have just lived through a nightmarish period of turmoil due to the atrocities of September 11, 2001, when murderous terrorists turned commercial airplanes into weapons of destruction. What more justification would one need for hating the culprits who planned and executed such a demonic act?

Our minds have been stunned by all the TV images of hate-filled zealots screaming "Death to all Americans." It's enough to make your blood boil. How does one process these emotions? Even if we wanted to forgive, how is it possible? This question has been asked and answered, but I will try again.

Jesus is the Way, the Truth and the Life. He answers such questions very directly: **"Learn of me for I am meek and humble of heart.... With man it is impossible, but with God, all things are possible"** (Mt 11:29; 19:26).

Once you admit that you are too enraged to love, much less forgive, then you are making progress. Turn immediately to the Lord for help.

He knows that your anger is justified. He doesn't ask you to deny your feelings. When He asks you to forgive, He is not saying: "What happened doesn't matter."

It does matter! He knows the evildoers must be stopped. But stopping them does not mean hating them. They may deserve our outrage, but they can't be allowed to turn us into hateful murderers. We have to pause to ask ourselves the question, why? Why does Jesus want us to forgive?

Because hate disqualifies a person from entering heaven, and He wants us with Him for all eternity. To become a child of the Light, one must live in harmony with God.

God is Unchanging Love. He causes the sun to rise and set on the good and bad alike. He wants us to love all His children, just as He does.

"If you love those who love you, what merit have you? Even sinners love those who love them. And if you do good only to those who do good to you, what merit have you?" (Mt 6:32, 33).

Once you accept the challenge, and understand that forgiveness is not a feeling, you can say, "Yes, I will forgive." Forgiveness is not in the feelings; it is in the will. The will has only one function: to say yes or no. Either you forgive the enemy, bad feelings included, or you do not.

Once you say, "Yes, Lord, I will obey you. I do forgive," the bad feelings will start to evaporate. It will take time, but they will recede. It's hard to believe for older Americans, but we now play baseball with the once hated enemy, the Japanese.

To truly forgive you have to surrender to God's power.

Sister Elizabeth of the Trinity once wrote: *"Love unites the soul with God; and the greater the love, the more it is centered in Him. When God's Love penetrates your soul's inmost depths, you become transformed into Christ."*

"Forgive them Father, for they know not what they do" (Lk 23:34). These words of Jesus spoken from the cross are there for us to ponder. He uttered them before his enemies asked for His mercy. He made excuses for them. Ignorance! They know not what they do.

Each and every one of us, with the help of God, can imitate Christ on the cross. We can learn to forgive our enemies, and even love them. Not all at once, but we can begin by praying for them.

The Joy of forgiveness is a sweet sign of our harmony with God's will. He asks us to forgive, so that our Joy may be full.

Father Paul Avallone, SDB, of Paterson, NJ, tells us how he ministered to a stranger.

My story begins in August 1990, on a train trip between Naples and Rome. I was returning from a short visit to some relatives living in a remote mountainous village south of Salerno.

Tired and a bit weary I settled in a window seat of the compartment and I began to doze when awakened by the call announcing the opening of the dining car — a welcome call! Making my way through several cars I arrived at the dining car and seated myself in a corner, eager for quiet and selfish isolation. God has his ways! Gradually the dining car began to fill up. Suddenly an elderly gentleman moved to the empty seat on my table. My false security was shattered!

"You are a Salesian priest," he said, before I could introduce myself. Surprised, I asked him how he knew — I had never met this man before. He simply answered, "By your smile I knew you were a Salesian, a son of Don Bosco." (St. John "Don" Bosco, a 19th century priest, was the founder of one of the largest religious orders in the Church. He devoted his life to the care of homeless boys, since he lost his father when he was two.)

I broadened my smile and gave a chuckle.

During dinner, my friend began to speak freely about his fear for the salvation of his soul: "Does God forgive? Is He merciful? Can I be sure about saving my soul?" The man was sincere and I could sense his fear and anxiety. From the general tone of our conversation I realized that he was a good man.

Our dialogue continued during the entire trip. His one focus was the MERCY of God. The poor man was seeking assurance that the mercy of God would be with him when he was called to eternity. I relied heavily on my theological background and recalled many scriptural passages assuring him of God's infinite mercy. I told him of the many saints who repented their sins, and who are now with God. Gradually he became more assured.

By now we were entering Rome and just before the train came to a stop my friend shook my hand warmly and said three kind words: "Thank you, Padre." I assured him that within a half-hour I would be celebrating Mass for him in the Sacred Heart Basilica.

Father Avallone kept up a correspondence with him for two years after he returned to the States, and said, "Hopefully, one day I will greet him in paradise."

9

THE JOY OF JESUS

"There will be more rejoicing in heaven over one lost
sheep who returns to God, than over ninety-nine
who have never strayed." (Lk 15:7)

In Chapter 10 of Luke's Gospel Jesus sent the Seventy-two out
on a mission. They were to go ahead of Him, two by two, to
every town. He would soon follow after they prepared the way
for Him. **"There's a great harvest,"** He said, **"but few workers
to gather it in.... I am sending you like lambs among wolves....
Heal the sick and tell the people the Kingdom of God is near."**

When they returned they were happy. Jesus, the Lord of
history, had given them powers they never dreamed of, and the
Holy Spirit radiated from them. Jesus had asked them to go out
on the highways and byways seeking the lost souls, and healing
the sick in His name. When they returned rejoicing, they said:
**"Lord, even the demons obeyed us when we commanded them
in your name."**

Here is the sentence that gives us a glimpse of the Lord's
inner life, **"Jesus was filled with joy by the Holy Spirit."** Jesus
expresses His delight: **"Oh Father thank you because you have
shown to the unlearned what you have hidden from the wise
and learned. Yes, Father, this was done by your own choice and
pleasure."**

He turned to His disciples and said, **"How happy you are

to see the things you see! For I tell you, many prophets and kings wanted to see what you see, but they could not, and hear what you hear, but they did not" (Lk 10:21-23).

In these passages we see Jesus rejoicing over His Father's intervention in the lives of His followers. Jesus was thrilled when His disciples obeyed Him, by allowing the Father's power to work through them. They went out to spread the Good News, and even the demons obeyed them. Jesus could not have been more delighted. He wants us to go forth as well. He wants us to proclaim the Kingdom. It pleases Him immensely when we obey by reaching out to the world.

The Apostles rejoiced a bit too much it seems, because Jesus decided to give them a little reality therapy: "Do not be glad because the evil spirits obey you; rather, be glad because your names are written in heaven" (Lk 10:20).

Ponder those words. Jesus does not want us to be too happy over the good we accomplish lest we get puffed up with our own importance. "When you have done all you have been commanded, say, 'We are unprofitable servants; we have only done our basic duty'" (Lk 17:10).

Look deeper at why Jesus wants you to rejoice. You have been chosen, and your name has been written in the Book of Life.

When people receive awards and honorary degrees, they feel good about themselves. They know they have done something outstanding, but Jesus says, "Don't be overly impressed with yourself."

True Joy come from recognizing the Divine Source of all you accomplish.

The Joy of Jesus arises from His union with the Holy Spirit and the Father. This union is the life of the Trinity within Him. It is the cause of our Joy as well. How wonderful it is to know that we have the Indwelling Trinity guiding us. All baptized people who love the Lord can take delight in their status as members of the Mystical Body of Christ.

When we attain salvation in heaven, we will experience what is called the Beatific Vision, which is far beyond anything we have ever experienced in this world. **"Eyes have not seen nor ears heard..."** (1 Cor 2:9).

Occasionally God gives us a glimpse of heaven in this world. It comes to those who become carriers of the Good News of the Gospel. Remember when He asked Peter the question, **"Do you love me?"** Three times he asked it, and three times Peter answered, **"Yes, Lord, you know that I love you."**

Jesus responded three times, **"Feed my lambs... feed my lambs... feed my little sheep"** (Jn 21:15-17). Jesus invited him to share His Joy with others. By getting the message out He wanted to reach His lost children. No one is to be left out of His love. He wanted people to know that however imperfect they may be, they can attain a high degree of intimacy with Him simply by asking for it.

A personal, prayerful relationship with the Lord will put you in touch with the mother lode of Joy. God wants to share Himself with you.

The Joy of Jesus is rooted in His union with the Father and the Holy Spirit, and in His love for each of us, He wants us to be part of that Love relationship.

On the night before He died, Jesus told His disciples, and indirectly all of us, that He wanted to give us the fullness of His Joy. He encouraged us to stay close to Him, **"Abide in me, and I will abide in you"** (Jn 15:4). By remaining in Him we will touch His Joy. Listen to His greatest sermon.

The Sermon on the Mount

The heart of Christ's Good News is found in the Eight Be-atitudes, which make up the core of His Sermon on the Mount. You can find them in Matthew 5:3-12, and in Luke 6:20-23.

"Blessed are the poor in spirit, for theirs is the Kingdom of Heaven." The word "Blessed" is translated in the Jerusalem Bible this way: **"How happy are you who are poor; for yours is the Kingdom of God."**

The French translation is even more emphatic than **"Blessed are the poor in spirit."** Their word for Blessed is *"bienheureux,"* which means very happy. Here is how it would look if we followed the French translation.

> **Very happy are the meek, for they shall possess the earth.**
> **Very happy are they who mourn, for they shall be comforted.**
> **Very happy are they who hunger and thirst for justice, for they shall be satisfied.**
> **Very happy are the merciful, for they shall obtain mercy.**
> **Very happy are the clean of heart, for they shall see God.**
> **Very happy are the peacemakers, for they shall be called the children of God.**
> **Very happy are they who suffer persecution for justice' sake, for theirs is the Kingdom of Heaven.**
> **Very happy are you when people hate you, drive you out, abuse you, denounce your name as criminal, on account of the Son of Man. Rejoice when that day comes, and dance for Joy, for then your reward will be great in heaven.**

It becomes immediately apparent that Jesus came with a message so radical that it turned the tables upside down on all our worldly presuppositions. How could a mourner be considered very happy? How could a prisoner who is unjustly arrested be filled with joy?

No way, just the opposite would be true. These people would feel anything but happy. The lepers heard this message, and were confused. They were outcasts. Everyone, including the Temple priests, considered them to be under God's condemnation. As defiled outcasts they couldn't even come to the Temple to be purified.

Jesus said, "NO!" He rejected that merciless interpretation, and proceeded to set the record straight. He came to fulfill the law. Imagine the astonishment of the lepers when Jesus, full of enthusiasm, came to tell them that they were not cursed by God, but blessed.

Their sickness, and their misery was not from God, nor was it His will for them. Far from it. Jesus said they should take delight in the fact that they were highly favored by God. **"Be very happy,"** he insisted.

How fantastic it must have been for them to learn that they are God's beloved when all along they felt like condemned rejects. Did they all believe Him? At first, probably not. How could they swallow it? But according to Scripture many did, and they experienced a true liberation.

The downtrodden are ignored, stepped on, and walked over. They do not feel happy. When life has always been unfair to you, can you imagine what a gift it must be to learn that true justice will triumph in your life? This is a message we need to take to our hearts. We must be among those who believe the Good News from the depth of our souls. God favors us. He tells us that those who persecute us are but a passing shadow. To believe this message of Joy you have to be humble.

Jesus said, **"Learn from me for I am meek and humble of heart"** (Mt 11:29). He saw His power as coming from above. He is likewise pleased with those who have the same vision. Depend entirely on Him for your strength. Do not be egotistical. Self-inflated people try to take all the credit. They tend to use people to satisfy their own needs, but they end up despised and scorned.

Happy are the meek. They see themselves accurately. They are free from egotistical posturing. This puts them under God's protection. The braggarts are out there on their own.

If you are merciful, you will receive mercy. This is good to know. When you need mercy, as we all do, it's nice to know that you have assurances of receiving it. Being merciful is a form of insurance. We pay the premium every day, because we need mercy every day. We give in order to receive.

In the Eight Beatitudes Jesus teaches us how to be happy.

It is almost too good to be true, isn't it? And yet it is true. It is the Good News of the Gospel. God is all about love and mercy, not legalism. The law considered the lepers to be moral outcasts, but Jesus told them to laugh at the law and rejoice because God favored them. What a monumental difference in interpreting the mind of God. The Joy of Jesus was in giving Joy.

Once you know these truths, you begin to realize that Joy is a choice. It is a gift first, but if you accept the gift, which is a choice, you control your own inner life. Your soul rejoices and your spirit soars.

Since the Lord came to bring Joy, there is no need to be afraid of God. If you are of good will, there is no need to re-proach yourself. In fact it would be better if you didn't judge yourself at all. Learn to be your own best friend.

Jesus said, **"Let the little children come to me"** (Lk 18:16). He invites the rich and poor alike to believe in Divine Providence, and summon up a spirit of optimism. Cancel the first sign of panic. Say "no" to fear, and say "yes" to Jesus. You are not in danger when you implore His help. The Spirit will guide you gently on what to do.

When you rely on your faith instead of your feelings, you can deal with all your nervous symptoms. There will be crosses in your life, but you don't have to make them any worse. Laugh at yourself for not believing the spiritual wisdom of the Sermon on the Mount, for not trusting the Lord who has promised to protect you, and guide you.

Perhaps the most difficult Beatitude to grasp is the final one: **"Blessed are they who are persecuted for my sake."** How can persecution be a sign of blessing? God knows we will be afraid many times in our lives, especially if we are persecuted. How can we come to know that His special favor rests on us even in the worst of times?

This is a matter of blind faith. Actually there is no other kind. Faith is blind trust. It is never easy to understand the truths we believe. However, the Lord wants us to count ourselves blessed, even when a malicious enemy is out to hurt us.

If a terrorist wanted to kill you simply because you are a Christian, Jesus says to count it a blessing. Is this possible? Yes, of course! We have thousands of martyrs down through history who were just as frightened as you, and who are now living in glory.

Be aware of God's loving Presence. The Holy Spirit is living within you. Rejoice whether you feel joy or not. Trust that God will come through for you.

I'd like to share a story with you. A scary but wonderful thing happened to me when I was marching in Selma, Alabama during the racial conflicts there in 1965. I was the president and founder of a local chapter of the Catholic Interracial Council at the time when we learned that a Unitarian minister, a peaceful protestor, had been murdered by "red necks" in Selma a week earlier. There was a national outcry. A few of us decided to go to Alabama in order to stand in solidarity with people of all faiths, in order to protest the injustices being done there.

When we got to Selma and went to the compound where

we were to be confined, a group of "red necks" were milling around with bats in their hands, taunting the new arrivals. They dared us to come out of the compound where we were told to remain under police protection. We were relatively safe as long as we stayed put, but the police were not always visible and we didn't know what would happen in the middle of the night if any of the Klansmen broke through.

They were members of the Ku Klux Klan, but were not in their white robes. It was a frightening experience. During the day they spewed insults at us. I was in a group that had many local black children and their parents. They were mostly Baptists. There were a few other priests, some nuns in habit, and a few Protestant ministers, and many college kids in the compound.

As we stood facing the Klansmen, at a distance of 15 feet or so, separated only by an invisible line, I wondered what would happen next. Somehow in the midst of all the confusion, I felt a warm glow. It was a joyful feeling. I was afraid, but I was also deeply contented.

This spirit of gladness stayed with me for several days. Granted, I was young and idealistic; perhaps it was the euphoria of youth, but I actually felt joyful about the fact that I might be martyred for a good cause. The Joy lingered for a long time. I remember it vaguely, but no longer feel it as I once did.

I'm not so sure how I would act in the same circumstances today. I would probably be a lot more prudent, maybe I would find an excuse for not going to Alabama. Who knows? What I do know is that the Holy Spirit was urging me forcefully to get involved. I was demonstrating to help the local African-American community secure equal justice under the law regarding voter registration, and the right to vote.

They were Americans who were virtually denied the right to vote by the scare tactics of the local politicians, and the culture of fear that surrounded their actions. It was a disgrace to realize that Americans in 1965 were still getting murdered in the South for standing up to the Ku Klux Klan.

I felt Joy because I was part of something great. I faced my fears, and by the grace of God felt courage and inner peace. God was right there with me.

They say that the early martyrs sang joyfully just before they were led to their deaths. I think I understand how that is possible. The Joy is directly given from above. By the grace of God we learn to control our fears, and live joyfully because of the knowledge of His love.

Enjoy your precious life!

Dismiss fear as fast as you can. Cast away the unhappiness that surrounds fear. Choose Life and choose Joy.

Sue Kluwe from Mason City, Iowa did just that. Here is her story.

In 1992 at the age of 51, I was faced with brain surgery to control and reduce epileptic seizures. I was petrified, yet the night before surgery I saw a priest and the day of surgery I put all my faith in God, and the doctors whom God would be guiding. The surgery was a success and I'm seizure free at age 60.

My mainstays have been prayer *and lots of it. God and I had many talks and walks together. Not that we didn't before, but I found out how 'special' a friend He was at that time.*

Without God in our lives we'd be like old ships without a rudder. Everybody has a place that's very special in this world. That place for me was Church choir (I'm Catholic).

When a lead position just was not in the cards, the director said, "We need someone to sing melody with the congregation." I was suddenly in seventh heaven, knowing I was needed by someone, somewhere. So by now it really didn't matter so much not being a leader. I was a happy follower.

So God has truly shown me how I am so very important in so many ways.

We all go through terrible moments in life. How wonderful it is to trust God and live joyfully.

10

FRESHEN YOUR PRAYER WITH JOY

"In praying, do not babble on as the Gentiles do; for they think
that by saying a great deal they will be heard. Your Father knows
what you need before you ask Him" (Mt 6:7).

God wants you to be joyful. Go to Him with the confidence of
a happy child, and trust His love at all times. Since God's love
and joy go hand in hand, we ought to lift up our hearts joyfully,
giving thanks. There is no need to babble.

What would happen if you decided to please the Lord by
being cheerful, rather than worrisome, when you pray? What
changes would you make? Would you relax more? When you
stand before God you know that He knows your needs before
you ask. Since you don't have to force feelings of any kind,
wouldn't it be nice if you simply calmed yourself, and decided
to be happy in His presence?

Many people have not been loved well in their lives. Their
basic human needs have not been met. They yearn for validation, acceptance, recognition, and affirmation. With this kind
of background it is virtually impossible for them to pray joyfully, unless they make a conscious effort to change.

With God's help this change is possible. Prayer time is a
time to practice the art of being joyful. The gift of Joy comes
from God, but you can anticipate His generosity. You can cheerfully accept the Joy that comes from the knowledge of His love.

Smile before you do anything else when you come to pray. The saints had the ability to rise above the character traits that held them back in the beginning of their struggle. Billions of people have overcome their childhood immaturity and gone on to great holiness.

The early slaves suffered miserably, and yet they kept their spirit of Joy alive. They contributed so much of the joyful music we now call jazz. Their secret was in their will to hold on to their dignity and their Joy.

They deliberately willed to be joyful in order to keep their slave masters from crushing them. All the joy in their spontaneous music came from the soul. It was not merely from their musical talents, but also from their holy determination to prevail over misery. They proved that Joy can, and often does, prevail over sorrow.

Persecuted people down through history haven proven that the human spirit is indomitable. So many of them have risen like the phoenix from the ashes, and so can you.

Freshen your prayer with Joy. This is not a suggestion; it is an imperative if you want to be a more joyful person. I think it is a Christian duty to proclaim Joy to the world. Dorothy Day called it the "duty of delight." Since we know that God wants to give us the fullness of Joy for all eternity, doesn't it follow that He wants us to experience His Joy here and now?

Trust Him and be glad in His presence. Most people miss the importance of this choosing to be a person of Joy. They do not think there is much to rejoice over, but that is self-sabotage, which is precisely the problem. Tunnel vision can blind one to the splendor of life.

Granted, life is difficult. We easily grow weary of the burdens and sorrows that befall us, but the important thing to remember is that we have the power to choose. The Joy we want and need will not flow unless we invite it into our hearts. We need to draw Joy forth from the living God. He abides in us.

"**The Joy of the Lord is our strength**" (Ne 8:10).

In order to enter the Joy of the Lord, all you have to do is knock. "**Knock and the door will be opened**" (Mt 7:7). To find Joy you must ask for Joy, and little Joys will come. Keep your eyes open for them, and they will lift up your spirit.

Suppose you are not in the mood to pray. The spiritual masters say you should not force feelings, but you should turn to God briefly and tell Him about your feelings. Just laugh at yourself when you feel nothing. There is a certain peace that comes from just knowing you are free. It doesn't matter. When you know by faith that you are in the presence of Infinite Joy, you can relax and just be there, without "praying." Being there is the best kind of prayer.

Give your bad mood over to Him, and gradually your mood will change. You only have to smile when you come into His presence, and He will do the rest. Keep your prayer personal. Base it on your unique personality. Don't try to imitate anyone else, not even any one of the saints. They did it their way, you must do it your way. Explore your own path to God. Whether you use a prayer book or not is irrelevant, just remind yourself to smile, and be still before the Lord. Give yourself to God as best you can.

The technique you use is not important, as long as you are grateful. Joy and gratitude are also two sides of the same coin. A simple smile will help to put you on the right path.

I am going to give you some ideas based on the writings of Abbot John Chapman. He was an English Benedictine Abbot who was an early Scripture scholar. He died in 1931, but he left this rich legacy on prayer.

Begin by praying as you can, not as you cannot. You do this by taking yourself where you find yourself. If you are angry about something don't try to become peaceful before you pray. Just bring your anger to Him. Be yourself. The only thing you have to give is yourself, and that is precisely what He wants.

Here are the steps to pure prayer:

- Stop everything else, and listen to your own breathing.
- Enjoy the inner quiet, and ignore the noise around you.
- Do not force feelings of any kind.
- When distractions come, just laugh at them.
- Pure prayer is not in the feelings, or the thoughts.
- Don't worry about your distractions; wave them away as you would a fly.
- Pure prayer is in the will.
- **Pure prayer is in your sincere intention and will to give yourself to God**.
- Simply keep giving yourself to God as best you can.
- Minimize your self-consciousness, and think of God's love.
- If your prayer is imperfect, accept it as such. God wants you, not perfection.
- If you feel stupid and speechless then offer God your stupidity.
- Do not try to be successful at prayer. God will do that for you.
- Delegate your desire to succeed at prayer to God Himself.
- Pray for the grace to want what God wants.
- Try with the highest part of your soul to trust God's mercy.
- Continue to relax your body, mind and soul.
- Enjoy the Lord in silence, and trust yourself to His mercy.
- Be happy bathing in His love.
- Always remember: *The only way to pray well is to pray often.*

Do not assume that God has to be told what you need. He knows your real needs before you ask. Try to be more concerned about pleasing Him. He wants your love, whether it is offered in joyful, public worship with your brothers and sisters, or alone behind closed doors. Either way He loves a cheerful giver.

Prayer and Service

Mother Teresa of Calcutta used to tell her sisters that the Lord Jesus comes to us in many distressing disguises. She prayed as a contemplative and drew forth God's Joy in order to give it to those most in need.

The poor and the hungry are not always pretty to look at, but Jesus is there, hidden in their distress. **"What you do for the least of my brethren you do for me"** (Mt 25:40).

Try to see the connection between prayer, contemplation and loving service. To love God living in the least among us is the great challenge of Christianity.

Prayer gives us the eyes, which enable us to see the face of God in the most unlikely places. We should try to pray well. But according to Abbot John Chapman, the only way to pray well is to pray often.

Prayer is essentially a meeting of the minds. It is more a spiritual communion than a list of petitions, though petitions are necessary too. There is no need to plead or argue with God. Simply ask Him to help those whom you love. Ask Him to deliver you from confusion, doubt and fear. He will answer you. Go for a long walk with Him, and pray; or just visit with Him quietly.

An Exercise of Silent Prayer

Prayer is an intimate, personal contact with the Almighty. Approach Him with respect and trust. Acknowledge that He is all Powerful, and you are powerless. Admit that He has a good and worthy plan for your life, and believe that it will unfold in time.

Express your deepest needs to Him. I'd like you to pause for a moment and put yourself in the presence of God. Imagine

that He is speaking directly to you. Think of Him as your special Advocate and intimate source of solace.

> **You do not have to be clever to please Me; all you have to
> do is want to love Me.** (Absorb the Joy of knowing that
> God is listening to you.)
>
> **Just speak to Me as you would to anyone of whom you are
> very fond.** (He is inviting you to intimacy.)
>
> **Are there people you want to pray for? Say their names to
> Me, and ask of Me as much as you like. I know all their
> needs, but I want you to show your love for them and Me
> by trusting Me. Give Me time to do what I know is best.**
> (You have a helpmate, a friend you can trust. Enjoy this
> awareness.)
>
> **Tell Me about the poor, the sick, and the sinners, and if you
> have lost the friendship or affection of anyone, tell Me
> about it.** (Love enfolds you, and your concerns are being
> respected.)
>
> **Is there anything you want for your soul?** (Ask for Joy, and
> smile.)
>
> **If you like, you can write out a long list of all your needs,
> and come and read it to Me.** (You are not alone; ask and
> you will receive. Is this not a reason to rejoice?)
>
> **Tell Me the things you feel guilty about. I will forgive you if
> you will accept My forgiveness.** (Say, "Yes, Lord, I will.")
>
> **Just tell Me about your pride, your touchiness, self-
> centeredness, meanness and laziness. I will love you in
> spite of these. Do not be ashamed, there are many saints
> in heaven who had the same faults as you; they prayed to
> Me and little by little, their faults were corrected.** (The pa-
> tience of God is infinite. Your past faults and failings mean
> nothing to Him, when you seek His forgiveness and rest
> joyfully in His arms.)
>
> **Do not hesitate to ask Me for blessings for the body and**

mind; for health, memory, and success. I can give everything, and I always do give everything you need to make your soul holier if you truly want it. (Speak up, pray for holiness and joy.)

What is it that you want today? Tell Me, for I long to do you good. What are your plans? Tell Me about them. Is there anyone you want to please? What do you want Me to do for them? What are your worries? Who has caused you pain? Tell Me all about it, and add that you will forgive and be kind to her or him, and I will bless you. (What a joy it is to be recognized, appreciated and affirmed by the King of Kings.)

Are you afraid of anything? Have you any tormenting, unreasonable fears? Trust yourself to Me. I am here. I see everything. I will not leave you. (Do not be afraid in the presence of Supreme Love.)

Have you no joys to tell Me about? Why do you not share your happiness with Me? (It pleases the Lord when you are joyful because of the knowledge of His love.)

Tell Me what has happened since yesterday to cheer and comfort you. Whatever it was, however big, however small, I prepared it. Show Me your gratitude and thank Me. (Imagine that God prepares your soul for joy, and offers countless little blessings to cheer your spirit.)

Are temptations bearing heavily upon you? Yielding to temptations always disturbs the peace of your soul. Ask Me, and I will help you overcome them. (There are no habits or inclinations that cannot be redeemed in His strength. Aim for holiness.)

Well, go along now. Get on with your work or play or other interests. Try to be quieter, humbler, more submissive, kinder; and come back soon and bring Me a more devoted heart. Tomorrow I shall have more blessings for you.

Visiting with your Lover can change your emotional state. Try repeating this experience once a day. You will grow in spiritual Joy, and you will project a more joyful image.

Once you feel comfortable in God's love, you can write your own prayer, and memorize it. *"Dear Lord, I know that You know what I need before I ask, but I am concerned about my present problem… (add here your particular needs). Remove my faults that I may serve You joyfully. Give me a grateful heart. Help me to forgive others as well as myself. Grant me that peace of soul, which the world cannot give, and help me to present a joyful presence to those I meet this day."*

St. Paul's great advice needs repeating: **"Rejoice always, and in all circumstances give thanks to the Lord, for this is the will of God for you in Christ Jesus"** (1 Th 5:16).

You can learn to rejoice, in spite of your feelings. Joy is in the will not the feelings. The reason for being joyful is God, and He is always present, no matter what you might be feeling at any given moment. "Rejoicing" is a way of practicing mind over matter.

Act the way you want to be, and soon you'll be the way you act.

If you want to be a joyful person, then act like one.

THE TRAGEDY OF SEPTEMBER 11, 2001

> On Sept. 11, 2001
> 36,000 children worldwide died of hunger.
> Where did this take place? In poor countries.
> News stories: none.
> Newspaper articles: none.
> Military alerts: none.
> Presidential proclamations: none.
> Messages of solidarity: none.
> Minutes of silence: none.
> Homage to innocent children: none.

The point is simple: we forget so many good people who are in pain. Being a good steward is a way of offsetting this problem.

11

JOY, PRAYER, AND STEWARDSHIP

"As each one has received gifts, use them to serve one another as good stewards of God's various graces." (1 P 4:10)

A disciple is not only a follower of Christ, but also a good steward.

It is your vocation, therefore, to use your gifts, talents, and your treasures in a responsible way. This is very important. The Lord has loaned you these gifts. He wants you to enjoy them. And He also wants you return them with interest.

Returning your gifts to God joyfully, can be an exhilarating life. This is not exclusively about payback, though we do have a debt to pay; it is also about giving glory to God and becoming fully alive.

Being a good steward brings about a state of self-respect and Joy.

You have been created to be a good steward, a channel of love. It is in giving to those in need that you will receive your happiest moments. Freshen your prayer with Joy, and then joyfully communicate God's love to everyone you meet. That's what a good steward does. When you take responsibility for using your gifts and talents well, you are a true disciple.

As the recipient and caretaker of God's bounty, you are accountable for the way you use your gifts. Use them intelligently, and you will bear good fruit. When you arrive at the pearly gates, you will still have to say, "I am an unprofitable servant," but the Lord will be pleased because you helped those He loved the most. In fact He depended on you to lessen their misery.

In the end, you can joyfully offer the homage of your entire life.

WE REAP WHAT WE SOW

Here is an old spiritual maxim: the only thing you can take with you when you enter the next world is what you gave away during your time on earth. Your talents and your treasures are only loaned to you in order to test your level of love. God wants to see how well you perform once you know what He expects of you.

Remember the parable of Lazarus and the rich man (Lk 16:19). When Lazarus the beggar arrived in heaven, the rich man was shocked to find himself shut out. He pleaded with God to be allowed to enter, but there was no way to cross over. God simply said, "You should have taken pity on Lazarus in your lifetime."

Had he done that, things would have been very different. Jesus gives us fair warning. The lesson may be frightening at first glance, but there is really nothing to fear. If you are open to good advice, a word to the wise is sufficient. **"Do not fear…. My yoke is easy, my burden light,"** says the Lord (Mt 14:27; 11:30).

A thoughtful person will begin to understand that the gift of Joy is there for the taking. To understand the concept of stewardship, listen to the Lord and control your negative thoughts.

A personal commitment to the Lord includes a willingness to be generous with your time, your talents, and your treasures. The way to the fullness of joy is through responsible stewardship. This doesn't mean that we are saved by "works." Jesus died on the cross to save us; that has already been done. Now He asks us to be good stewards.

FUNDAMENTALISTS

Fundamentalist Christians are our brothers and sisters in Christ. I love them for their zeal, but they have a contrived understanding of Scripture, always insisting on the literal interpretation.

For instance, they don't really believe that Herod had a tail and four legs even though Jesus called him a fox. They know it is only a metaphor.

They don't really think that the Lord wants them to cut off their right hand if it offends Him. Jesus told us to do that, but they know He was using hyperbole.

They know that metaphorical, figurative, and allegorical language is used throughout Holy Scripture. Jonah in the belly of a whale was not literal history. They know that, but they still insist on the literal interpretation. They only do this when it suits them, however. Then they badger people who do not agree with them.

It isn't really honest. Their literalism makes them exceedingly judgmental. The words of Jesus, **"Judge not that you be not judged"** (Mt 7:1), are disregarded.

Fundamentalists maintain that Catholics are not saved, because they are not "born again." They insist on the idea of accepting Jesus as Lord, and ignore the fact that Catholics must be baptized, and then confirmed when they come of age through the Sacrament of Confirmation. Catholics do accept Jesus as Lord.

I remember the statement of a TV Evangelist who said, "Mother Teresa isn't saved because good works can never save anyone." The implication was that she never accepted Jesus as

Lord. Unbelievable! Of course, she accepted Him. She lived and died serving Him in the least of the brethren. The idea behind this insult is the false belief that Catholics think they are saved by acts alone.

Nonsense! Catholics have never believed that actions alone will save them. However, they know that Jesus definitely wants His followers to get involved in helping others. In a world filled with injustice and suffering, He wants us to be active.

Fundamentalists are blind to the social Gospel. They even scorn it. Jesus was very definite about the importance of social action: **"Woe to you, for when I was hungry you did not give me to eat.... I tell you solemnly, insofar as you neglected to do this to one of the least of these, you neglected to do it to me.... Go away to eternal punishment"** (Mt 25:46). Accepting Jesus as Lord is not enough; He wants obedience.

"Why do you call me, 'Lord, Lord,' and do not do what my Father in heaven wants you to do?" (Mt 7:21). Fundamentalists have a lot to answer for in their self-righteous attitude.

They like to jar Catholics with loaded questions like "Where in the Bible does it say there is a Purgatory?"

Many Christian words are not in the Bible. The words Easter and Christmas are not in the Bible. Does this make them unbiblical? The important thing is the concept that the words express.

Fundamentalists believe that either you're saved, or you're cast into hell. They make no provision that a person who was a murderous felon his entire life, might make a deathbed acceptance of the Lord out of fear of hell. Is he on the same level as Billy Graham when he meets God? It defies reason.

The idea of purgatory is biblical. It goes back to the Old Testament. **"They begged prayerfully that the sins of those who had fallen might be fully blotted out.... For if we had not expected the fallen to rise again, it would have been superfluous** and foolish to pray for the dead, whereas in fact it is... holy and devout" (2 M 12:42, 44-45).

Why would this be true if a man is going straight to hell for his sins? Why would the sacred texts say it is a holy thing to pray for him?

Fundamentalists may be sincere, but their beliefs are misguided. They are disruptive and shallow. By minimizing the importance of charity, which Jesus emphatically required, they teach serious errors to well-meaning disciples. This won't help them when they meet God face to face.

They never stop to think that on judgment day the Lord might say to them, "Just because you called me Lord, doesn't mean you did what I wanted you to do."

Pray for Fundamentalists. They need enlightenment.

The Catholic Church may be far from perfect. We admit we are the sinful people of God. But the Church teaches us to believe **all** the words of Jesus, not just a few isolated sentences like, "Unless you are born again... you will not be saved." This is true, but alone it is an incomplete synthesis of Christ's teaching.

Catholics who have abandoned the Church, and given up the Blessed Eucharist for the Fundamentalists' bowl of cold, lumpy porridge, have been mightily deceived. Pray for them all, that one day they will **come to a knowledge of the truth and be saved**" (1 Tm 2:4).

Cultivate a Joyful Presence

We are permitted to enjoy a good meal, and take Joy from our bodily senses. We can also thrill at the idea of the happiness of heaven. We can turn to the Holy Spirit, and continually draw from His Joy.

The soul needs faith, hope and love in order to live joyfully. There are skills needed to perfect the instrument we have been given, the body and the soul. Being a good Christian presupposes that one has made a decision to bear discomfort with courage. The will to push forward when the going gets rough is a common trait of the saints.

Christianity is not about "me." It is not "Me-ligion." Christianity is about sharing, and community life. We believe in the social Gospel. We care about the poor. Other Christian Churches do as well.

The Reformed Church excelled among Christian Churches in actively supporting the "Underground Railroad," which helped escaping slaves in the 19th century. They understood, as we do, their Christian "Re-ligion." It had nothing to do with "Me-ligion," the exaggerated individualism of the Fundamentalist. The word "religere" is from the Latin, meaning "to bind back." Religion binds us back to the community of God's people, and to God Himself. It brings us back to the reality that we are our brother's keeper.

You bind yourself back to God by changing from individualistic thinking to group awareness. For example, you know how to relieve your thirst, and warm your body when it is cold. You must also know how to care about your neighbor when he or she is thirsty or cold. Not merely care about them, but do something to help them if they are not able to help themselves.

The body knows instinctively how to attain greater comfort; the soul also knows how to give comfort. It is in giving that we receive.

Comforting your soul is not difficult. Clothe yourself with Joy, and drink in the spirit of gladness. The soul craves Joy and meaning. It does not want to be held hostage to the body's self-destructive instincts. It must find purpose and direction before it can enjoy that peace which the world cannot give.

If you want to win an Olympic gold medal you train. If

you want to be a saint, you must put on the will to practice being a saint whether you feel like it or not. This is the law of cause and effect. It's very simple.

To feed Joy to the soul, you begin with prayer. Love and service are really the fruits of prayer. Prayer wins the graces you will need to carry out your loving service joyfully, instead of grudgingly.

Jesus told us that the supreme law is love. He does not ask us to perform great deeds. He doesn't ask for a constant flurry of activity. He asks only that we go forth and become a light in this world of darkness, an instrument of His love.

I love this quote from Pope John XXIII: *"Every believer is called by Christ to be a spark of light, a center of love, a vivifying leaven in this world. And this can be accomplished all the more perfectly when each one lives in deep intimacy and communion with God."*

"To be a light," means that you have to do little things well, for the love of God. In order to preach the Gospel with your life you will need to see, feel and taste the love of God. The important connection between prayer and action is indisputable, because prayer makes you into a new creation. It teaches you that charity begins at home.

Mother Teresa of Calcutta gave us this sage advice:

"Each person's mission is a mission of love. But you must have time for your own first, and after that you can work for others. Begin in the place where you are, with the people closest to you. Make your homes centers of compassion and forgive endlessly. Let no one ever come to you without coming away better and happier."

See how gently she encourages you. Charity begins with self, and with those closest to you. Growing in your ability to love God is a skill that begins with self-love. That doesn't mean indulging your every whim. We are all growing to full maturity. Young people tend to be self-centered. Some teenagers are monsters in their demanding ways. As they mature they learn to let go of their egotism, and gradually they grow into healthy, loving adults.

Let me tell you a story about a woman I know. I'll call her Ann. She is now full of joy, and blesses God every day for her good fortune, but it didn't start out that way. She was a typical, lazy teenager, who loved to sleep in whenever she could. She claimed she needed nine hours of sleep, or she would be miserable all day long. After Ann married, and had her first child she was extremely agitated. Trying to cope with the demands of her new infant seemed overwhelming. She dreamed of escaping.

Ann loved her infant son, but at the same time she resented the absolute demands he placed on her. Before she gathered herself together, she was shocked to find herself pregnant again. As it turned out, she was not only pregnant, but expecting twins. This put her on the verge of a breakdown.

She prayed for strength to accept her new challenge, and her prayers were answered. When I met her two years after the twins were born, she was bubbling with joy, and was bragging about her children, and how happy she was. As she spoke one of them ran over to her for a hug. She was smiling, and said, "I'm glad I had the twins. I find it easier to deal with the three of them, than it was when I only had the one."

Amazing! Ann grew up overnight. She learned to accept her vocation. It wasn't easy, but she became a mature woman. The old days of sleeping nine hours became a thing of the past. I tell you it was prayer that got her through. She was given the grace to meet the challenge of love. And, as a result, she found peace and joy.

The old Catholic wedding ritual put it nicely, *"Marriage can be difficult and irksome, but love can make it easy, and perfect love can make it a joy."*

Love, service, and joy go together. Be patient with yourself when things get rough. The Lord will help you through each crisis one day at a time. In the process don't make matters worse by complaining.

DON'T BE TOO HARD ON YOURSELF

I would like to conclude this chapter by acknowledging our old friend, human weakness. Sure it would be nice if we could easily accept our mission in life, and accept God's will without a whimper, but we are all human. It isn't easy to smile when you feel like crying. Do not be too hard on yourself when you feel discouraged and fear failure. According to Vince Lombardi, the Green Bay Packer coach of happy memory, "When the going gets rough, the tough get going."

He was a bit of a slavedriver with his players, but they all loved him because he drove them on to victory. Yes, it would be wonderful if we all had a coach nearby to remind us to fight the good fight. If we could actually see the face of God in everyone we meet, it would spur us on. If we could be filled with jubilation because we believe God is present within us, it would be wonderful. But alas we have to proceed on faith.

Life is difficult. We cuss and fuss, and succumb to weakness. We suffer humiliations every day, and it can be downright miserable. And yet isn't it true that some of your greatest memories are ones where you persevered, and did the right thing in a painful situation?

You are capable of greatness. You are a saint-in-training. That means when you fall down, you pick yourself up. You will do whatever it takes to get the job done.

This book is not designed to make you feel guilty for not being perfect. Of course you will have your bad days, but don't make too much of them. This book is only intended to lift you up so you can enjoy life as God intends it.

Your burdens may be heavy at times, but you are strong

in the Lord. He is your Strength and your Joy. He wants you to enjoy your precious life.

The familiar quote from Blessed Julian of Norwich, which I use so often, catches the spirit of it: *"The greatest honor you can give to Almighty God, is to live joyfully because of the knowledge of His love."*

This insight is a mystical revelation. She believed she was hearing the voice of Jesus speaking to her. I believe it is an authentic revelation. You don't have to believe it, if you prefer not to, but her writings are in complete harmony with the Gospel message.

Here is another example of Jesus speaking to her:

"I know you want to live for My love, gladly suffering all the trials that may come to you. But inasmuch as you do not live without sin, you are depressed and sorrowful.... Yet, do not be vexed too much about those sins that fall to you against your will.... I keep you close to my heart most securely."

These words of comfort help me to understand the compassionate heart of Jesus. He did not come to condemn us. Remember the mercy He showed to the woman taken in adultery: **"Has no one condemned you? Then neither do I condemn you"** (Jn 8:10-11).

Be at peace. Your union with God depends more on His love for you, than on your love for Him. Moral perfection is not what the Lord seeks. It is impossible to be perfect anyway. What He wants is for you to be an instrument of His love.

He claimed you as His own, and placed an indelible sign on your soul at Baptism. He wants your joy to be full as you find little ways to be a good steward of the gifts He has bestowed upon you.

Trust Him and don't be too hard on yourself. Accept yourself warts and all, and enjoy your precious life of loving service.

Darleen Primamore of Clifton, New Jersey described an unforgettable moment in her life.

> *1983 was the best year of my life. I felt something was missing however, and I began to realize I was missing God in my life. My parents weren't religious but when I was younger I would go to a Protestant church with my grandmother. The first thing I did was to go back to that church and it just didn't feel right, so every Sunday I would go to another church. One Sunday I walked into a Roman Catholic Church and the most wonderful feeling came over me. It felt like I had come home!*
>
> *I made my profession of faith in the Church. The day before this profession of faith, I was at work, and as usual I was about to bring the daily reports upstairs. I was about to head to the elevator when something made me feel like taking the stairs.*
>
> *I was all alone in the stairwell when all of a sudden I felt myself going into the most beautiful light and I felt completely full of joy and love with no problems. I felt a peace I never knew before.*
>
> *I thought to myself, "I want to stay here," but a voice said, "You must go back!" All of a sudden I felt my soul go back into my body and there I am still standing on the stairs with the reports still in my hands.*
>
> *I felt myself glowing and I thought, "God must be happy with me!" A few months later, my life changed even more when I prayed for a child and God showed my husband and me the way, and we adopted a baby from Korea who is now 18. She has been such a joy in my life.*
>
> *Since then there have been several storms to get through, but I think back to that day in the stairwell, and I know the truth and I keep my faith.*

Darleen came to believe deeply that God truly loved her in a personal way, and it made a tremendous difference in the way she lived her life.

12

THE JOY OF CONTEMPLATION

"Joy is the fruit of the Holy Spirit." (Gal 5:2)

Contemplation is wordless prayer. It can be both simple and joyful. St. John of the Cross loved to teach his disciples about contemplative prayer: *"There is a place within the soul which is inaccessible to the devil and the world."*

As his union with Jesus deepened, his prayer became more satisfying. There is a secret chamber of the soul where God gives Himself to you. Jesus invited you to go within and experience a deep, spiritual intimacy with Him. Jesus said, **"Father, I will that where I am, they... will be there with me. Those whom you have given to me will then be able to see my glory"** (Jn 17:24).

Abiding in the Lord is not simply a matter of offering an occasional prayer. It is more a permanent mind-set. You are united with Him in work and play, in joy and in sorrow. Even when you are not consciously aware of praying, His divine presence is always with you.

"Without faith it is impossible to penetrate this mystery" (cf. 1 Cor 2). Faith enables us to experience here and now, what will be our future destiny. We are given a foretaste of the beatific vision. The Lord wants us to find Him within ourselves: **"The Kingdom of God is within you"** (Lk 17:21).

The Holy Spirit is the Soul of your soul. You can speak to

the indwelling Spirit. The grace of Baptism puts you in touch with the Joy of Jesus, which is the Joy of the Holy Spirit.

Here is a prayer by the late Cardinal Mercier of Belgium, which has always helped me to understand this mystery: "Holy Spirit, *Soul of my soul*, guide me, console me, strengthen me."

The Holy Spirit is the Soul of your soul. God is Love, and God is Joy. At the center of your being is Joy in abundance. All you need to do is awaken to Joy. Once you do, you will be able to understand Christ's teaching.

Since Joy is the fruit of the Holy Spirit, you would do well to go directly to the source. Joy is the infallible sign of the presence of the Holy Spirit.

Turning to the Lover within will give you the strength you need to follow the demands of love. There is no question about it, love is demanding. However, we are never left alone, like helpless children lost in the wild. God is our strength. He wants our trust, and he tests our trust every day.

This Joy that comes from within is not a case of mind over matter. I am not telling you to smile when you feel like crying. That would be contrived.

"To exhort people to be happy, to be positive in thought and deed, to smile when they do not feel like smiling can be helpful, but it does not tap into God's Joy, which is available on an entirely different level. The Joy and Peace of God are gifts to those who open their hearts to Him, those who encounter Him in prayer, those who say yes to Him in all circumstances of their lives, those who are in right relationship with others, who are givers and helpers. I hope this does not sound as if God gives His Joy to an elite group! The Good News is so simple and can be understood by anyone, but it requires a listening heart, an attentive heart. People with brilliant minds often do not hear the Word of God, while countless people through the ages, little ones, illiterate ones, have opened their hearts to the Lord and experienced His Joy" (Catherine de Vinck).

Do not think about your limited understanding of this mystery. Think more about the privilege you have been given, and rejoice in the knowledge of His love. Be happy with God. The highest form of prayer is to love God and live your precious life joyfully.

The Lord teaches us that our prayer can be both simple and joyful. He created us to be creatures of love and joy. Believe in His unchanging love. Give yourself to Him often. He loves you, and He wants to be happy with you.

Resting in His love is the highest form of contemplation.

In this way we touch the Joy of heaven. Without words we enter the Holy Presence of God. He in turn gives us His supreme Love and Joy.

Our spiritual Joy begins with the gift of faith. It is a gift because it is offered free of charge to everyone. The Lord opens the door, but we must enter it. Once you make that leap of faith, the Holy Spirit will invite you into His Joy.

"Enter into the Joy of the Lord" (Mt 25:21).

If you have read along this far, I am certain that you have accepted the gift of faith, and have already received the Holy Spirit. The struggle for a deeper understanding of this mystery will never end, so don't be surprised if you feel like a beginner. Every skill needs to be learned and practiced. No one promised it would be easy. Be patient and day by day you will make progress.

REVIEWING THE BASICS

Prayer is communion with God, and since His essence is Love, Mercy, Joy and Peace, the closer you get to Him, the more you become filled with His attributes. Living in the Holy Communion of the Trinity will enable you to live your life at its highest level.

Some people think that prayer is nothing more than a laundry list of petitions, but pure prayer is so much more. It is entering the furnace of God's Love. By uniting with Him we enter His hidden world. Occasionally a flame of love, a feeling of delight will flare up within us during this prayer time, but not often. When it does there are no words to describe it.

One day, when I was twenty-four, I was wrestling with God, trying to understand what He wanted me to do with my life. I was a soldier kneeling in the Post Chapel at Fort Sam Houston, in San Antonio Texas. For many years I felt the urge to be a priest. Sometimes the desire was irresistible, but at the same time I felt an aversion to the idea. I feared that I might only be imagining the whole thing.

The inner conflict drained me of energy because I also wanted to marry and have a family. I couldn't get myself to believe that I had a calling from God. I wanted a normal, happy life in the world. I saw the life of a priest as a big risk. At times, it attracted me, then all of sudden I was overcome with doubt. I wanted to help people as a priest, but quite frankly, I didn't want to pay the price. The idea of celibacy turned me off completely.

So I clung to the dream of having a beautiful marriage with wonderful children, and a successful career. Apparently, my plan for attaining happiness was not God's plan because I couldn't shed the feeling that I had a vocation to the priesthood.

The Holy Spirit was communicating with my soul. I was struggling at prayer. A desire arose deep within me. I wanted to preach, and offer Holy Mass. I wanted to comfort the sick, and counsel the afflicted. I had a longing to give myself away, but I kept telling myself these thoughts were crazy.

This battle within me raged through most of my college years. I obtained a Bachelor of Science degree in Business Administration at Fordham University in 1953. The Korean War was winding down, but in September after my graduation, I was drafted into the Army.

They sent me to do my basic training in Camp Gordon, Augusta, Georgia.

When I completed the first eight weeks, they sent me for eight more weeks, in training for the Military Police. When that was finished, I was an MP, and they assigned me to San Antonio, Texas where I spent the next two years.

As I mentioned above, one evening, in the Post Chapel at Fort Sam Houston, a strange thing happened. While praying for guidance about a half hour had passed when I felt myself being lifted slowly out of my body. It was eerie. I felt like a banana leaving the skin, and was soon looking down on my own body kneeling in the first pew.

A great inner peace came over me. I was suddenly liberated from all my worries. I knew I was in the Presence of God, and the special feeling ended in a matter of seconds. I returned to my body, and sat back in a state of wonder, and deep contentment. This quiet time lasted for another thirty minutes. I thanked God. It was all I could do.

The memory of that experience has never left me. Whether it was a manifestation of my own imagination or a mystical experience I do not know, but it had a powerful effect on me. My desire to be a priest was decidedly advanced.

For that brief moment, I felt touched by God in a way I had never felt before or since. It took me another year before I actually made plans to enter the seminary, but I was happy that entire year, and no longer tormented by doubts. I knew I was going to be a priest.

Everyone experiences God in their own unique way. Whether we sense His presence in prayer, or in the beauty of nature, we know that God is near.

Blessed Julian of Norwich said, *"The fullness of joy is to behold God in everything."* She didn't need a mystical experience to see God, though I'm sure she had many such moments. Her faith helped her to see Him in the majestic display of autumn, in the laughter of a tiny child, and in the roar of the waves crashing on the shore. She saw God in all her fellow human beings.

When I ran a soup kitchen in Paterson, New Jersey, I can honestly say I saw the face of God in our clients. They weren't much to look at, but the eyes of faith can do wonders. I was privileged to serve them. Don't ask me what attracted me to that work, I really couldn't tell you, but humanly speaking it was a delight. With the exception of a few mentally sick people they were all polite, grateful, and respectful. I saw the human dignity beneath their tattered clothing, and felt grateful for the gift of my vocation.

Though it has not always been easy being a priest, it has given me a life full of Joy and celebration. It certainly fulfilled my dream of living a meaningful life. By following my holy desires, my soul has prospered.

At the time I didn't know if that out-of-body experience meant anything at all. I only knew that it gave me the assurance that God was calling me. Some might say I was deluded, but if so, it was a magnificent delusion. You can't argue with forty-one years of basic happiness. The occasional thorns were not so bad. All in all, I'd gladly do it again.

In his book, *Surprised by Joy*, C.S. Lewis speaks of an experience he had when he was eight years old. He writes that it happened next to a flowering currant bush in his family garden.

"Suddenly there arose in me without a warning, as if from the depths not of years but of centuries… it is difficult to find words strong enough… a sensation came over me. Milton's enormous bliss of Eden comes somewhere near it, suddenly there was a sensation of desire, but desire for what?"

He goes on to say that this ecstatic moment passed quickly, and *"the world turned commonplace."* He never forgot that day. Though he doesn't tell us how that moment influenced his life, we know that he went on to become one of the greatest spiritual writers of the 20th century.

Are such experiences rare? I suspect they happen to more people than we might imagine. Believers know that God loves them whether they have a mystical experience or not. However, many have had an experience of God's love that transcends blind faith.

Billions of people down through the ages have never had any sign of a mystical experience, but they have known God nevertheless. We all have to depend on faith in the day-to-day struggle of life. Extraordinary graces are few and far between.

Contemplation helps us to gain insight. We get closer to the Holy Spirit, the source of our Joy. Wordless prayer gives us that Joy, which the world cannot give. The Holy Spirit becomes a real partner. The Spirit also helps you to get out of your self. You can stand apart from yourself without leaving your body. You can look at yourself as though you were an observer. Watch yourself acting out the role you've decided to play in life. This may seem like a curious psychological feat, but it can be done.

Recently, I came across one of my baby pictures. I couldn't help but wonder, was this really me? Seeing myself as an infant was a different kind of out-of-body-experience. My father was an amateur photographer, and I had seen many of my baby pictures before, but this time I really stopped to examine myself as an infant in my mother's arms.

I am the baby in the picture, and yet my tiny body no longer exists. I then had the sobering thought that my present adult body would also one day disappear. So too would the world in which I am presently living. It will all disappear one day.

Someone sent me a copy of *The New York Times* on the day of my birth, September 8, 1931. The great depression was well under way, and the headlines read, "President Herbert Hoover Hears Labor Leaders Demanding Job Relief." On that day, "The Assembly of the League of Nations opened for business." In the ads I saw that a 12-day cruise to Bermuda cost $110; and a brand new six-cylinder Chevrolet would only set you back

$475. Mind-boggling! A different world. Did I actually live in that ancient time? Yes, apparently I did.

The person in that baby picture has now grown old. Here I am observing the way I looked more than 70 years ago. All the cells in the body have changed. They have changed completely every seven years or so. That means that part of me has been disappearing, while another part has been coming to life. My soul has remained basically the same through it all, though I advanced in wisdom, learning and grace.

The soul is the "observer," and the soul remains essentially the same. I can look at myself as an infant, and know that I, the real me, once lived in that tiny body. That body no longer exists, but I do. I am still here.

This brings me to the obvious distinction between the "I" who observes, and the "me" who is observed. What can our baby pictures teach us? They can help us to do the same act of objective observation with respect to our present body.

For instance, you can observe yourself reading this book. You can become a silent observer of yourself as one who is searching for wisdom. I invite you to practice the art of observing yourself as St. Teresa of Avila did. She thanked God for giving her the grace of disidentifying herself with herself. The mystics are constantly urging people to disidentify with their transient selves.

In his wonderful book *Awakening* (A Doubleday Image Book, NY, 1992), the late Father Anthony de Mello wrote about the importance of being aware. You don't have to know exactly who you really are at any given moment. That isn't always so easy to do, but you can observe yourself objectively. There is a purifying effect in seeing yourself act out your role in life.

A recovering alcoholic once told me that his conversion came one night when he was on his hands and knees in the rain, drunk, sick, and homeless. At that moment he saw himself from afar and said, "This is not who I am, this is not who I was born to be."

His soul had been held hostage by his bodily cravings, and his very soul was crying out to his sick personality. That moment of awareness changed his life. He made up his mind to sober up, and he never looked back. He went on to be a successful, happy family man.

Father de Mello claims that you will never succeed in knowing fully the mystery of who you are, but *"the important thing is to drop the labels, and not identify with your body or your present state in life."* You can disidentify with yourself.

The person you appear to be at the present moment is not necessarily the real you. If you identify with your money, you may feel devastated when you lose it, as your personality became impoverished. Some people actually commit suicide because in losing their wealth, they think they became a failure.

They were unaware of who they really are. According to Father de Mello it is wrong to identify with your success or your failure. You are an eternal being. The present world will pass away. The "I," who is the observer in the now of time, is distinct from the "self" who is being observed.

You are not a label that others put on you. You are destined for glory. You are preparing for a new and higher level of life. You are a saint-in-training, a sinner at times, but a potential saint.

If you are successful in the eyes of the world, remember it is only a snapshot of your passing life. Everything changes. Tomorrow you may lose your job. Then who are you? Have you changed into a failure? Nonsense! If I said, "Money can't buy everything," you would probably agree. So if you lose your money, why let it ruin your life? Choose Joy in all circumstances. If you made money before, you can make it again.

Most people want respect, validation, and affirmation, but

they miss the mark. They make bad choices. They become greedy, or lustful, or resentful. If you see yourself as a failure because you are not as rich as you would like to be, you are selling yourself short. You are rash judging yourself.

Tomorrow you may be on top of the heap, and the next day on the bottom. Success and failure are passing things. Do not identify with your present status, or with your money. Identify with Joy, your unchanging center. The real you can abide joyfully through all the seasons of your life.

SHEDDING FALSE ILLUSIONS

The ancient religions of the East have always taught the necessity of attaining this higher level of awareness. Contemplation will help you to reach it. By becoming more aware of who you really are, and what you really need, you can more easily shed false hopes and illusions.

Contemplation can help you to cancel all the negativity in your life. Rejecting self-sabotage becomes automatic. As you open yourself to the source of your Joy, you can remain the same sacred person on good days and bad. That sacred self, your soul, is distinct from your transitory self, your present personality.

For instance, *anorexia nervosa* is an illness in which dieting is carried out to excess. An anorexic girl will have a morbid fear of being fat. By her practice of severe dieting she is left with a deep hunger, which in turn occasionally compels her to binge on food. But being fearful of becoming fat, she forces herself to vomit. The cycle is repeated over and over.

If she agrees to accept professional treatment she can make progress in shedding her false notion that she is unacceptable, or ugly. People with this condition are in need of validation. Food is not the real issue. When she blames her feelings of inadequacy on her weight, she is locked into the dangerous compulsion of fasting. Even though others may see her as being thin, she clings to the fear that she is fat. It gives her something to blame for her desperate feelings.

To escape from ridicule she will do anything, including starving herself. In other words, to alleviate her fear of being rejected, she engages in a radical dieting regime that could threaten her life if she is not helped.

When asked why she is sad, she might say "because I feel fat." "Fat" is not a feeling, but for her it is. She uses it as a code word for "ugly." She is expressing her inner distress. Being thin becomes an obsession because for her it means, being pretty instead of being ugly. Well-meaning friends will try to convince her to eat more as though food was the main issue. She refuses, and the battle lines are drawn.

Psychiatrists tell us, "It is not about food." The girl has a deep insecurity. She is afraid of being rejected. She already sees herself as a failure. Her state of mind must change if she is to get well, but this is easier said than done. She chooses to believe that she's too fat because this belief gives her something concrete to blame for her feelings.

Sadly, this medical condition can happen to children from loving homes. We don't know the actual cause. It is just part of the human condition to believe some of the negative thoughts and feelings that pop into our heads. Insecurity is almost universal. Negative thoughts like these are not facts, but they can cripple us if we allow them to take hold.

Unless you take control of your thoughts, life can become needlessly miserable. Most of us give ourselves the benefit of the doubt in these matters. But those who identify with the negative thoughts and feelings that bounce around in their heads are vulnerable to mental illness.

Each person is precious in the sight of God, and beautifully made.

Contemplation can help you to get rooted in the truth, in

the simple awareness that you are a tiny creature and that God is the creator of the universe. You are tiny. Everyone is tiny by comparison to Him. It is OK to be small and humble. He will supply what you need in the way of love and approval. Love yourself, because He loves you. See yourself as lovable.

Meditation is not the same as contemplation. Meditation is a way of thinking about certain truths or events. If you daydream about the parable of the Prodigal Son you will get the sense of God's goodness. He is like the father in the parable. He embraced his wayward son when the boy returned from a life of irresponsibility. It can be a comfort to meditate on positive, uplifting stories if you are insecure.

Contemplation even goes a step further. It lets you sink into the arms of God. You say nothing, and feel only gratitude.

There are a series of ideas I wrote for myself to keep my mind oriented to the truth. I meditate on them whenever I feel tempted to put myself down. They awaken in me a feeling of abandonment to Divine Providence, and I go with the flow.

Instead of thinking negative thoughts, I repeat these ideas over and over to myself.

> *I am not alone, for God is with me always.*
> *I am not afraid, for God is my strength and my joy.*
> *I am forgiven all my sins, for God is mercy and love.*
> *I am bearing good fruit, for God is working through me.*
> *I am steadfast for God is strengthening me.*
> *I am happy, for I swim in an ocean of God's Unchanging Joy.*

These ideas have the power to cancel negative thinking. You no longer believe that you are unloved, unattractive, or inadequate. You cancel all the negative thoughts, and replace them with positive affirmations. Being aware that you are alive and well and happy is the essential thing for your soul to prosper.

You Are a Temple of the Holy Spirit

Fill your soul with the Joy of the Holy Spirit.

If a woman identifies with her body, she will always see flaws. She is not her body. She inhabits a body, which is changing all the time. Her soul is filled with a spirit. If the spirit is holy she will be happy. If the spirit is not holy she will be confused and full of self-doubt. Pray for the Holy Spirit to flood your soul with blessings.

If a man identifies with his success, he will think of himself as above average. This is a sure way of setting himself up for a fall. In the best-case scenario he will have to step down one day, if only to retire. Then he will lose his position and his power. Stepping down to the level of the average human being may not be so easy, especially if he has indulged his superiority illusion for a long time. Above average expectations can lead to above average disappointments.

Self-confidence withers at the first sign of loss, unless your confidence is rooted somewhere other than in your own imagination. If you find your strength in God's unchanging love you will always be safe. If you live in His Joy, you will go through the trials of life with greater ease.

When you realize that you are a temple of the Holy Spirit you will learn to thrive: in Him, with Him, and through Him. You can feel safe in His love. Put your faith in the Joy and Strength of the Holy Spirit, and all will be well.

Contemplation is a time for entering into the Joy of Jesus. His union with His Father and the Holy Spirit can become the mysterious center of your personality. Jesus has communicated the Holy Spirit to you, and spiritual Joy is the result. The Blessed Trinity is living within you.

Spiritual Joy is permanent. Human happiness is often a passing thing. The passing experiences of happiness are enhanced when you know that you have spiritual Joy.

A man celebrating at a party on New Year's Eve can sing for joy, but soon the glow of the alcohol wears off. Then he sinks into sadness. Later he has a headache. Is this happiness?

Spiritual Joy, on the other hand, is long lasting. It is God's life abiding in us. It permeates and pervades your whole being in good times and bad.

You are much more than your present state of mind might indicate. Your personality can be shaped by the evil one, or by the Holy Spirit. If the Holy Spirit is in you, you can be sad and still have Joy deep within your soul. If you want to cope well with all that life throws at you be aware of the Spirit living in you. Bad things will happen to you in life, but they need not undermine your confidence in God's Love and Joy.

True believers do not become desperate when tragedies come. They may be deeply shaken and even wounded, but they rebound, and remain steadfast in the faith. They rise in the strength of Christ. Joy and peace are always in the soul; therefore joy will always prevail over sorrow.

Jesus, dying on the cross, was in misery, but He was also in His glory. In the eyes of most of His contemporaries, including many of His followers, He was seen as a failure. To His Father in heaven He was a total success.

Nothing is as it appears. God's ways are not ours.

Jesus was always pure of heart. His presence in you makes you pure of heart as well. There is a corner of your soul that has never sinned. Do not drag the past and all your guilty feelings into the present moment. Do not identify with your sinful self. Ask, and your sins will be forgiven. Shed the memory of them, as you would take off an old coat. Once you repent and amend your life you have become a new creation.

Your true and noble self is alive and well. Let go of what is in the past. Concentrate on the all-important truth that God loves you. If you have been hurt by anyone, turn the bad feelings and the justice issue over to the Lord. Let Him take care of the crimes and punishment. Let go! Forgive as best you can. Laugh at yourself for holding on to grudges.

At times you may be like a dog with a bone, refusing to let go. Remember you are not a dog. You are a noble Christian. You can walk away from your anger.

Do not poison your chances for happiness by thinking negatively. Do not let the past destroy your present moment. God knows who you are, and He loves you. That's all that really matters. Pray for the grace to become your own best friend, instead of your own worst enemy.

Jesus told the lepers not to be sad. He taught all of us to respect one another because all life is sacred. Each person is precious. No matter how you may look or feel at any given moment, the real you is in God's love. You are precious to God.

Sad or happy, rich or poor, you are the child of a great King. Your true self is always loved. The "I" that is you is always under the protection of a merciful God.

No label can define you. Your soul cannot be sullied by passing events. It is wrong to be unhappy because you lost something you thought was vital to your identity. You are not your body, or your job. You are not the person in your baby pictures. You are not what you did in the past. That bad deed is not who you are. You are a good person who has been forgiven.

Now you must forgive yourself. You have grown in wisdom, age, and grace, and the essential you is still pure. Try to identify more with your true self, the one that is permeated by God's life. Think less about your past imperfections.

Respect yourself. Become your own best friend. Love your soul. Treat it kindly. Guide it to safe shelter; resuscitate your spirit with Joy.

Part Three

BEING JOYFUL

Anne Boyle of Clifton, New Jersey tells how the Lord brought her through her problems.

My aunt, who is subject to depression, recently asked me why I am always so happy. I related to her that as a teenager I was very quiet and shy. I did make friends easily, but it seemed whenever I had a close friend, she would move away and we would lose touch. As a result, I was often lonely.

I can relate to teenagers who contemplate suicide. As a Catholic, I never considered suicide but often wondered why I was born.

Then, one Sunday at Mass, I was following the Gospel in my missal. Suddenly, I realized that what Jesus was saying was just as true almost 2000 years later, and He was speaking to me. Thereafter, whenever I went to Mass, I began to pay attention to the readings. Gradually, I came to the realization that God really loves me and cares about me. Thus, Jesus became the friend who was always there and would never leave me.

My life has been blessed with an ever-increasing awareness of God's presence. He has led my husband Gerry and me through many ways of increasing our faith. God has brought us through crises and illnesses and has given us many wonderful gifts, including our five children and six (so far) grandchildren. We are truly blessed.

At a day of recollection some years ago, a priest told us something that I have never forgotten. He said that each person is born with a God-hole and we cannot be truly happy until this hole is filled in. People try to fill it with drugs, alcohol, sex, entertainment, etc., but the only thing that can fill the God-hole is God. If we can fill up with the Lord's love, we will find more happiness than we could ever imagine.

One of our daughters once asked me why I cry in Church. I asked her if she cried when she saw a movie with an emotional scene, or read a story with a happy ending. She said, "Yes, but Mom, you cry in Church!" I tried to explain that the Gospel readings, the homily, the fact of the bread and wine becoming Jesus all touch my heart. God is truly the source of all happiness.

Our other daughter just gave us a CD, which contains the song, "My Happiness." The last part of the song can be used to describe my relationship with God perfectly: Whether skies are gray or blue, anyplace on earth will do, just as long as I'm with you, my happiness."

Anne Boyle refers to the Lord as, "My Happiness," and so can you. Dismiss fear. Exercise your will power, and say yes to joy.

13

YOU ARE RESPONSIBLE
FOR YOUR JOY

"Whoever sows sparingly will also reap sparingly,
and whoever sows bountifully will reap bountifully. God
loves the cheerful giver." (2 Cor 9:6, 7)

Everything depends on God and His grace. St. Paul tells us that it is up to us to sow bountifully, if we want to reap a rich harvest. In other words, pray as if everything depended on God, but act as if everything depended on you. In the end we will all be judged on love.

That means that you are responsible for your own Joy, both here and in the hereafter. Even though Joy is a gift, you must do your part to exercise your Joy muscles. Practice being joyful.

It is important not only to hear the words of Jesus, but also to act on them. He wants to establish a Kingdom of Love, Joy and Peace. If you cooperate with Him in His plan of salvation all will be well. Seek first the Kingdom.

The word "seek" is a verb. It implies action. The connection between prayer and action is obvious. There is no secret to this. Jesus spoke plainly: **"Do unto others as you would have them do unto you"** (Mt 7:12). The word "do" is the key to being a good steward.

It is possible for you to swim in an ocean of Joy if you plan ahead. You will be rewarded in this world, as well as the next by sowing bountifully, and setting your sights high.

You have to decide what kind of person you want to be. Will you go for the gold, or will you sabotage any chance you have at happiness? Will you aim high, or will you become a burden to yourself and others? My hope is that you will choose Joy over sorrow.

Commit yourself to making this a better world. If you help others, it will give you more human joy than you ever dreamed possible, and if you pray for the grace of the Holy Spirit you will be flooded with supernatural Joy. Your self-respect will soar, and others will look upon you with a new admiration.

When you respect yourself, you are likely to be more sensitive to the needs of others. You will be more accepting of the weak and wounded of this world. However, accepting your neighbor in a nonjudgmental way can only happen if you are not judgmental about yourself. It takes a certain generosity of spirit to love yourself enough to aim at becoming a messenger of Joy.

Once you arrive at this level you will be a noble human being. Doubts will come for sure, and fears will still plague you at times, but not in the same way. John the Baptist, whom Jesus called the greatest man born of woman, had doubts toward the end of his life. He sent his followers to ask Jesus if He was truly the Messiah. These misgivings were easily quieted by the words of Jesus: **"Tell him that the blind see, and the deaf hear"** (Mt 11:4-5).

If you are already living life at this level of Joy, then you have become a blessing to everyone you meet. You are a gift of God, a beacon of hope to everyone you meet. You are another Christ, and you have found your true mission. To be a carrier of God's Love and Joy is to be a true Catholic Christian.

You have become an optimist, offering a hopeful vision

to everyone you meet. You carry a vision of good cheer, and holy hope. You understand the deeper meaning of life. Your gentle demeanor exudes an inner contentment. Your smile is an authentic blessing. You are holy.

Jesus wants you to claim this Joy. When you do, He will say: **"Well done good and faithful servant"** (Mt 25:23). He will thank you for trusting His love.

Change Is Never Easy

How can you bring yourself to this higher level of harmony with God? How can you live joyfully because of the knowledge of His love? Simply by willing it.

"If you want to be a saint, will it" (St. Thomas Aquinas). This needs to be interpreted properly. Thomas is not saying that sanctity is merely a matter of will power. He is however insisting that you must make an act of the will to be in harmony with God, or you go nowhere. Nor is he saying that holiness is a matter of correct thinking. Right thinking is essential for the grace of God to work, but the grace of God is the essential thing.

Sainthood is a gift, and sainthood is the result of cooperation with that gift. Our holiness is God abiding in us. He gets the glory because He supplies the gift. He also holds us accountable. We are saved by Jesus Christ, and He asks us to help Him save others. We have to make a return on the gifts He bestows on us.

Jean Pierre de Caussade made an interesting comment. He was the famous 18th century French Jesuit who wrote *Abandonment to Divine Providence*. He said that, *"happiness and holiness are found in our fidelity to the duty of the present moment."* Doing one's duty is a way of practicing obedience to God's will. Since duty is always a matter of acting in the present moment, the path to Holiness and Joy, according to de Caussade, is found in being faithful to the duties of our state in life. That means doing the dishes, mending socks, filling out your tax forms, taking the children for a walk, and all the other mundane things of life are all opportunities for growth in holiness and happiness.

The additional duty of delight also impels us to take Joy from the little things that make life meaningful. Even when tears begin welling up because of some tragedy, we can keep an inner smile alive within us. It is possible to be joyful in the midst of sorrow. We can always come to the One who comforts and sustains us.

GOD'S LOVE IS UNCHANGING

"In this world you will have many troubles, but I have overcome the world, so be of good cheer," says the Lord (Jn 16:33). All may not be well in your life, but your soul can be swimming in Joy when you know God is near.

It seems ridiculous to those who dismiss the words of Jesus, but it is true. If you want to be a messenger of Joy, you must rely on faith, not feelings. You must will it. If you want to be a joyful person you must choose Joy.

So many people make themselves miserable by the unconscious choices they make. Learn from them, and make better choices. Since you are responsible for your own happiness, you will be wise to think positively. Cancel your self-pity. Cancel all your negative thoughts. Your feelings will evolve slowly and they will eventually follow your will.

Anger can be a terrible obstacle to change. Why do so many people use their anger against themselves? Perhaps they think it gives them some kind of validity to remain outraged over some offense. The truth is that anger debilitates the soul's strength, and unsettles the body's emotional system. The genuine Christian knows that a joyful life is God's will for us. An angry life needs to be managed and controlled. Anger defeats God's purpose.

It's not that you do not have a right to be angry. Of course you do. You have been hurt, violated, betrayed, and abused. You are furious. All of these horrible things are despicable. They cry to heaven for justice. But sustained anger only burns up your energy, and leaves you wilted.

Decide to drop the excess baggage of anger, and turn the justice issue over to the Lord. Take care of your soul. Pray for the grace to surrender to your Father's will. It takes much more energy to remain angry than it does to turn your anger over to the Lord. The emotional pain of sustained anger is a form of heat that you generate by holding on to the grudge. Accelerating your car engine in neutral only burns gas, and overheats the engine. You go nowhere in the process.

When repressed anger burns enough energy, you become exhausted, and eventually you fall into a depression. How do you get out of it? Just stop pressing the accelerator. Let go and let God. Do not cling to your anger. Emotional exhaustion is not worth it. You deserve better.

Many people sabotage themselves with their repressed outrage. Peace of mind is only a step away. It won't come for a couple of weeks, because you have to slow down before the remedy takes, but when it does the dark clouds blow away.

For greater emotional comfort, let go of your anger. Turn the justice issue over to God, and let Him worry about getting even.

The choice is yours. Either you decide to cancel self-sabotage, and get on with life, or you will persist in making yourself miserable. This is a no-brainer. Don't say you can't do it because you can. Millions of people have. Sometimes you just have to forgive in order to free yourself. It doesn't mean you let the guilty party off the hook. It means you give the responsibility of attaining justice to God. Even if you can't forget, you can forgive. In time the raw memories will fade away. This change in your thinking can begin right now.

What About Sadness?

If there is sadness in your heart, do not try to force feelings of Joy. Just work within your limits. I love this prayer by Father Walter Ciszek, S.J.

Lord Jesus, I ask for the grace to accept the sadness in my heart, as your will for me, in this moment. I offer it up, in union with your suffering, for those who are in deepest need of your redeeming grace. I surrender myself to your Father's will, and I ask You to move me on to the next task that You have set for me.

Lead me away from dwelling on the hurt I feel: to thoughts of charity for those who need my love; to thoughts of compassion for those who need my care; and to thoughts of giving to those who need my help.

As I give myself to You, help me to provide for the salvation of those who come to me in need.

May I find my healing in this giving.

May I always accept it as God's will.

May I find my true self by living for others in a spirit of sacrifice and suffering.

May I die more fully to myself, and live more fully in You as I seek to surrender to You.

May I come to trust that You will do everything for me.

Many people fear change. They love the status quo, and refuse to believe that prayer can change everything. But it does! Prayer enables you to see the light: God will do for you what you cannot do for yourself. You can will to be joyful, and ask God to make you into a cheerful giver. Let God help you, and remember too that God helps those who help themselves.

A JOYFUL LIFE HONORS GOD

We are more pleasing to the Lord when we are fully alive to all that is beautiful around us. Joy is the highest expression of human life. A grateful heart is full of joy. A resentful spirit is full of anger and frustration. Envy is defined as sadness over the good fortune of another. Reject envy and dismiss sadness if you want to live a joyful life. It is your choice.

A successful athlete has a winning attitude. He or she gets in the flow of the game confidently playing to win. The fearful opponent plays defensively, and tries to keep from losing. The fear of losing inhibits the athlete's skills. A somber mood develops when one is afraid of making a mistake. The troubled athlete plays too cautiously, and by not taking risks, misses opportunities to score. The game can be lost in the second half, by timidity and fear.

A happy pianist delights in the sounds he creates for his audience; whereas a tense pianist pounds away at the piano worrying about what the critics might say if he makes a mistake. He worries about failing, and brings on failure.

A happy physician exudes confidence in his skills. In the process he or she gives much needed assurance and comfort to all. A greedy physician sees dollar signs in his service. The patients are seen more as units of income than suffering human beings. This attitude translates into a spirit of arrogance and disinterest.

A confident, happy teacher enjoys the children. She or he loves their active, engaging curiosity. A bored, disinterested teacher is always on guard against discipline problems. The confident teacher is happy and effective, the bored one is uninspiring and frightened.

Love is the motivation that makes the difference. With love comes joy and freedom.

You sabotage yourself when you do not strive to create an

atmosphere of emotional comfort for yourself and for others. To achieve this goal you deliberately have to choose Joy. With faith, Joy will follow. Spiritual Joy follows natural joy.

Decide whether you want to be a healer or a victim. Adopt the attitude of a healer; and reject the idea that you are a victim. This is essential if you are going to enjoy the Lord, and enjoy your precious life. You will have to make the choice.

Happiness and joy are virtues well worth developing, but it takes courage and hard work to change. It takes will power to strive to remain happy within yourself when others you encounter are making life miserable for themselves and everyone around them.

You must be vigilant about holding on to your joyful spirit. Put on the will to cling to Joy. Bring healing to each situation that faces you. Hold back your egotism as best you can. Be calm. Speak wisely. A healer knows how to remain joyful. A healer knows how to love.

You can do this by God's grace, even if you have been wounded earlier by life. If you have suffered a miserable childhood for instance, your wounds will be deep, but they can heal. Turn them over to the Lord, and bathe them in His healing light.

A healer does not absorb the emotions of others. Do not try to help those who are emotionally upset by becoming miserable with them. If you become too empathetic, in the end there will be two miserable people instead of one. Stay detached in the pure sense, even as you try to help. Like a good nurse or doctor, hold on to your professionalism so you can be of help to the next patient, and not wasted by the one before.

If someone is outraged, even if it is justified anger, don't absorb that anger. You can show your concern in other ways. Compassion is a skill. It is not adapting to the mood of the person you are helping; rather it is acknowledging their right to be angry, and holding on to your Joy at the same time. Just be willing to listen.

Did you read that carefully? **Hold on to your Joy.** Remain self-possessed. You can help the other person move through his or her pain without becoming part of the problem. You can do this by asking questions. Questions have a way of distracting the other person from the misery at hand. Help the distraught person to think about the feelings that are welling up.

If someone is throwing a tantrum, let the steam blow for awhile then ask, "Why are you so upset?" Follow up, "Why does that make you so mad?" Then ask, "Is there anything that I can do to be of help?" Questions deflect the emotional flow, and get the person to calm down. You don't have to solve the problem. You just have to be there with your compassion, by being willing to listen.

Here are a few questions to keep in reserve.

"Why do you think this is happening to you?" They may say something like: "I think God is punishing me." Ask them "Do you really believe that?" If they say "Yes," then ask, "Why do you believe that when you know that God is Love?" If they say "I don't believe He loves me," ask, "Do you really believe that you are the only exception to God's universal Love? Why would you think that?"

Helping people to explain their feelings and beliefs can be a big help in the process of clarification. Sifting feelings from fact is an important contribution to emotional peace. It is good to help people to think about their feelings. Held up to the cold light of reason, negative thoughts and feelings can be rejected more easily.

If you're dealing with an obstinate person, keep asking questions anyway. Here is a scenario that may be useful. You have just listened to a young woman complain bitterly about her mother. You respond, "So you're furious with your mother. What is it about her that makes you so mad?" Listen for a while and then ask, "Is there a part of you that still loves her? Is there a part of her that still loves you?" If she says she hates her, ask,

"Why?" If she admits that she loves her, and hates her at the same time, then let her talk it out. Focus on why she loves her mother.

If she has a modicum of faith, remind her of the words of Jesus: **"Don't worry about tomorrow. Today's worries are enough. There is no need to add to the troubles each day brings"** (Mt 6:34).

Overcoming Fear

The Book of Proverbs says that **"fear of the Lord is the beginning of wisdom"** (Pr 1:7). But fear in this context must be understood correctly. The Book refers to a reverential fear, which is a kind of respectful awe. We experience awe in the presence of the majesty of God. Since God is unchanging Love and unbounded Joy, we don't have to fear Him.

It would be better to trust Him and absorb His Spirit than indulge our fears. Canceling fear is the beginning of real wisdom. Fear keeps us from trusting God, and trust is the most important message that Christ came to proclaim.

Through trust, change is really possible. For instance, the word "repent" is repeated over and over again in the New Testament. John the Baptist proclaimed it as the *sine qua non* of admission to the Kingdom. To repent is to change. When you repent everything changes. Let me put it another way. When the sun comes out the snow begins to melt. Everything gets brighter and warmer.

Some would argue that preserving your joy, and working to create an atmosphere of emotional comfort around you might be a little bit selfish. Not so! A joyful person is one who does not let others take over. Do not let any sick patient, or any demanding neurotic drain you of Joy. Learn to preserve yourself for the next person who needs you.

Put an invisible glass wall between you and the complain-
ers. Let everything they say hit the glass, and drip down harm-
lessly without touching your spirit. Smile, listen, be there, be
kind, but do not wallow in the mud with them. They are working to have their needs met through a pattern of self-pity and
complaint. The more you give in, the more they will see that
their method is working.

Sometimes it is a close relative, and you can't walk away.
Then it is all the more necessary to hold on to your Joy. You do
not have to answer every question or counter every woe. Let
them speak until they tire, and remain silent. Stroke their fore-
head gently. Say nothing. You do not have to swing at every
pitch. Occasionally ask a question.

For example, if they say, "I'm such a burden, my hospital
bills are costing a fortune. It would be better if I died for
everyone's sake," you may feel there is some truth in that, but
simply ask the question, "Do you really believe that?" They will
say, "Yes," and you say, "After all the good you've done for us,
how could you believe that?" Don't sweat it, if they persist. Just
smile.

Make an intention to be stronger and more energized when
you leave the patient than when you went in to see them. Hold
on to your Joy, and give comfort by your presence, not by your
emotional surrender to the mood of the moment. You are there
for them, but you will not allow yourself to be drowned emotionally by them. If you do, you will soon become an enabler.
By letting them take advantage of you, you will become depressed.

Usually fear is the underlying problem in all these encounters. If you assign yourself the role of a rational friend who asks
rational questions, rather than an emotional punching bag who
groans with every complaint, you'll be much better off.

After they say their piece, if it is appropriate you might
ask, "What are you going to do about it?" Think with them as

they plan their escape. Guide them in keeping it within moral perimeters.

Everyone has greater energy and conviction when they take positive, constructive action. In matters that seem to be beyond one's control, all anyone can do is pray. Pray with the patient for deliverance from fear. Pray for the grace to trust in God's loving power.

Helping someone to cancel their negative thoughts is probably the most important thing you can do for them. If they resist, give them time to figure it out for themselves. If after a good period of time they are still clinging to their misery, you may have to step back and simply remain silent.

Happiness is a choice. You can't choose it for others. Protect yourself from assuming guilt for not solving their problems. They are responsible for their joy and you are responsible for yours. That distinction is very important. If you want to preserve your joy stay detached enough to be objective, but remain interested enough to be an instrument of love.

Pray for those you try to help. Tell them you will continue to pray for them. That may be about all you can do at the moment. In the more difficult cases, accept your limitations.

You cannot alter the thinking of others. They must do that for themselves. You can only guide them. By deciding to be a healer, you mustn't think that you will always succeed in healing. It does mean that you will not allow yourself to become emotionally involved to the point of losing your Joy. Hold on to Joy, and all will be well.

Don't Let the Past Drag You Down

Leonardo da Vinci was working on the face of Jesus, the centerpiece of his great painting "The Last Supper," when an argument broke out among his assistants. It so disturbed him, and distracted him that he became furious. After rebuking them he calmed down, and returned to his painting. For a long time he couldn't concentrate. His conscience disturbed him about the way he had reacted. He wasn't the cause of the disturbance, but his reaction to it weighed on his mind.

To get rid of the emotional block, he went over to the men who had created the disturbance and apologized. He gave them each a piece of fruit to make amends. When his good feelings returned, he was able to get on with his work.

The importance of repentance cannot be exaggerated. It is not merely a matter of feeling sorrow for what you did; one has to make amends. When that is possible, joy returns to the soul. Making amends is the key to regaining the joyful spirit. If you can't get up the courage to apologize and make amends, then at the very least you should turn to the Lord for help.

"Draw near to God, and He will draw near to you" (Jm 4:8). In order to create an atmosphere of emotional comfort, do not let the past keep you down. Do not let the memory of some past trauma cloud your joy in the present moment. Now is all you have. The past is over. Don't let it dominate your present mood. Let it die, and it will not hurt you. In many cases, the only way to deal with these bad feelings is to repent and make amends.

Don't Let the Future Frighten You

Just as past events can linger in your mind and upset your emotions, so too can your fear of the future. The future is hidden from your eyes. We all have a way of imagining the worst. If you let this kind of thinking go unchecked, it will poison the joy of your present moment. Fear of the future can be deadly.

Some people think that God is punishing them for something they did years ago. Actually they are punishing themselves.

They came to the conclusion that they do not have the right to be too happy, never accepting on faith, that God is unchanging love.

This attitude actually makes them afraid of being too happy. Consciously or subconsciously they expect the worst from God. This is so sad. God's Divine Providence is there for them in the future, as well as in the present moment. They can rely on His promise to protect them, no matter what happens.

God is nothing but mercy and forgiveness. If you ask for forgiveness, He will forgive. Don't allow yourself to feel that God is ready to punish you at the drop of a hat. Once you express sorrow for what you have done, God forgives.

However, you must understand that while God forgives, nature does not forgive. If you smoked cigarettes for thirty years, there will be lung damage, even though God loves you. So if you have cancer of the lungs later in life, don't blame God.

The Lord God will be with you through all your trials and tribulations, but don't blame Him for everything that goes wrong.

If you have done something bad, try to make amends, if possible. By that I mean it's never too late to give up smoking. But forgive yourself if you can't do that. Make each day count as best you can. Get on with your precious life. Be as happy as you can be.

You can only do that by abandoning yourself to Divine Providence, and living in the present moment the best way you know how. Let go and let God. Choose Joy, and learn to laugh at yourself more. Joy is the state of a contented soul. Coming to terms with the reality of death is never easy, but since we are all in the same boat, there is no choice. Accept it or go crazy trying to deny or evade it. Joy is not the same as having all the answers. We will never be privy to the mysteries of life and grace. Neither is Joy the feeling of bodily delight. Earthly pleasures are desirable, but not lasting. Like the animals, we too enjoy bodily pleasures. A refreshing cold drink on a muggy day is enjoyable for all of God's sentient creatures. However the animals are not capable of attaining spiritual Joy. A cat will purr when it is petted and loved, but this is not Joy. It is contentment.

Spiritual Joy is God's gift to his children.

St. Paul spells out the faith dimension of this Joy: **"The fruits of the Spirit are charity, joy, peace, patience, kindness, goodness, faithfulness, and self-control"** (Gal 5:22).

He calls Joy one of the fruits of the Spirit. A fruit is the product of a higher form of life. Therefore, in the theological sense, Joy is the product of something holy beyond our capacity to comprehend. Joy flows from the Spirit. The person must also be grounded in a meaningful life, which is lived under the influence of the Holy Spirit. Repentance is one way to cleanse the soul of joyless feelings. Turning to the Holy Spirit for help is the only way to repair the damage.

This Joy in turn produces an inner glow, a glow that is found in all the saints. Artists try to depict it visually as a halo. You can have the glow of spiritual health, simply by not sabotaging yourself. Do not let the past drag you down.

Be more accepting and respectful of yourself. See yourself as a blessing to those you meet, and let your smile be a blessing to everyone you encounter.

Sow, not sparingly but generously, so that you may reap a rich harvest of Joy.

God grant me the
Serenity to accept the things I cannot change,
Courage to change the things I can,
And the Wisdom to know the difference,
Living one day at a time,
Enjoying one moment at a time,
Accepting hardships as the pathway to peace;
Taking as He did, this sinful world as it is,
Not as I would have it;
Trusting that He will make all things right
If I surrender to His will;
That I may be reasonably happy in this life
And supremely happy with Him forever.

Rev. Dr. Reinhold Niebuhr

14

DO NOT POSTPONE JOY

"Do not hide your light! Let it shine. Let your
good deeds glow for all to see, so that they will praise your
heavenly Father." (Mt 5:15, 16)

Joy is being your best self.

Deciding to be joyful is an act of the will. You decide to please God by living gladly because of the knowledge of His love.

You decide to be joyful, and you do not have to force feelings to do it. Let God do the work for you. That means even if you don't feel joyful at any given moment, you simply claim Joy.

Smile confidently when you catch yourself being gloomy. Know that the Lord is working in you, supplying you with His eternal Joy.

St. Paul was a wonderful messenger of Joy. He trusted the Lord, and conditioned his will to embrace the teachings of Jesus. I have paraphrased some of his ideas on the subject in the following synopsis of what it means to be a messenger of Joy: **"This grace has been given to me to enlighten all people to the fact that Joy is the fruit of the Holy Spirit. Remember your present afflictions are only for the moment, but they are achieving an eternal glory for you. Be thankful therefore in all circumstances. God will comfort you in your afflictions. Eye has not seen, nor has ear heard, nor has it so much as dawned on anyone what God has prepared for those who love Him."**

Paul conditioned his thinking by writing and teaching these truths. He knew that by remembering the truths of faith he would prosper. Finding meaning is so important. Faith supplies the wisdom to do this. God made each one of us for a definite purpose. We were created to use our gifts, talents and treasures to help build up the Kingdom.

This type of "building up" is not the same as signing a generous check for some Church building fund. Building up the Kingdom is more a matter of cooperating with God's plan of salvation. Understanding who you are in the great scheme of things is one of the by-products of a vibrant faith.

Cardinal Newman's magnificent words on the subject are worth reviewing.

> *God has created me to do Him some great service.*
> *He has committed some work to me*
> *which He has not committed to another.*
> *I have my mission…*
> *I am a link in a chain,*
> *a bond of connection between persons.*
> *He has not created me for naught.*
> *I shall do good, I shall do His work.*
> *I shall be an angel of peace,*
> *a preacher of truth in my own place,*
> *even while not intending it,*
> *if I but keep His commandments.*
> *Therefore I will trust Him.*
> *Whatever, wherever I am,*
> *I can never be thrown away.*
> *If I am in sickness,*
> *my sickness may serve Him;*
> *if I am in sorrow,*
> *my sorrow may serve Him.*
> *He does nothing in vain,*
> *He knows what He is about.*

Newman instructs us to trust the Lord. This is the basis of true Christian holiness. However, holiness is more than mere almsgiving and fasting. Those are admirable Christian practices. Holiness is intimately tied into the idea of self-giving. Going outside of your inner life, and seeking first the Kingdom of God is a matter of loving others.

We do this by living as instruments of God's love. Every kind gesture, every gentle act of caring, all that we do to make others a little happier is part of our vocation: to love and be loved.

Live in the present moment, and become a good steward of all the talents and treasures God has given you. Decide to honor God with your joy and your generosity. Bring a smile to the face of your neighbor. Live a Spirit-filled life. Live your life in Him, with Him and through Him.

Be aware of God's love flowing through you.

"I am the vine, you are the branches. Remain in me and I will remain in you and you will bear much fruit, for without me you can do nothing" (Jn 15:5).

Holiness is abiding in the holy communion of Love. Divine Life is in you. God supplies the holiness and the joy, you are the raw material. He will make you into one of His great masterpieces if you let Him.

Don't postpone Joy. Put a smile on your face today. You are called to seek first the Kingdom, and you can do that by putting one foot in heaven right now. Live as an instrument of God's love. Every kind act you perform is God expressing His love through you. The whole legacy of your life will be rich because of God's grace.

All that you do for others to help them be a little happier improves the well-being of the world. It is a way of finding meaning and joy for yourself as well. The secret once again: *"Pray as if everything depended on God, and act as if everything depended on you"* (St. Ignatius).

The fruit of prayer is charity and loving service. The Holy Spirit leads us to become the good stewards of all our gifts. To live in the Holy Spirit is to rejoice in the knowledge of God's unchanging love.

Striving to live joyfully is a noble ambition, an ideal, and a sublime goal. We cannot get there all at once, I assure you. So please dear friend, do not be discouraged if you seem to be at odds and ends at this particular moment. It will get better. Meanwhile, **"Ask and you will receive,"** says the Lord (Mt 21:22). It is amazing how prayer can move mountains.

Once you find meaning and purpose, life is as easy as following your heart.

As the recipient and caretaker of God's gifts, you are accountable for the way you use them. You will know your gifts by your desire to use them. A disciple is not only a follower of Christ, but also a good steward of the talents he or she feels from within. St. Peter put it well: It is your vocation to use those gifts, talents and treasures in a responsible way, for the glory of God, and for your own delight. This is the way you will find your bliss.

Put Your Faith to Work

The Lord has loaned you these gifts. He wants you to enjoy them now. He wants you to share them now. One of the joys of being a Christian is to be found in the belief that by returning your gifts to God with interest, you are pleasing Him hour by hour.

"Every believer is called by Christ to be a spark of light, a center of love, a vivifying leaven in this world. And this can be accomplished all the more perfectly where each one lives in deep intimacy and communion with God" (Pope John XXIII).

To be a light, and a vivifying leaven, means doing little things exceedingly well for the love of God. This skill requires an awareness of the important connection between prayer and action. St. Francis of Assisi saw this connection clearly. He prayed for the strength to love others in such a way as to strengthen them and bring them Joy. He taught his followers what real evangelization was all about: *"Do you want to know one of the best ways to win people over, and lead them to God? It consists in giving them joy, and making them happy."*

There is not only Joy in spreading Joy, for those who share their faith, there is sheer bliss.

Jesus said, **"Do not be afraid. My yoke is easy, my burden light"** (Mt 14:27; 11:30); and it's true.

A thoughtful person will begin to understand that the gift of joy comes to those who have faith enough to accept His teaching. It takes courage at first to be a cheerful giver, but after a while, it becomes easy. Everything you have has been given to you, so you might as well be cheerful about sharing your gifts.

Jesus meant what He said, **"I came that my joy may be in you, and your joy may be complete"** (Jn 15:11). The way to this fullness of Joy is through prayer and responsible stewardship. There may be a price to pay. The challenge is clear.

"If you wish to come after me, you must deny yourself and take up your cross every day. For if you wish to save your life, you will lose it, but if you wish to lose your life for my sake you will save it" (Lk 9:23, 24).

This is an invitation to become the best you can be. It is a call to meaning, not necessarily a call to suffering. No one wants to suffer. Jesus didn't want to suffer. It was thrust upon Him. In the meantime, we can delight in the use of all our senses, and all our talents. We can thrill at the splendor of spiritual happiness. We don't want to allow ourselves to become self-absorbed to the point of losing our sense of mission, but that is unlikely in one who has faith.

In the wake of the Twin Towers disaster, we were confused and frightened. Added to the shock of the destruction of the Towers and the attack on the Pentagon were the reports about germ warfare. The word "Anthrax" was on everyone's mind. Other threats related to the possibilities of more terrorism began to poison the atmosphere.

We Catholics have also suffered a monumental shock related to the scandal involving sexual molestation by the clergy. Grave misjudgments by the hierarchy have occurred in the past allowing pedophiles to remain in the active ministry. The whole scandal has been despicable.

We can't deny our anger. What we have to do is control it. I don't want to oversimplify the problem, but at some point you have to protect yourself from cynicism.

Americans have shown great courage in dealing with these unimaginably dark events. We can't deny that we are still wounded, but Jesus has the right tonic for each and every one of us: **"Do not put on a gloomy look.... Stop worrying about tomorrow... tomorrow will take care of itself. Take it one day at a time"** (Mt 6:16, 34). He also said: **"In this world you will have many troubles, but cheer up, I have overcome the world"** (Jn 16:33).

You can't postpone joy by waiting until you are out of the slump. Don't spend your life waiting for someone to bail you out of the doldrums. You must take charge of your own joy. You must not only listen to the words of Jesus, you must act on them right now. Turn the justice issue over to the Lord.

Repeat this mantra of St. Paul often: **"Rejoice always! In all circumstances give thanks to the Lord, for this is the will of God for you in Christ Jesus"** (1 Th 5:16).

St. Paul went through hell and back as a missionary, and all the while he demanded Joy of himself. In spite of all his afflictions, he insisted on being visibly joyful. You can do the same. You can be a messenger of Joy right now.

Even though it may seem impossible to rejoice always, especially when you feel beaten down, you have to remember that with Christ all things are possible. It is precisely when you are the most downhearted that you must pick yourself up.

You cannot allow yourself to become dominated by the dark feelings of the moment. Snap out of it, and carry on with courage. Joy is a decision, not a feeling. You can decide to be joyful because of the knowledge of God's love. Don't drink yourself into oblivion. No matter how you feel, it is better to take control than to turn your life over to a state of chemical dependence. Men and women are perfectible. This is a belief which is deeply rooted in our Catholic Faith.

Pope John Paul II echoed the challenge of Jesus: *"Christ came to bring joy.... Go, therefore, and become messengers of joy."*

SHARE THE GIFT OF FAITH

We are all called to be messengers of Joy; the sick and the handicapped are not excused. The worse off you are, the better and more impressive your witness will be. A messenger is one who speaks up in whatever way he or she can. This is a faith issue. Being a good steward is a faith and obedience issue. A recent poll of 6,038 American adults, randomly chosen by a *Barna* research project, showed that Catholics are in last place when it comes to inviting outsiders to share in the benefits of their Catholic Faith. No doubt the scandals have taken their toll.

60% of all Pentecostals go out of their way to share their faith with outsiders. Among Baptists that number is 43%; Presbyterians, 23%; Lutherans, 21%; Methodists, 20%; and Episcopalians, 14%. Unfortunately, Catholics come in last with only 10%.

There is something disturbing about these numbers. After all, the apostles and saints, down through the ages, all possessed the missionary spirit. It is not quite enough to go to Mass and Holy Communion to fulfill your obligation to worship. You should think about inviting others to join you.

Catholics go to study groups and prayer meetings to deepen their faith, but they rarely introduce an outsider to the club. The best way to hold on to your faith is to share it.

Spiritual hunger abounds out there, people are swimming in fear and confusion, but we are so respectful of their privacy that we fail to share our deepest feelings.

Holding on to your faith without sharing it, is like keeping fresh fruit in a bowl without ever eating it. Soon it rots, and you have to throw it away.

How does one keep that from happening? By sharing your good fortune with others. Share the Faith. There is Joy in this if you do it tactfully, and gently.

Think about it. When a friend tells you a sad story, do you ever ask him or her to pray about it with you? Have you ever introduced a person who is grief-stricken to Mary, the Mother of Sorrows? She, who stood courageously beneath the cross, might offer some comfort. She has comforted millions of others. It is beyond our power to explain, but Our Lady of Consolation is there for Catholics and non-Catholics alike.

Do you ever invite a non-Catholic to Mass. Why not? If you believe that Jesus is truly present in the Eucharist, why not share that belief? If you don't believe it, you are out of step with the official teachings of the Church.

If you are hesitant about bringing anyone to your parish because there is no welcoming committee, why not volunteer to start one yourself? I say this because Joy comes from being a conduit of love. You can think of yourself as a storehouse or a pipeline. A storehouse stays bottled up under lock and key. A pipeline is always active, carrying valuable commodities to those in need. The active life is a joyful life.

Many years ago the late Cardinal Suenens appointed me to be his representative in the U.S. and Canada for the FIAT Evangelization Movement. I wrote about this in the second book of this Joy Trilogy, *God Delights In You.*

"*Fiat mihi*" is Latin for: "Be it done unto me," Mary's words to the angel Gabriel at the Annunciation. **Fiat** stands for the word **Yes**. We want to say yes to the Lord with the same courage that Mary had. We want to accept our vocation to make Jesus known and loved as she did.

The members form prayer groups and meet at least once a month. They come together for prayer and mutual encouragement. The aim is to call on the Holy Spirit, as Mary did, for new miracles of all kinds. They leave the meeting energized and go out to make Jesus known and loved, not on a soap box, but in gentle ways.

At these meetings, which last for about an hour or so, the group unites in spirit with Mary and calls upon the Holy Spirit for an increase of strength and Joy. This is in imitation of the Apostles who were once gathered in the Upper Room with Mary at Pentecost. She knew how to pray to the Holy Spirit, because He had come to her many years before, and the miracle of the Incarnation was the result.

The Apostles were at their lowest when they came together, and behold, after praying in the Spirit, they were revived. Not only revived, but emboldened to go forth and proclaim the Gospel at the risk of life and limb.

FIAT prayer groups begin by praying the rosary. Many use a shortened version of the traditional rosary, the FIAT rosary, which has only three decades, one for the Joyful Mysteries, one for the Sorrowful Mysteries, and the third for the Glorious Mysteries. When I pray it I use the Birth of Jesus, throughout the decade of the Joyful Mysteries, the Crucifixion for the Sorrowful Mysteries, and the Resurrection for the Glorious Mysteries. There is no need to complicate it. The point of the rosary is to meditate on the mysteries of the life of Jesus.

Sometimes I say the entire rosary focusing on one mystery, like the Descent of the Holy Spirit upon the Apostles. This is the gift of Jesus to us all. I call upon the Spirit for Strength and Joy.

After reciting the rosary, the members have a spiritual discussion. Chit-chat can precede the meeting, but once it is under way, everyone stays focused. The members report on their efforts in the past week or month to help make Jesus better known and loved. No one is pressured to speak.

Those who do report, tell how they carried Jesus to others. For instance, "I visited my neighbor in the hospital. At first I just listened, and then I had the courage to say: 'Can we pray together for good health?' I thought she might be uncomfortable with the idea, but she was delighted."

This type of example gives the others the idea of doing the same thing. You only do what feels right for you. No one is forced to do anything that makes them uncomfortable. No assignments are given.

Each FIAT prayer group is independent. The group elects a leader, and the members make their own rules. You can begin a group of your own, simply by deciding to do it. You only have to find one other person to join you. In time more will come. Prayer groups should not grow beyond twelve. If you have more than that, you should start a second group.

Cardinal Suenens used to say that FIAT was not a movement with an organizational structure; rather it is an "Inspiration." The idea is to call upon the Holy Spirit, asking Him to enflame the hearts of the members with love and zeal. Uniting with Mary is important because she became the mother of Jesus, our Master, by uniting with the Holy Spirit.

The twelve frightened Apostles were transformed by the Holy Spirit. We too need courage to be a little bolder about bringing Christ to the world. The meetings help to embolden the members to overcome their natural shyness. In a short time, they are only too willing to share their stories. It soon becomes easy, and then it becomes fun. You need the support of others. Cardinal Suenens once said to me: "Alone you are finished."

By taking evangelization seriously, we do the work of the

Church. There is Joy in being a member of such a group. Each member may choose to participate, or not. Some just come to pray and listen. Everyone is free.

Telling others your story may seem like bragging at first, but it isn't. After awhile, the members commend and applaud one another.

If you would like some more information on this anointed ministry write to me: Box 172, Clifton, NJ 07011. Both Pope Paul VI and Pope John Paul II gave Cardinal Seunens full permission to promote this apostolate. The international headquarters is in Belgium at Kardinaal Sterckxlaan 117,8-1860, Oppem-Meke, Belgium, Europe.

You can also log in on my website at:

www.fatherjohncatoir.com

or www.stjudemedia.com

or www.MessengerofJoy.com

Be proud of your Catholic Faith, and try to be a messenger of Joy.

God made you for a definite purpose. You were created to use your gifts, talents and treasures in such a way as to help build up the Kingdom. It amounts to a personal ministry of your own. Giving a generous check to some charity is good, but it does not give you as much personal fulfillment as an active ministry, which is personally tailored to your own conscience.

It is a gift of God's grace to participate in the ministry of Christ. It is also a way to be our own best self.

Live in the present moment, and become a good steward of all the talents and treasures that God has given you. Decide to honor God with your life. Live a Spirit-filled life. Live your precious life joyfully.

In Him, with Him and through Him you will find your bliss.

Steven Yim from Honolulu, Hawaii tells us how he manages to integrate prayer with his difficult counseling career.

> *In my first two years as a school counselor, a rosary and a whistle got me through. They were gifts from two school principals. The rosary reminded me of God's guiding hand, and the whistle called to mind my freedom to respond to God's love call.*
>
> *I have carried the rosary to work everyday for twenty-one years. Whenever I felt discouraged, I touched the rosary. Feeling the pain of children and families who were dealing with divorce, abuse, abandonment, retardation, muscular dystrophy, was overwhelming at times. The rosary's cross reminded me that being a school counselor wasn't going to be easy. But the Lord would be my strength.*
>
> *I also placed a whistle in my pocket before going to work. I thought about the choice before me. Shall I get mired in the world's suffering or shall I become a Christ-centered, playful school counselor? I chose to smile, relax and be gentle with children because I knew God loved me and He would be my shield. I hugged the children at recess; I listened to their stories and participated in their sports and games.*
>
> *The Lord had given me the courage to care for children joyfully. God had put a rosary and a whistle in my hand to remind me to pray always and never to take myself too seriously. My work had become a ministry. "I lift up my eyes toward the mountains, whence shall help come to me? My help is from the Lord, who made heaven and earth" (Ps 121:1-2).*

Steven commanded his mind to think positively. He decided to control his thoughts, so that his emotions would carry him forward and not drag him down. He used the whistle and the rosary as reminders of his good intentions. Once he decided to make his career a joyful experience, he asked for God's grace, and became an instrument of Joy.

All authentic spiritual help is from the Lord, but to make it effective in our lives we must will it. The will directs the mind to accept the Lord's Joy.

15

JOY AND CONSCIENCE

"Rejoice always, and be grateful in all circumstances, for this is
the will of God for you in Christ Jesus" (1 Th 5:16).

St. Paul was right. You can be grateful in all circumstances, and
you can rejoice in the knowledge of God's love at all times; all
you need is the will.

Commanding yourself to be joyful takes will power. You
can't rely on feelings. After all, who can "rejoice always"? Life
is so full of tragedy that we automatically rule out joy as a permanent feature of our personality. Why is that?

If Christ came to bring Joy, why shouldn't you notify your
face accordingly? The will is in charge, not the emotions. By developing the will to bear discomfort with a smile, you will be
able to make a giant leap forward in your spiritual journey. You
will also improve your mental health, and sweeten your daily
existence.

REMOVING OBSTACLES

The spiritual life is an adventure in practicing the art and
virtue of joyful living. Start with your tendency to complain and
criticize. If you find yourself complaining all the time, stop it.
Stop being so negative, and get on with the job at hand. If there

is a serious wrong that must be righted, take steps in a rational way to do something, but stop carping. Actions speak louder than words.

Granted, you may have to take action to correct a wrong in order to serve a greater good, but complaining day in and day out is a sign of immaturity. Remain faithful to your decision to be joyful no matter what, even if it hurts.

Where's the joy in being a grouch? Focusing on the negative cannot help anyone, least of all yourself. Sometimes it's better to grin and bear it. All of this will require courage, and in some cases heroism. It will certainly take will training to perfect the skill. You will have to stick to your guns, and fight the good fight, but it is so worth the effort.

FOLLOW YOUR GRACE

St. Teresa of Avila is a perfect example of someone who had to struggle to follow her grace. She knew exactly what God wanted of her. To follow her calling she had to use gifts she never knew she had. Controlling her fears was never easy for her; but she forced herself to persevere in what she believed was a calling from God.

Teresa was born in Avila, Spain, in the year 1515. At the age of 21 she entered the Carmelite convent in her home town. Because of her poor health she had to return home. However, the urge to give herself to God continued, and two years later she returned to the convent, this time for good.

There were many abuses in the discipline of religious life in her time. The vow of poverty was often compromised. Nuns from wealthy families had privileges that the others were denied. More luxurious living, and better food enjoyed by a few, had replaced the ideal of equality in the strict observance of the vow. Teresa saw the injustice as a betrayal. She was seething with discontent, not because she wanted to have more luxuries for herself, but because she saw religious life descending toward greater corruption.

Her poor health continued to cause her distress, but she was determined to do something about the problem. She wanted to reform the Order; however, her inner doubts stopped her from taking any decisive action. When she finally did act, she brought down the wrath of her superiors upon her. For daring to question the status quo, the superior accused her of pride. The other sisters joined right in, and spoke harshly against her.

"Who does she think she is, this upstart who questions her superiors?" Faced with daily persecution, she became filled with doubt. Her inner demons began tormenting her. She questioned her own motives, "What am I doing? Who do I think I am? Maybe I am filled with pride. Maybe I am making a fool of myself."

The doubts only got worse when she tried to suppress them. "You're going to fail miserably. One day you'll be thrown out of the Order. They will make your life miserable. You're going against Jesus who said, **'Judge not that you be not judged.'**" She saw herself dividing the community, and perhaps hurting the Carmelite Order, and feared that God might punish her if she persisted.

These thoughts made her sick. Nevertheless, deep down she knew she was right. So she put on the will to bear the pain and discomfort, and decided to go forward. Her idea of reforming the Order consumed her. She understood it to be her destiny. She accepted the mantle with courage and admitted she was a reformer, come what may. In 1555, recognizing the need to control her negative thinking, she wrote a little prayer for herself, which she repeated over and over again until it became second nature. It was her mantra, her pep talk, her way of setting her will to move forward.

Let nothing disturb you.
Let nothing cause you fear.
God is unchanging.
Patience obtains all.
Whoever has God needs nothing else.
God alone suffices.

This prayer sustained her all through the period of rejection and harassment. She kept fighting the good fight, and appealed to higher authorities. Eventually she prevailed, and in 1562 obtained the approval of the Superior General in Rome to break away from her community and start the first convent of the Reformed Carmelites.

In spite of continuing rebukes and false accusations she won. She was accused of being proud and stubborn, but she willed to resist, and kept saying her prayer. By ignoring her own doubts as best she could, she was able to bring widespread reform to religious life.

With the help of St. John of the Cross, she got permission from the head of the Carmelite Order to carry her reforms to the male members of the Carmelite community. In 1567 she opened the first Reformed Carmelite house for the priests and brothers. Before her death on October 4, 1582, she had established 16 new Reformed convents, and 14 new communities for the men of the Carmelite Order. When she received praise for her accomplishments, she gave God all the credit, but those who understood knew that it was her indomitable will power that made it possible. Her cooperation with God's grace was essential.

Where did her inner commitment come from? It was God's grace, but also it was her will that carried her through those stormy years. How did she do it? That's simple. She willed it!

It might be a good idea to make her prayer your own.

Let nothing disturb you, let nothing cause you fear. God is unchanging. Patience obtains all. Whoever has God needs nothing else. God alone suffices.

St. Teresa of Avila was canonized in 1622. She was the first woman to be made a Doctor of the Church, and her feast day on the calendar of saints, is October 15th.

When St. Paul says: **"Rejoice always, and be grateful in all circumstances, for this is the will of God for you in Christ Jesus,"** he doesn't mean that it will be easy (1 Th 5:16-17). Each one of us has to write our own mantra, and set our own will to the task. Holiness is God living in you. To be really holy you must decide to change into the person God wants you to be. It's a bit of a paradox. You must first realize that you are nothing, and that you will accomplish nothing on your own. Then you must decide to let the Lord lead you.

At some point however, you have to dive in, and act as though everything depended on you. Trust the Lord, and He will support you, but you must have the courage to follow your conscience and act. I am trying to get you to commit yourself to the art of living joyfully.

In a way, this decision to be your true self, accepting the Lord's call to Joy, is not unlike the call of St. Teresa. You won't be reforming a religious order, but you will be reforming your inner life. Moving away from a gloom and doom type of spirituality to one of Joy, begins with prayer. From prayer you move to love and Joy.

Mother Teresa of Calcutta took her name from St. Teresa of Avila. She too prayed to be a carrier of Divine Love, in fact that is the title she gave to her community: Carriers of Divine Love. She used to say: *"It's not how much you do, it's how much love you put into the doing."*

Love takes discipline. The ability to carry the burdens and obligations of love can wear you down. You have to put on the will to bear it if you hope to make progress, but don't do it out of doleful resignation. Do it with style. Live joyfully as you become a carrier of Divine Love and Joy. Jesus assured us that His yoke is easy and His burden is light. The trick is to let the Lord do all the worrying for you. Concern about success or failure should be left at the door. Call on Jesus and the Holy Spirit to help you become an instrument of love and Joy, and leave it at that. Become a channel of God's Joy in spite of your imperfections. The goal of the spiritual life is holiness, and this is essentially a gift of God. Ask for it and trust the Lord. Don't do anything you know is seriously wrong, and Joy will flower in the garden of your striving. Very often it takes great strength of character to follow your conscience, but that is what a saint aspires to do, and you are a saint-in-training. Which brings us to the matter of following your conscience.

CONSCIENCE

Ultimately, we all have to have the courage of our convictions if we are to achieve holiness. It takes courage to be fully alive.

The Second Vatican Council states that *"conscience is the most secret core and sanctuary of the person... where one is alone with God, and there in one's innermost self, perceives God's voice"* (*Pastoral Constitution on the Church in the Modern World*, #16).

We all know right from wrong, and there is usually common agreement on the basic moral questions. For instance, no one questions the validity of the Ten Commandments. They are meant to be commands not suggestions.

Moral theology is the study of the meaning of divine revelation, and it is a complicated science. For instance, "Thou shalt not kill" is an absolute statement. However, if a thief comes into your home at night and threatens the life of your loved ones, do you have the right to protect yourself by shooting the intruder? The answer is yes, you can take a life in certain circumstances. Since justified killing is possible, perhaps a better translation of the Commandment might be, "Thou shalt not murder." Murder implies an unjust killing. It would be better not to aim to kill, but in the heat of a robbery, simply firing the weapon might involve a killing.

The semantic problems that arise from the Ten Commandments could fill volumes. Interpretations differ. As a result you are left with your own conscience to decide what God is saying to you. Not that each of us can come up with our own version of the Commandments, but each of us can see nuances that the others cannot.

It is good to remember that Jesus opposed the legalists of His day with fury. They despised Him for it. When He attacked the Pharisees for imposing laws on the faithful that were too heavy to bear He awakened their wrath. They completely missed the point that the Supreme Law is love, not legalism.

The people of Christ's day were overburdened with hundreds of rules and regulations. When strictly enforced, they made a drudgery of life. Jesus came to bring liberation and Joy. Both He and the Pharisees were being faithful to the Ten Commandments as they understood them.

Jesus said He came to fulfill the law, not to destroy it. He respected the Supreme Law, and taught others to do the same. And yet He attacked the Pharisees because they had manufactured laws, and enforced them as though they were all on an equal level. Jesus opposed this legalism, and offered freedom of conscience as a remedy.

The Catholic Church teaches that when there is a doubt of law, we are free to follow our consciences. When you stop to think that Jesus came to bring Joy, you can see that there is a certain amount of personal freedom available to you. People who are always worried about displeasing God may be scrupulous because of the teaching of strict legalists. This dreaded mental condition can turn life into a nightmare.

Jesus came to liberate people from the oppression of fear about the binding power of various laws. Jesus always stressed mercy over moralism. For instance, Jesus favored the lepers.

They were a despised class. They were not only quarantined, but were morally ostracized. Their disease was thought to be the direct result of their sins. This made them spiritually defiled in the eyes of the law. They were forbidden from coming to the Temple to be purified. As a result, they were regarded as condemned by God. A good Jew would have nothing to do with them.

Jesus flew in the face of this injustice, and went to them, straightaway. He preached the Good News of the Gospel, telling them they were not cursed by God, but blessed. They were blessed in such a wonderful way that the Kingdom of God was theirs.

This was His Sermon on the Mount. The Eight Beatitudes are the core teaching of His Sermon in Matthew 5:3-10. Jesus told the lepers to disregard what they had been taught. They were to think of themselves as loved by God, not cast out. He said in effect, "Your disease has nothing to do with your worthiness or unworthiness. You have found favor with God, you are blessed."

For those who got the message it was music to their ears, indeed the best news they ever heard. The Pharisees reacted fiercely. Their authority was challenged. Jesus counteracted with courage, and continued to go against the tide. Almost at every turn He challenged the Hebrew traditions.

Remember the Samaritan woman at the well? She was a half-breed, an outcast. The Jews despised all Samaritans for that reason. Their Jewish ancestors had virtually defected from Judaism by intermarrying with foreigners. Consequently, they were thought to be under God's curse. By law, a good Jew could not even speak to a Samaritan.

Jesus came up to the Samaritan woman with complete freedom, and engaged her in a conversation. Eventually He chose her to be His messenger, and sent her back to her village with the news that she had spoken to the promised one of Israel. It is interesting to note that the word Apostle, from the Greek, means messenger. She was an early Apostle of sorts.

Jesus always followed His conscience. The letter of the law often violated His conscience and He resisted it. He understood the true nature of the moral order. He knew that God is love. He wanted to make God's will relevant to the lives of all people, especially outcasts. In doing this He was defending the Supreme Law not violating it. The people who crucified Him didn't see it that way.

Lawmakers of every age try to envision every circumstance when they make universal laws, but this is impossible. There will always be exceptions to the universal law. Hard cases, it is said, do not make good law; but when such cases come up, the usual legal presumptions are difficult to sustain.

For example, a thirty-year-old man with the emotional maturity of a twelve-year-old may get married legally, but soon his behavior destroys the marriage. The disaster showed that he was incapable of assuming the burdens and obligations of marriage, even though he publicly declared the vows. The legal presumption of validity for that marriage stands however, until it can be overturned in a court of law. The annulment process in the Church attempts to do just that.

People have human rights in every society, and one of the most important human rights is the right to follow one's conscience. To be guided by the truth, and to act honorably with love, is the goal of an upright conscience. One has not only the right, but also the duty to obey one's conscience. It should be an informed conscience, but that doesn't mean that freedom is canceled.

The Church serves us by pointing us in the right direction. However, in the final analysis, it is the individual's conscience, which is the proximate norm of morality.

There are many times in life when a conflict arises between the law and one's private sense of what God really wants. St. Augustine once said, **"Love God and do as you please."**

Giving yourself the freedom to act according to your conscience is not laxity. You have the right and the duty. Escaping from one's duty however, through cheap rationalizations is not a noble Christian response to life. However, there are circumstances where it is necessary to follow freedom, and at those times, it may be best to get the advice of a mature spiritual advisor before acting too hastily.

When it comes to choosing the path that is right for you, be courageous, and follow your conscience. Joy is a choice, and you have the right to an informed conscience when it comes to finding peace and joy in your life.

Stories About Ordinary People Doing Extraordinary Things

Here are some stories I wrote when I was in charge of The Christophers in New York. These are stories taken from newspapers, and reworked for brevity purposes. They are each about one person making a difference. When some good needs to be done, or some correction to a problem made, good people accept the responsibility, and change things for the better.

When you take positive action, you often run into misunderstanding and opposition. You may have to give up certain freedoms to follow your calling. This will take the will to bear discomfort. Will power is the *sine qua non* of spiritual maturity. Jesus had an abundance of it.

The heroes among us all have it. They set their sights high, and move forward no matter what the obstacles may be. Here, then, are a few stories about people who decided to change the world for the better. **"By their fruits you will know them"** (Mt 7:16).

1. Walter Turnbull has a Ph.D. in music, a field he obviously loves. And he also had a fulfilling musical career appearing as a soloist with major orchestras. Yet he felt something was missing.

What Dr. Turnbull really wanted was to be able to inspire and encourage youngsters to love music and to grow through music the way he had. So he organized a group of young singers whose talents have been showcased worldwide.

The renowned Boys Choir of Harlem, under his direction, sings every form of music from Bach to Pop to Gospel.

While many of these choir members are growing up in inner-city poverty, scholarships send ninety-eight percent of them to college.

A lot of youngsters and audiences are enriched because this one man loved music and decided to share that love with others.

So you see it's true — **one person can make a difference.**

A happy person is one who knows his or her purpose in life. Purpose and direction give life meaning. Joy is the by-product of a meaningful life. Choose to be more joyful.

2. When Catherine McMullen was injured in an accident, a two-year-old came to her aid. The 79-year-old New Jersey woman was alone in the house with her two-year-old grandson, Sal, when she tripped on the basement stairs and broke her leg.

When the toddler saw that she couldn't move, he brought her a blanket to keep her warm. The child didn't know how to make a telephone call, but when his mother phoned home, he answered.

He told her to come right away because his Nana couldn't get up. Thanks to Sal, Mrs. McMullen was kept warm and out of shock while the ambulance came to the rescue. The family was amazed that a two-year-old was smart enough to keep his grandmother warm. Sometimes grown-ups don't know how to act in an emergency situation.

Knowing what to say or do in a crisis is just common sense. Whether you're 2 or 92, if you keep calm and use your common sense, the results of your actions are likely to amaze you.

If a child can do the right thing in an emergency, so can you. Pray for the grace to be able to stay calm and use your common sense in any future emergency. Decide to be more helpful and less prone to panic. Choose Joy.

3. A New York City dentist and his wife were dismayed when they learned that their newborn son suffered from Down's Syndrome and would be mentally retarded. But they quickly came to love their infant as a beautiful gift from God.

The father said, "I realized that we all have problems and handicaps of one kind or another." So, no longer feeling hopeless, he began thinking about how modern medicine and education could help his son.

"It won't be easy," he said, "but God gave us our son and will give us the strength and understanding to help him lead a happy life."

Whatever this baby's disability might be, he will have one great advantage: the love and encouragement of a caring family. And isn't that the kind of love all of us need? To be there for one another is the essence of charity.

The challenge of love can be daunting. Put aside any fear of the unknown and learn to trust God. Decide to be more trusting and less fearful. Choose Joy.

4. If you think about the scourge of homelessness, it can

seem overpowering, but it tends to become more manageable if you look at it in the context of a local problem.

Bettie Hilbreath of Sulphur Springs, Texas asked herself how she might help homeless people. She decided there was at least one thing within her power to do. She could help them keep warm by making them quilts.

So on a regular basis she and some friends gather for quilting bees in one of their homes. Then, once a month they bring their completed handiwork to the Senior Citizen Center where the quilts are distributed to those in need.

Maybe one person can't solve the vast problem of homelessness, but one person can certainly make the world a warmer place for a few homeless individuals.

Living only for oneself can be so boring and joyless. Selfish people are usually the most jaded and unhappy people on the planet. Decide to be more generous. Choose Joy.

5. In a remote area of California, there's an unlocked cabin for travelers to enjoy. It's known as Winkler's Cabin. The shelter is furnished with a table and chairs, bunk beds, two mirrors, a stove and some canned goods.

Years ago, a miner named James Winkler built the cabin in a beautiful valley and then welcomed strangers to use it at no charge.

A sign was placed over the cabin door which read: "Take What You Need — Leave What You Can." Over the years, hundreds of travelers have accepted the invitation. One of them wrote this sentiment in the guest book:

"Thank you for this beautiful experience where one can draw closer to God and nature. You will not be forgotten."

There are many reasons to be generous to family, friends, and strangers, but one of the nicest is that people who do things for others are remembered and cherished.

Thinking of others more, and of yourself less, enhances

your self-respect. It draws a harvest of gratitude. Decide to be more thoughtful. Choose Joy.

6. It's hard to imagine what Thanksgiving Day is like for the homeless, but Marilyn and Bernie Ziller decided to find out.

What the Zillers did was to take their family to a San Francisco soup kitchen for Thanksgiving. Because they aren't destitute they also left a generous contribution after the meal.

The Zillers found that the experience gave them and their children a greater understanding of what it means to be poor. They also came away with a fuller appreciation of how much they have. One of the first fruits of confronting the misery of others is gratitude. "There but for the grace of God go I."

Bernie, the father, pointed out, "It's easy to sit at home with your family and blot out the rest of the world." His wife, Marilyn, added, "I see myself differently now. I feel humbled and grateful for what we have."

Saint Paul once said, **"Rejoice always, in all circumstances give thanks to the Lord"** (1 Th 5:16-17).

Joy comes to those who care about others. They expand their own horizons in the process. Decide to be more giving. Choose Joy.

7. In Oakland, California, a group of senior citizens wanted to escape from self-pity and idleness, so they decided to form a theater company for their own enjoyment. Known as the College Avenue Players, they put together five original plays and staged them for interested audiences of all ages.

In discussing the program, one of the members made this observation:

"When most people think of the needs of senior citizens they usually think about food and shelter, but never about entertainment. What we do at the College Avenue Players is provide another kind of medicine for the elderly, an evening's entertainment."

Recreation and entertainment are basic to the enjoyment of life. A good laugh is sometimes the best medicine. Our thanks go out to all those performers who give so much time and talent to bring others a little more happiness.

Use your gifts and talents to make this a better world. Join with others and create enjoyment for the good of all. Decide to be more open to giving, and less open to self-pity. Choose Joy.

8. Perhaps you've heard of Alan Paton, the South African author who died at the age of 85. His novel *Cry, the Beloved Country* was his most famous book. It sold more than 15 million copies and helped to expose the evils of apartheid, South Africa's now defunct system of racial segregation.

Paton, a white man, was a critic of the South African white regime. He rebelled against the censorship and unjust laws imposed by racial tyrants. In crying out against this evil system he put his life at great risk. Paton once said, "Man was not created to go down on his belly before the state." What courage that must have taken!

Challenging the evils in our world often involves enormous risks. But remember, with God's help all things are possible. Jesus said, **"Take courage for I have overcome the world"** (Jn 16:33).

The dignity of the human person from conception to death is inviolable. Don't let people trample on human rights. Decide to be courageous. Live one day at a time, and try to be true to yourself, so that you can be there for others. Choose Joy.

I shall pass through this life but once.
Any good, therefore that I can do,
Or any kindness I can show to any fellow creature,
Let me do it now.
Let me not defer or neglect it,
For I shall not pass this way again.

Etienne de Grellet

16

JOY AND TOUGH LOVE

**"Blessed are those who hear the Word of God
and put it into practice."** (Lk 11:28)

The interesting thing about love is that it requires will power. Love is not a romantic emotion. Feelings wear away with time, but true love lasts because it is in the will. For a marriage to last beyond the first few years it takes the will to bear discomfort, the willingness to forgive, and a good sense of humor.

A growing number of physicians, nurses, psychologists and therapists are using mirth and laughter to reduce stress, and ease pain. Norman Cousins, a famous editor, wrote about his recovery from a crippling spinal disease by the use of daily doses of humor. He treated himself to a hotel suite, brought in funny movies, and took large doses of vitamin C. The whole project was less expensive and more effective than going to the hospital, and a lot more fun. He said he owed his recovery to laughter.

Getting along in this big bad world requires both grit and a good sense of humor. There's no doubt about it. It also takes tough love.

Let me give you an example. The state of Matrimony is essentially a relationship between two incompatible people. They bind themselves together for life in a covenant that takes courage, prayer, and will power to sustain. Remaining faithful to their promises, and raising children can sap all their energy.

Since every human being is unique, it follows that every couple is basically incompatible. Even if both parties like the same music, read the same books, and support the same political party, they still remain utter mysteries to one another. They still have to respect the privacy of the other party.

Learning how to navigate their differences with grace takes perseverance, patience, and the will to keep the love alive. Even when feelings of love have been all but obliterated by anger, successful partners still hang in there. The will to endure all things keeps the marriage from falling apart. The emotions cannot be trusted to do that.

Existential love is not the love of dreams and poetry. "Love is a harsh and dreadful thing," wrote Feodor Dostoevsky. When you look at the crucifix, you understand how true that is.

When true love is present an atmosphere of joy can prevail. And interestingly enough, the promotion of joy and laughter makes it easier to love.

All caretakers and all parents know what true love requires. They may not always know how to create the ambiance of joy, because there are times when the ingratitude of the other party, or the children they are trying to serve makes momentary joy impossible. For love to flourish, one must often pay a heavy price.

There's no question about it, becoming a loving person requires the will to bear discomfort. This discomfort can be a sweet thing, but often it is a bitter pill. When you know that your will is going to be tested every day of your life, you gain a quiet satisfaction out of not allowing yourself to be filled with self-pity. A whiner only gets contempt from others, not sympathy.

The will has only one function, to say yes or no. If you say yes to love, even when your feelings do not lend support, you are in command of your life. However, a person is not required to become a doormat. It is wrong to let someone walk all over you.

In a marriage contract the duty of mutual respect is part of the bargain. When violations occur out of inadvertence, human error, or ignorance, you can make excuses, and carry on with courage. However, systematic, repeated abuse can make a marriage intolerable. It would not be Christian to accept physical, and/or psychological abuse on a regular basis. You then become an enabler. If you allow someone to debase you saying things like, "I think you're garbage, and if you accept what I do to you, you must be garbage, so I'm going to treat you accordingly," then shame on you. You only get what you ask for.

The will should say yes to a difficult marriage, and no to a chronically abusive one. Joy will never flow if one party is a tyrant. We used to tell women that their vows require them to take anything the husband decides to deliver in the way of abuse, but no more. Thank God women have become too wise for that.

True love tries to protect the joy of the other party. Being joyful even when your emotions are down is one way to express love. It is a courageous way, and it isn't phony. Joy begets joy. Joy is an important way of becoming a better instrument of God's love. Why is that? Because the only thing you have to give is yourself.

Who wants to be around someone who is joyless? A person who is driven by compulsions is seldom able to project joy, even if that person is a do-gooder. Compulsive activity is unnerving. This is especially true for the clergy. Parishioners are quick to spot a preacher who talks the talk, but doesn't walk the walk. A joyless pastor who doesn't practice what he preaches turns people off.

Who wants to learn from a teacher who is not emotionally comfortable with herself? Or, who wants to work under a boss who is always impatient and quick to criticize?

The answer is no one!

On the other hand, doesn't everyone enjoy the company of a person who is happy? Everyone wants to learn from a teacher who is kind and joyful. Developing a curiosity about learning can either be fun, or drudgery, depending how the teacher presents the material.

Most people prefer a person who is calm, self-possessed, and joyful. Good humor and laughter go a long way. A nervous taskmaster who never laughs will not succeed at anything, unless he decides to change.

The truth is that children and adults alike respond better to someone who exudes a spirit of peace and joy. So why not dig in and bite the bullet? Put on the will to do what it takes to love well, and to enjoy yourself in the process. It takes a strong determination to put up with annoyances. Grin and bear it. Fighting the good fight takes grit. Sometimes tough love is the only remedy available.

In a moment I will present some cases where tough love is needed if you are going to save a loved one. This approach deserves a little background information.

Marshall McLuhan was right when he wrote, "the medium is the message." He meant that the way you communicate with people is the key to reaching them. If you give books away to illiterate people you won't be doing them a favor.

In the matter of love, you are the medium of every message you present. If you want to be a good parent, teacher, boss, or counselor, you would do well to examine the state of your emotional life. Are you a joyful person or not? The answer to that question is crucial.

There are many hard-working mothers who are compulsive, driven by a need to be perfect. The compulsion to work and clean in order to be the perfect wife is a sure way to forfeit joy. The compulsive need to demonstrate your competence in order to protect yourself against criticism is a no-win strategy. Such a woman becomes the victim of her own fears.

The fear of failure and rejection can surely ruin your life. Underlying the visible symptom of perfectionism is a deep insecurity. It needs to be examined and exorcised as soon as possible.

Many people have neurotic ways of coping with their fears, but unless they see them for what they are, and confront them, they will continue to be dominated by them. If you always do what you've always done, you'll always get what you always got.

Fear is the enemy of joy. It makes people ineffective. Fear makes parenting a misery. Love on the other hand makes it a joy.

"Stop worrying about tomorrow. God will take care of your tomorrow. Take it one day at a time" (Mt 6:34).

The issue, as far as Jesus is concerned, is one of trust. Are you able to trust Him? Can you turn yourself over to the Holy Spirit? Divine Life is within you. When you catch yourself out of sync with God's Peace and Joy, the first thing to do is try to calm yourself down. Turn to prayer. Call on the name of Jesus right away and be still in His presence. Contemplation will help you do this.

Listen to your own breathing. Feel the relaxation moving up from your feet, to your legs, to your stomach, to your neck, and to your face. Ask yourself, "Where have I not let go?" And then let go. Rest in that state. Be happy with God who is deep within you. Draw from His Joy.

Give yourself at least five minutes a day for this visit to your personal spa. This is contemplation, wordless prayer at its best. Simply give yourself to God and let Him worry about the rest. Do not be too hard on yourself. You're human, and it's normal to have everyday worry. You will never be entirely free of it.

Some worry is necessary, like putting food on the table. This kind of fussing keeps you on your toes. But needless worry turns into sustained anxiety, which can be damaging to your health. You can do better by trying to be free of fear.

Children react better to a parent who carries a sense of joy through all the fussing. Discipline, correction, and instruction go down easier in a joyful household. If the children react negatively to the messenger, maybe they are missing the message.

Whether you are a parent, a clergyman, a teacher, a counselor, or a businessman, the person you are makes a far bigger impact on those around you than the words you speak.

Therefore, cultivate joy as a tool for winning friends and influencing people. Joy is an important parental tool, and an indispensible pastoral tool. It is also empowers a person to be effective in dealing with others in business or in social events.

All successful people possess something called good character. A person worth knowing is one who has a set of values, and who lives by a set of principles. Those who are driven by their fears and feelings eventually lose power, joy, purpose and direction.

Joyful people are not upset by the emotional state of others; nor are they easily sidetracked from their goals. In the art of parenting, leading or counseling, the skill of staying calm is most important. When such a person comes to the assistance of someone in need, whether it is a child or an adult, they do not enter into the emotional climate of the upset person. They empathize, but they do not cry along with them. They hold on to their joy.

Some misguided parents, in the name of compassion, identify with the emotional distress of their child, weeping along with them instead of lifting them up emotionally. One can be empathetic without losing self-composure. If you identify too closely with the pain of your child, you may end up with two highly excited or upset people, instead of one.

Your job is to stay calm. Objectivity and patience can be more helpful than a knee-jerk reaction. Parents and counselors should not allow themselves to be manipulated by a distraught child. Doing their bidding too quickly may have you rushing off to school to complain before all the facts are gathered. This is a sure way of forfeiting respect, power and joy in the long run. It also teaches the child that his or her tears can command action in the adult world. The realities of life will soon shatter that idea.

Some incidents require good investigating skills to get to the bottom of the problem. And some problems require tough love, not appeasement. If there is a justice issue, then of course you must take the appropriate action. But in the process, always hold on to your joy. Your emotional center should not be turned over to another.

Skilled counselors remain self-possessed. They listen, offer advice if asked, but at no time do they surrender their objectivity. There is a silent prayer I offer when I am counseling.

"Here I am Lord. I am at peace. I am joyful. Help me to communicate your love with my eyes, and my smile. Help me show this person that there is light at the end of the tunnel. Help me to help them to trust You, and reject all fear."

Professional golfers learn to stay within themselves. If they try to do more than their natural abilities allow, becoming over-ambitious, and trying to hit the ball farther than ever, they end up swinging too hard. This makes them lose control of the ball's direction. To win they have to relax, and hold on to their composure.

Playing for the fun of the game produces the best results. Staying within yourself as you try to be of help to others takes the same kind of skill. The object is to help the person move through his or her problem, and come up with alternative solutions. You shouldn't try to do that for them, but you can listen.

Show them that you understand their pain. Offer a glass of water, a tissue, or move them to a more comfortable chair. Express your understanding that this problem must have been a terrible blow. But all the while, hold on to your joy.

The attitude you maintain will be more reassuring than any advice you might give. Problem solving is not your goal. Each person has to do their own problem solving. However, offering a loving hand in friendship can help them through the storm.

Joy is so elusive and so uncertain at times. We always want to be more loving, more helpful, and more joyful, but our very exposure to the problems of others makes us vulnerable. "There but for the grace of God go I." Keep in mind that you are limited. We are all, in a real sense, powerless. Only God can help us. He is the only one with real power. Turn to Him. Stay calm, and enter into His Joy as you try to help others.

Weather the storms of life without losing your connection to the Spirit of Joy. Your Joy is the best thing you can give to a person in need. This is not a feeling you are communicating, but a presence. Your inner knowledge of God's Presence is your best gift. You can bring them this joyful Presence, which comes from the knowledge of God's Love. You can allow the Lord to bless them through your smile and your kindness.

Never turn anyone away who comes to you for help.

Now, having said that, I realize that there are times when you have to be tough. Some people need reality therapy before they wake up. We cannot live in a fantasy world. Life is consequential, and people have to be held accountable. Everyone must take responsibility for his or her own happiness and safety.

If you are working with someone who is bent on self-destruction you will have to talk straight. Get between the victim and drugs.

THE DRUG SUB-CULTURE

Over half a million Americans die each year from drug and alcohol related causes. More than $56 billion dollars is spent on illegal drugs in the U.S. alone. A recent survey indicated that only 14% of parents thought that their children had ever used drugs. They are wrong because 38% of the teens surveyed admitted that they were using.

What begins as harmless fun, like smoking a little pot, can

blossom quickly into a life-threatening addiction. Marijuana is stronger today than it was in the 60's and 70's. The dealers want kids to get hooked early so they can move on to more serious drugs. Teens go from experimentation to addiction in about 6 to 18 months. More kids are smoking pot in grammar school today than ever before. The average age for first use is 14, but some start in the fifth grade and earlier. By senior year in high school, 1 in 20 use drugs on a daily basis.

When they begin using drugs their learning skills diminish, and their concentration is impaired. In addition, their interest in sports and other school activities fades away. Watch for warning signs like changes in behavior or appearance, a big drop in grades or a decrease in energy. A sure tip-off is any unexpected disappearances of money or possessions. At a certain point family conflicts become more intense.

Set your will to take action. The will says yes or no. You must say no and mean it. Do not tolerate disobedience, no matter what it takes. Involve the police if necessary. Tough love is the only love you can give to a rebellious addict. Pampering is a delusion. It can only lead to disaster. The following case deals with the drug problem and tough love. I have changed the names to protect the family.

CASE ONE

Maggie and Tom were beside themselves with worry. They found their son Tom Jr. hiding his drug paraphernalia. He admitted using, and was already addicted at age seventeen. They made rules to correct this situation, but he would not obey them. He was sneaking out of the house from his bedroom window in the middle of the night on a regular basis.

They wanted to know what they could do to put a stop to this self-destructive behavior. Obviously, there is no room for a Pollyanna approach to this problem.

Get involved in the battle to get your child off drugs, and stay involved. Make your expectations known. Do not let them travel in the company of questionable people. Network with other parents, and join a support group.

Setting a good example is essential. Don't use drugs yourself, and be aware of your drinking habits. You may have to set a better example.

Do whatever you have to do to save your child. Above all, pray for God's wisdom and strength. Ultimately prayer will be your strongest weapon.

Tom Jr. is either open to entering a recovery program or he is not. Normally, parents can't force their children into treatment. Normally, it just doesn't work that way. The average treatment center will not accept an unwilling client. However, do not wait for them to come to talk to you. Go to them, and talk straight. Do not tolerate evasive answers. Take a stand and mean it. Be ready to listen, but don't let them hold you hostage to their self-destructive behavior.

You have to act.

Find out what they are thinking about as far as their future is concerned. Consider using random drug-screening tests right in your home. Testing their urine is one way to be sure. If they lie to you and test positively, punish them severely. In advanced cases you will need to enlist trained professional help. They may leave home and try to make it on the street.

Anyone in charge of a youngster at risk cannot make decisions for him. He has to want sobriety, or you're in for a rough ride. In the worst case scenario there are crisis intervention centers that might work when everything else fails. They will arrange to take him against his will, and deal with him at their treatment center. Angry, resistant clients are not impossible to tame. In such a place he would be virtually in prison, and there are no guarantees about the outcome, but they do have success stories and it may be worth the risk. Be advised, they are usually very expensive.

This answer may be frightening, but it is the only honest one I can give. Tough love is true love even though all the warm feelings are missing.

While you can't make them stop, your children must know that you have a zero tolerance for drug abuse. Tell them you love them, but warn them about the consequences of drug use.

Tell them they will one day have to spend time in jail, perhaps years. In spite of everything, keep your sense of humor. Tell them you'll visit them, and bring them comic books. Immature brats like comic books. Tell them they are also risking the possibility of a miserable death. Ask them what kind of a casket they want.

Let them know your displeasure in no uncertain terms. Be prepared to face the fact that your best efforts may not be enough. If the child leaves the house, all you can do is pray. You may even have to throw them out to protect your family. That may be the only kind of love you can muster, if all else has failed. Stand firm, and pray.

There is no joy in tough love, I admit. But through it all there is grace. God is with you every step of the way. Tap into His strength and Joy.

My heart goes out to parents who are dealing with headstrong teens. Do not be discouraged. They will fight you tooth and nail, but if you persist, your chances of prevailing are very good. With God's help all things are possible. Keep praying, and learn to laugh at your own powerlessness. It will teach you how much you need God. There are problems that only God can solve. It's good to know that He is on your side.

Domestic warfare can be a plague, but if you set your mind on positive results, you will maintain your self-respect, and probably succeed in your goals. Once you have done all that anyone could do, just knowing that you tried can bring a measure of joy and peace to your soul.

A less serious but potentially dangerous problem is the one dealing with adolescent rebellion.

CASE TWO

A woman named Sarah was deeply distraught over the behavior of her daughter. It was not drugs, but college drinking and partying. The girl was sullen, inconsiderate, self-centered, and at times defiant. Sarah feared for her future.

I was more optimistic about the girl's future, because I had seen immaturity before, and I know it is universal. I told the mother to be patient. Maturity takes time; mistakes will be made. Once you grasp this fact you will be able to see that all is not lost when they begin testing their own freedom.

College drinking is widespread, and a young girl is at great risk if she doesn't wise up fast. The parents cannot be passive. Even though this is a stage that will pass, the parents must be firm. The vast majority of college drinkers are merely showing off, and the boys are sowing their wild oats. It can be a dangerous environment for a girl.

However there is reason to be hopeful. Even the wildest girl or boy will grow up.

Let me tell you a true story about a man who gave his father fits when he was a boy.

These are his own words:

> *"I was born stubborn. I was also tough, not in the polite sense of the word, but in the sense our neighbors used that word in Shenandoah, Pennsylvania where I grew up. They shook their heads and called me "tough." This is nothing to be proud of, but it shows as honestly as I know how to state it, what sort of raw material God had to work with.*
>
> *"I was a bully, the leader of a gang, a street fighter, and most of the fights I picked on purpose, just for devilment. I had no use for school except insofar as it had a playground where I could fight or wrestle.... Things were so bad in fact that while I was still in grammar school, my father actually took me to the police station insisting that they send me to reform school.*

"And yet my father was the kindest of men. He was simply at his wit's end. Talking to me did no good. Thrashing me only gave me an opportunity to show how tough I was."

The writer is the late Father Walter Ciszek, SJ. He was my confessor for a few years when he was living with the Jesuits at Fordham University. Fr. Ciszek's character was so unlike the boy he described in his book, I had to wonder if he might be exaggerating. But no, he assured me. He simply credits God for the miracle of changing his heart.

If you do not know his story read his autobiography, With God In Russia, a Doubleday Image Book, published in 1964. The book tells of his years of hard labor with barely enough to eat. He had been arrested under false charges in Poland where he was serving as a missionary priest. Soviet authorities accused him of being a spy for the Vatican on the grounds that he had offered Mass in public.

They put him in solitary confinement. For five years he was beaten and interrogated continually until he was so weak that he signed a confession in a daze, against his will. As a result, he spent 15 more years doing hard labor in Siberia; accused falsely of being a Vatican spy.

After Father Ciszek's death he was proposed for canonization. His extraordinary charity and perseverance, in the face of cruelty, made him exceptional. His real character came out during his ordeal, and it turned out that he was down deep the gentlest and sweetest person you could ever imagine. If faith and grace can move mountains, changing hearts is no problem.

This brings me back to the distraught mother in my story. I would ask her to get involved and stay involved in her daughter's discipline, and be patient. God writes straight with crooked lines. He draws good out of evil. He transforms personalities. Don't think the worst. Don't ever give up on your child, pray always.

Your teenagers will grow up one day. Young adults eventu-

ally mature and become sane again. There is always hope. Put your trust in the Lord, and keep praying. One day, with the help of God, all will be well. Your patience will be rewarded.

The problem of losing one's sense of purpose is serious. If you lose your self-respect you are finished. Getting control of your thoughts is key, and this will take tough love.

CASE THREE

Antoinette was slightly depressed, thinking dark thoughts about how useless her life had become. She was afraid she was wasting her potential as a wife and mother. She wondered if her total absorption with her little family made any difference at all in the grand scheme of things. She felt unappreciated, taken for granted. "Is it worth all this effort?" she wondered. "Is this where I'm supposed to be?"

There can be many reasons for the bad feelings. Sometimes the inner turmoil is nothing more than the tyranny of the super-ego. People browbeat themselves. Their subconscious mind constantly brings up hurtful memories, which torment them. It's like a tape-recorder playing poisonous messages in the mind. The inner demon puts fear in the heart of such people. Even the strongest individuals find it exceedingly difficult to change a negative pattern of thinking that has become habitual. They don't know how to erase the tape.

Fortunately there is another voice that also speaks to us. It is the voice of the Holy Spirit. This woman can also hear the Spirit saying, "Pay no attention to your doubts. Laugh at them. You are a wife and a mother. You are doing the best you can. I have called you to be a mother. Don't be discouraged. What you do is hidden from the gaze of the world, but I see all your sacrifices and they are pleasing to me. Your life gives meaning to my grand purpose. I will reward you in due time. Trust me and don't be afraid."

Perhaps the problem is rooted in the husband-wife relation-ship. The best thing to do is go for counseling. If the Lord would speak to you He might say: "Your husband cannot be the man I want him to be without your support. Your influence upon him is beyond anything you can see or imagine. I bless you both and honor your love. Your children are precious to me, more precious than you know. I have entrusted them to your care. What you feel unable to do for them or for your husband, you can turn the problem over to me. I will be living in you, and will care for all of you in ways that you cannot see or know.

"Your life of love and service may not seem spectacular to oth-ers but it is to me. Count on me to be there for you. When you try to please me, I delight in you, but even if you forget all about my presence, I still love you with all my heart. Be at peace. Laugh at that discouraging inner-voice. You are my beloved. Trust me."

It is much better to listen to the Holy Spirit, the source of love, strength and joy than to focus on sadness and self-recrimination. Pray for the serenity to accept the things you cannot change, the courage to change the things you can, and the wisdom to know the difference.

Standing up to hardships can be difficult, but tough love enables you to surmount your fears.

CASE FOUR

George was a retired lawyer. He was in his early seventies and began thinking that it was time to start preparing to meet his Maker.

He was a perfectionist. In his youth he suffered from scrupu-losity. It was a problem which tormented him. He came to me hop-ing that I would be his spiritual director. Even though he was a successful professional, he was filled with self-doubt.

He wanted me to take some responsibility for his spiritual state so he could be sure he was on the right path. He was afraid of displeasing God.

He didn't consciously ask me to think for him, but it was his hidden agenda. I began by instructing him about the nature of spiritual direction.

It is important first of all to know the distinction between counseling and spiritual direction. Counseling or guidance is a process aimed at stabilizing the person's mental and emotional well-being, and pointing them in the right direction. It is a good and necessary service at times, but it is not spiritual direction. Spiritual direction involves an interpersonal relationship in which the director listens to the person who comes for help.

However, it is more than listening, and more than counseling. Spiritual direction is also about discernment. Counseling and spiritual direction are not mutually exclusive.

True spiritual direction involves a bit of counseling, as well as the gift of discernment. The director tries to recognize the stirrings of the Holy Spirit. Discernment requires prayer. Discernment is a gift from God. One does not become a spiritual director by getting an academic degree, though it helps to study the spiritual masters. Since grace builds on nature study is important, but knowledge is not enough. A spirit of humility before God, asking for His help enables the director to discern what the Holy Spirit is asking. The essential question is this: What is God asking of me?

Discernment starts the moment the dialogue begins. The director needs to clarify the person's level of faith, hope and charity. The process is similar to psychological counseling, but the goal is different. The psychologist is trying to restore emotional and mental health. The spiritual director will want the same thing, but he or she may lack the competence to be a skilled counselor. The spiritual director is concerned about increasing faith, hope and charity.

The first task is to examine the person's level of faith, by asking questions like these: When do you pray, how often, and in what way? What do you experience during prayer? What is the fruit of your prayer-life? What are you doing for God and neighbor as a result of prayer?

The clarification process continues with questions about the virtue of hope: How strong is your trust? Are you anxious about many things? How well do you see the relationship between a strong faith and a high level of trust in God's mercy and goodness?

Needless worry about the past or the future can destroy peace and joy. It is a sign of weak hope. God wants us all to be loving and joyful, and free of fear.

Then move on to questions about charity: Are you a generous person? Do you forgive those who hurt you? Do you have real compassion, or is it a strained sense of obligation?

Good spiritual directors do not direct. The director never says, "Be more joyful." I may be able to do that in a book as a matter of general direction, but when I am the spiritual director of an individual I would never say, "God wants you to do more volunteer work." Even if I thought it would help, I would try to elicit the idea from the directee.

What I would do is ask this question: "Do you believe that God wants you to be happy?" If the answer is yes, fine; if it is no, then I've hit on a serious obstacle to joy. "Why?" I would ask. "What reason do you have for saying this?"

If she gives a reason or two that doesn't make sense, I would ask: "Do you really believe what you just said? Really?"

Eventually the person may figure it out. God does not play favorites. No individual is an exception to God's universal love for His children.

The process of spiritual direction is not primarily advisory or informative, though the director might impart advice or knowledge from time to time. Nor is the goal primarily therapeutic, though emotional relief is often a valued by-product of the service.

Spiritual direction attempts to listen to the soul of the person. Sometimes a soul is held hostage by the personal ambition of the subject. Spiritual direction is an adult-to-adult relationship, not a *parent-child relationship, so the director never speaks for God, or presumes to know God's will for the person. The director always gives the client the space and freedom necessary to discover the voice of God arising from within.*

The person must find the Inner Light himself.

It is good to remember that Joy is the infallible sign of the presence of the Holy Spirit. A joyless, fearful person needs to be reconnected with God's Joy. That means getting rid of envy, which is sadness over the good fortune of another; and jealousy, which is a state of fear and suspicion that someone is getting what you should have.

Helping someone to think about his feelings can be liberating. The tough part comes when you try to discern where the Holy Spirit is leading this person. The Spirit often leads us in directions we would not have chosen for ourselves. The call may lead to difficult decisions.

Why? Because the Spirit moves us to love, and love always involves the cross in one way or another. Love also brings with it great joy and exhilaration.

As Mother Teresa put it, faith leads to love, love leads to service, and service leads to the cross. But at each stage we are being led home to heaven.

Now having said all that, I asked George what form of service would he find enjoyable? I let him explain an idea he had about serving in a soup kitchen. He lit up as he told me about his dream, but he was afraid of acting on his idea.

Then I asked him what changes could he make in his life to make the dream come true. He understood, and said he would make the call to the local soup kitchen.

To live more joyfully one has to take some action. Presuming that you have accepted Jesus as Lord, the next step is to do what He asks: **"When I was hungry did you give me to eat?"** (Mt 25:35).

That doesn't mean we should all get involved with soup kitchens; there are many kinds of hunger.

The greatest honor we can give to God is to trust Him, and live more joyfully because of His love. It is possible to be free of worry and fear.

George said his wife was always after him to loosen up, and enjoy his retirement years. I asked him what he thought of that, and he agreed he had work to do on this.

Before we were finished he wanted to do a better job of caring about his wife's happiness. He agreed to reward her for a lifetime of loving service by taking her out more. This I think is a high spiritual goal because it is love in action.

Our first visit ended happily. He made some good resolutions. He agreed also to offer God all the joy that resulted from his new resolutions. Offering joy and thanksgiving can be done in a variety of ways.

The following case is a bit technical in that there are legal questions involved. Nevertheless, the spiritual well being of the woman in question cries out for kindness.

CASE FIVE

Betty, a divorced Catholic was raising two children, and she wanted an annulment so she could marry again. But she was reluctant to go for one because she believed incorrectly that a Church annulment would make her children illegitimate.

The truth is that the children born of an annulled marriage are not illegitimate. In fact, canon law specifically declares them to be legitimate. Illegitimacy, a term no longer in widespread use, is the state of one born out of wedlock. All children are precious in the sight of God. All children are miracles of his creation. Children of an annulled marriage were not born out of wedlock, and can never be declared illegitimate.

Betty read Sheila Rauch Kennedy's book Shattered Faith *that took issue with the Catholic Church's annulment process. Mrs.*

Kennedy was raised in the Episcopal Church, and therefore always believed that a divorce is morally permissible. She objected to the invasion of her privacy when the Catholic Church took up the annulment case initiated by her husband.

Sheila Kennedy's problem was basically the same one King Henry VIII raised nearly five hundred years ago: Why isn't a civil divorcing enough? Why should a marriage be nullified by the Catholic Church? The answer is: because the Roman Catholic Church tries to be faithful to the words of Jesus found in Matthew 19:6, "What God has joined together let no one put asunder."

Divorce puts a marriage asunder by severing an existing bond, and legally bestowing the right to remarry. On the other hand, an annulment, whether civil or ecclesiastical, finds the original contract to be invalid, negating the need to sever the bond. There was no bond in the first place. If there was no valid contract, either because true consent was never given, or one of the parties lacked the capacity to marry, then there is no divorce per se, but rather an acknowledgment of the invalid contract.

You can't sign a contract to build a skyscraper if you don't have the money or the materials to do the job. Some people simply lack the capacity to enter into and sustain the burdens and obligations of marriage.

In an ecclesiastical annulment, the marriage bond is not severed, as in a divorce. The annulment declares that a true contract never existed. The Church is not saying that the annulled marriage never existed. We acknowledge its existence, and respect the memory of it. We also state that the children born of the marriage are precious and legitimate.

All the annulment does is state that the marriage contract itself was defective from the beginning due to some imperfection in the nature of the consent or in the capacity of at least one of the parties. When there is an essential defect of this kind, the contract is declared null, and is no longer binding. The presumption of validity is thus overturned.

Some Catholics find it emotionally impossible to dredge up the painful memories of the past. As a result they never apply for an annulment. A certain percentage of those who do apply are rejected because they have no grounds.

Catholics who take matters into their own hands, and remarry without the benefit of a Church annulment are forbidden to receive Holy Communion. Some go to Communion anyway believing that the new marriage is a blessing sent by God, and that the prior marriage was the false marriage.

The Church teaches that you have the right and the duty to follow your conscience, as long as it has been informed by the Church's teachings. What does that mean? Must we always conform? No, an informed conscience is not necessarily a conformed conscience.

What is the role of the teaching authority of the Church in these matters?

"The Magisterium *(the teaching authority of the Church)* **fulfills the aspirations of conscience by enabling it to find the moral good at which it aims... for Catholics the Magisterium is one, but only one informant of conscience."** *These words of Avery Dulles, SJ, were delivered before he was made a Cardinal of the Church, in a talk given to 400 prelates including cardinals, archbishops, and bishops at the 10th Bishops' Workshop, Dallas, Texas, 1991. I was on the program as well that day, and heard him deliver this talk, which the Bishops peacefully accepted.*

The conscience is an inner faculty, which enables us to distinguish good from evil. The Church guides us in our search for truth, but the Church is not the only source of information to help form the conscience. It sometimes happens that one is not able to conform to the Church's teaching because of some extraordinary circumstances. Freedom of conscience means that we must respect their decision in the matter.

People have honest disagreements with the Church. They reason that there are many ways of knowing God's will. Difficulties often arise in these matters affecting one's marital status.

When a marriage is presumed to be valid, though in fact it was a disaster because of physical abuse, alcoholism, infidelity or some such malady, the question arises: should we regard it as valid? The annulment process attempts to answer that question.

When the rights and obligations of the husband and the wife no longer have any practical meaning due to the fact that the marriage is dead, the situation cries to heaven for some remedy. If the parties break up and reconciliation is no longer possible, the parties can seek an annulment. All the Protestant Churches, and the Easter Orthodox Churches, permit remarriage without the benefit of an annulment.

The Good Conscience Marriage

The Roman Catholic Church will not allow remarriage without the benefit of an annulment. When there is a marriage still in possession, still on the books, the Church does not permit a party to enter into a new union. The annulment process is available to examine the claim that the prior marriage or marriages were not valid because of some defect of contract, or intention. If this fact is uncovered, and the annulment granted, the parties are free to marry again.

Here is where the idea of a good conscience marriage comes into play. If a woman marries again after her divorce without the benefit of an annulment, she is considered by the Church to be living in sin. Actually only God knows whether or not there is a sin involved. It might be better to say she is living in an uncanonical marriage.

Let's say her conscience is clear. She believes she is not living in sin. In fact she believes strongly that God wants her to marry her new husband for her sake, and for the sake of the children. She is in good faith, believing that the first marriage was bogus and untrue.

This means she has entered what we call a "good conscience marriage."

She may be deluded, or she may be right. Just because she has disagreed with the Church's teaching, which forbade her to re-marry without the benefit of a divorce, doesn't ipso facto make her wrong. It could be that she is exactly right, but the tribunal has not yet verified her deepest conviction.

She may refuse to go through the elaborate ordeal of an an-nulment because she doesn't want to dredge up the past. She knows her former spouse would be a hostile witness anyway. Can anyone blame her?

Since priests are required to respect the consciences of their people even if they disagree with them, the local priests will not refuse her Holy Communion if she approaches to receive. Or she may de-cide to go to a church where she is not known.

We can only urge people to try to do what the Church recom-mends, i.e., to go through the annulment process, but if someone prefers to trust God's love, and omit the legalities, so be it.

Most Catholics would rather have an annulment than follow the "internal forum" or good conscience solution because it officially releases them to begin their new life.

The Church tribunals offer a ministry of mercy.

I advised Betty to try for an annulment. She preferred not to. I respected her conscience and turned her over to God's love and mercy.

The joy of following one's conscience is a basic right. The Church is here to guide you, but the Church also tries to be emi-nently reasonable in dealing with difficult pastoral problems.

Nancy Paola of Cranston, Rhode Island tells a fascinating story of how she fought the good fight to save her marriage.

After five years of dating, I was SURE I found the right man to marry. I consulted with God time and again, since my faith was an active faith, but my lover's faith was dormant and I wasn't confident that we would see eye-to-eye. But I was in love and I was certain that he loved me, so in 1979 we married.

He had not made his Confirmation, but because I was such an active member of my Church the priest married us anyway, with the promise that he would be confirmed within a year. In 1981 our first child was born and in 1982 the second.

Our marriage began to unravel, crumble, and sour. The financial feast of the mid-1980's was swallowing my husband, the political scene of our small city lured my husband, and a woman in his office had snatched his desires.

After months of heartache, I gave him to the Lord. I was tired of the fighting, the lies, and the deception. My self-esteem was at an all time low. The stress was affecting my health, my parenting skills; every single person, I mean anyone who knew my situation screamed, "Divorce the bum!" except for my beautifully faith-filled mother, sister and best friend.

They advised me to continue to be a "prayer warrior." I prayed every free moment and some that weren't free. The message was always the same, "be calm, patient, loving, understanding, be the teacher of unconditional love and forgiveness." Three days before Christmas in 1992, my husband returned home, crying because he could not believe how merciful the Lord is, that unconditional love truly exists, that the world offers fleeting joys, while the sacrament of marriage is a lasting joy. He made his Confirmation during the Easter vigil in 1998. He still cries at every Mass, I cry with him, the Joy is overwhelming.

The power of prayer is enormous. Those who go the extra mile are often rewarded in this life as well as the next. This is not to say that a woman should accept abuse and remain in a dead marriage if her dignity and safety are at stake, but it does say that miracles are possible.

17

JOY AND THE LITURGY

"They worshiped Him, and then went back to Jerusalem full of Joy." (Lk 24:52)

The liturgy of the Church is the place where we all come together to admit to one another that we need God in our lives. It is where we worship, where we offer the Divine Sacrifice of Jesus on the Cross. It is all about loving God and one another. The vertical dimension is essential to the Holy Sacrifice of the Mass, but so too is the horizontal dimension. By that I mean the way we interact with one another.

Father James Moroney, a liturgist for the American Catholic Bishops, wrote this interesting commentary, *"It doesn't matter if you have a presider who is a professional liturgist, or even one who understands what the liturgy is all about theologically or ritually. What we need is a priest who believes in loving God."*

It is important that the celebrant at Mass is willing to empower the people to worship in the correct spirit, the Spirit of Love. Moroney says we also need in our Masses a sense of the people loving one another, of the priest loving the assembly, the assembly loving the priest, and everyone loving Christ.

To accomplish this, and thereby to avoid the perfunctory routine of heartless repetition, we need a welcoming hospitality. If the Mass is not a celebration of Joy, it is not fulfilling its purpose.

The entrance rite should be a joyous form of welcome to one and all, an invitation to unite as one in giving ourselves to God. No one should feel like a stranger. Hospitality means that there is a spirit of kindness to the newcomer. This is the natural outgrowth of an authentic belief in Jesus. If you have really met the Lord, and understood His loving nature, you cannot help but be hospitable to the newcomer.

The point of all this is that the community is "the Mystical Body of Christ," worshiping the Father, and loving one another. We become one with Christ as we unite with Him in offering ourselves to the Father.

A good liturgy occurs when you can see the effects of it in people's lives. Do you see the people becoming more and more Christ-like? Are there signs that people care about the less fortunate in the community? Are there food collections for the local pantry or soup kitchen? Are there other signs that the community is becoming more unified in their prayer?

Holy Mass is not a place for individuals to come together and dial "G" for God, so that each person can have a private conversation with God. The Mass is a ritual in which people give worship to God as a living community. We stand together in His Presence. Group prayer is more powerful than individual prayer. Together we pray for the intentions of others, and they in turn pray for your intentions.

In addition to worship, the liturgy gives purpose and direction to our lives. It refreshes the spirit, and reminds us to banish fear. All of these elements taken together help us to experience the joy of belonging to a 2000-year-old family that is still thriving in the name of Jesus Christ.

Besides serving as a unifying activity, the Mass infuses us with the strength we need to carry out our duties and obligations to those we love. It helps us maintain what Dorothy Day called the duty of delight. We have an obligation to give back a joyful presence to the Lord for all that He has given to us.

Public worship is a perfect antidote to the excessive, unbridled individualism of our age. The privatization of religion is not what God wants. We are taught to say, "Our Father" not "My Father." The Lord wants us to worship Him as a family. Let's try to do that with joyful hearts.

THE FORMULA FOR JOY

At Holy Mass we obey the supreme law, **"To love God with all your heart, with all your soul and with all your strength... and love your neighbor as you love yourself"** (Dt 6:4-6).

This is the formula for true Joy. A truly happy life begins when you believe this law and obey it. This law of love is more than a suggestion. We have to love or we will perish. The *sine qua non* of real human happiness is found in a meaningful life. Nothing but love will satisfy the hunger of the soul in following its true calling.

This brings us to the personal application of the law. Unless you love yourself, you will never be able to enjoy your precious life. Charity begins at home in more ways than one.

Jesus wants you to love yourself, and be happy with Him beginning now. This is not to say that He wants you to be comfortable and aloof in a world desperately in need of help and healing. The world needs you, and what only you can give.

You have gifts and talents that are unique to you. Using them wisely, generously will be your greatest crown in heaven, and fulfillment here on earth.

A prayer by St. Ignatius Loyola will help you develop this spirit.

> **Dear Lord, teach me to be generous,**
> **Teach me to serve you as you deserve,**
> **To give and not to count the cost**
> **To fight and not to heed the wound,**

To toil and not to seek for rest,
To labor and not to seek reward,
Save that of knowing that I do your will.

Very few of us have reached this level of spiritual gener-osity. In fact St. Ignatius hadn't reached it when he wrote that prayer. That's why he put it down on paper, to remind himself of his lofty goals. Human nature always pulls back, counts the cost, cares for the emotional wounds, stops to rest, and looks for recognition. We are human. It's the most natural thing in the world to be less than generous. Therefore, we must pray for the grace to transcend our shoddy egos, and become saints.

Christian discipleship is the call to greatness. The Lord wants us to share our gifts, talents and treasures with those less fortunate.

This is what it means to be a good steward, and the lit-urgy is a ritual in which we publicly profess our noblest aspira-tions. To love is to be caring. The Scriptures go so far as to sug-gest that we tithe a portion of all we receive.

"Who then is the faithful and prudent steward whom the master will put in charge of his servants to distribute the food allowances at the proper time? Blessed is that servant whom his master on arrival finds doing so. Truly, I say to you, he will put him in charge of all his property" (Lk 12:42-44).

The Catholic Bishops put it this way: *"A Christian stew-ard is one who receives God's gifts gratefully, cherishes and tends to them in a responsible manner, and then shares them in justice and love with others, and returns them with increase to the Lord"* (From their Pastoral Letter on Stewardship, 1992).

Our first pope, St. Peter, taught that this principle is an integral part of being a member of the Church. Everyone who belongs to Christ is challenged to be a cheerful giver. From the very beginning, we were called to live a life in imitation of Christ, and we understand it to be an invitation to Joy. The only thing we can take with us when we arrive at the pearly gates is what we have given away during our life here on earth.

Here is a little story to bring home the point.

A rich woman died and went to heaven. St. Peter greeted her politely and escorted her to her new home. As they passed by the lovely estates with beautiful flowers and flowing lawns, she was feeling wonderfully alive. Gradually the houses and lawns became smaller. Soon they were in a run-down tenement district with dilapidated apartments. As they traveled on, she became noticeably uneasy. When Peter showed her a shack in the woods with no indoor plumbing, he said, "Here Madam is you new residence." She protested, "I can't live in this hovel." St. Peter calmly replied, "But madam, this is all we could build for you with the materials you sent ahead."

Good stewardship is planing ahead. Apart from the security of knowing that we will be judged on what we did for the least of our brothers, there is a side benefit to this idea of tithing.

You get to keep 90% of everything you own. You can spend it any way you like. Spend it on yourself, for your needs here and now. Once you have given your tithe to the poor, to the parish, to those doing good work throughout the world, you know you have pleased the Lord. What you have left is yours to enjoy.

It is important that you recognize where all your possessions come from, **"Do not be deceived, every good and every perfect gift is from above"** (Jm 1:17). **"Whether you eat or drink, or whatever you do, do everything for the glory of God"** (1 Cor 10:31).

Here is my favorite quote from St. Paul, **"Bear one another's burdens, in that way you will fulfill the law of Jesus Christ"** (Gal 6:2). This quote so inspired me when I was Chief

Judge of the Marriage Tribunal for the Diocese of Paterson, New Jersey, nearly 35 years ago, I put it on our Tribunal letterhead, and I'm happy to say it's still there.

STEWARDSHIP AND THE LITURGY

How does this idea of stewardship relate to the liturgy? The better question is: How does it not?

Participation at Holy Mass is an indispensable way of loving yourself enough to show God that you love Him. When you become obedient to Him, He notices.

Worship is the Spirit of love at work in each community. The liturgy is one of the best ways to surrender to the Lord. You come to Mass as a way of showing respect. You also open yourself to the community at prayer. It exposes you to the needs of others, and teaches you to be a good and faithful servant.

Any inconvenience involved is soon rewarded with a feeling of belonging to something larger than yourself. If you have faith in the Real Presence, there can even be a deep sense of awe as you kneel before the Blessed Eucharist. The Presence of God is made palpable at Holy Communion. What a privilege!

"Serve the Lord with gladness; come before Him singing for Joy" (Ps 100:2)

A good pastor teaches his people that the parish is accountable to God as a unit. The community also has to be a good steward of its gifts. The weekly income should be tithed to some mutually agreed upon charity.

I was in charge of a poverty program in Paterson, New Jersey for nearly three years. It was called Eva's Village. We fed 700 meals a day to the poor. We also had several shelters for homeless men, women, and children. Donations came in from Catholic, Protestant and Jewish people from all over New Jersey, and beyond.

Community giving, however, should not merely be a matter of sending money. Food pantries, clothing collections, recreational events, and other kinds of creative activities can be sponsored to help the needy. A few parishes have little theater clubs; they put on performances for the sick and elderly.

There are gifted individuals in every community who can serve in their own unique way. A good pastor searches the talents of his parishioners. He then invites them to share their gifts with the community. God is well served by those who share their gifts with the community.

"When God loves me, He desires nothing else than to be loved by me; He loves me in order that I may love Him because He knows well that all who love Him find in this very love their joy and happiness."

St. Bernard of Clairvaux

"To love God as a friend, that is the secret of happiness and the secret of the saints."

Sister Elizabeth of the Trinity

"A cheerful heart is the best medicine."

Proverbs 17:22

"In everything we call a trial or a sorrow, believe me, an angel's hand is there, and the wonder of an overshadowing, loving Presence."

Fra Angelico

18

ENJOY YOUR PRECIOUS LIFE

**"I have told you all of this so that my joy may be in you
and your joy may be complete."** (Jn 15:11)

As I conclude this trilogy, I once again turn to those beautiful
words of Jesus: They inspired me to begin this project, and they
enabled me to see it through to the end. It is in His will that I
have found the fullness of Joy.

In this chapter I want to review the qualities that promote
Joy: charity, gratitude, courage, cheerfulness, self-love (which
includes care of the body), generosity, holy desires, forgiveness,
and humility. Learn of Jesus who was meek and humble of heart,
and learn of Mary who by her humble trust brought the Joy of
Jesus into our world.

The Mother of Jesus understood the primacy of Joy: **"My
soul proclaims the greatness of the Lord, and my spirit rejoices
in God my Savior"** (Lk 1:47). She is the truest embodiment of
Joy, and the perfect model for Christian living. Imitate her, and
your spiritual life will flourish. The key word in her life was trust.
Mary trusted the promises of the Holy Spirit, and thrived in that
trust. She knew the Hebrew Bible well and lived it: **"The words
of the Lord are true, all His works are trustworthy"** (Ps 33:4).

You can imitate her spirit of Joy. You can trust the Lord
to send you His Joy, and when Joy begins flowing in your heart,
please notify your face. Smile because you are a temple of Joy.

Your energy level will perk up; your step will become bouncier; and your smile will brighten. Your sensations will all be heightened because Joy will make you a new creation.

Don't begin by looking for the feeling of Joy. Begin by believing in the Spirit of Joy within you. Be one with Him in spite of your feelings. Sooner or later you will realize that you are part of God's life. This knowledge will fill you with a peace and a Joy that this word cannot give. It will awaken your whole body to a higher level of existence.

Believe in your own Joy. This is not a conceit. You know you are an average person, but you also know that you are an instrument of God's Joy. Just as Jesus accepted the life that God had chosen for Him, so will you. The Lord wants you to live in His Joy.

Pope John Paul II called us all to be messengers of Joy. The words of Christ give us the encouragement we need to be messengers of Joy. Human happiness is a legitimate spiritual goal. Indeed Christ's invitation to Joy is a religious calling. We are all challenged to accept the **duty of delight**.

Jesus came to bring us Joy, and this is the basis of all human happiness.

It is up to us to fulfill God's plan. We are called to live our precious lives as joyfully as possible, and to do this we need to claim Joy as our baptismal right. We have to pray as if everything depended on God, and act as if everything depended on us.

Here are the virtues I have stressed throughout this book.

CHARITY

"Help carry one another's burdens; in that way you will fulfill the law of Jesus Christ" (Gal 6:2).

Jesus made Joy the reward of self-giving. One of the best

ways to give yourself to another is by listening to them. It is charitable to become an attentive listener.

Dr. Karl Menninger of the Menninger Foundation in Topeka, Kansas, asked his resident students to identify the most important part of the treatment process of the mental patients assigned to them.

Some said it was the relationship between therapist and patient; others spoke of the necessity of contact with families; another group thought it was the correct drug prescription. Menninger said no to all of the above. "The foremost task of any therapist" he said, "is to listen."

After years of doing therapy on countless patients, he believed that the experience of not being listened to was one of the strongest influences that made people unwell. The experience of being listened to made them well again.

Listening doesn't seem like much of a gift, but it truly is. It is a way of affirming a person who is in desperate need of validation.

Good parents make countless sacrifices for their children, and they receive precious little credit for all they do. However, some of them do not realize how important it is to have the patience to listen to their children.

One woman I know put an old sofa in the kitchen, and when the kids came home from school, they would alternately flop on the couch talking endlessly while she was preparing dinner.

Jesus sees all, and knows all. He assures us that everything done in the name of love will receive its reward. He promises an abundance of joy to those who give themselves away to others. However small or trivial the service of listening might seem, it is one of the most important things you can do for another. Charity begins at home with the children.

The simple act of listening can reap a legacy of healing and contentment.

GRATITUDE

"**Rejoice always, and in all circumstances give thanks to the Lord, for this is the will of God for you in Christ Jesus**" (1 Th 5:16-18).

With Christ all things are possible. To be grateful in all circumstances will take God's grace, and a little imagination. There is an ancient spiritual maxim: "Joy abounds in a heart filled with gratitude."

Joy and generosity are intimately connected. In Luke (17:11-19) we read about the leper who returned to give thanks. "**When he realized he had been healed, he returned glorifying God in a loud voice and he fell at the feet of Jesus and thanked Him.**"

You don't have to be cured from leprosy to find a reason for being grateful. I don't know who wrote the following, but it spoke to my heart,

> *Be thankful for the clothes that are too snug because it means you have enough to eat.*
>
> *Be thankful for the mess you clean up after a party, because it means you have friends.*
>
> *Be thankful for the taxes you pay, because it means you are employed.*
>
> *Be thankful for the heating bills because it means you are not out in the cold.*
>
> *Be thankful for the laundry chores, because it means you have clothes to wear.*
>
> *Be thankful for the lady who sings off key, because it means you can hear.*
>
> *Be thankful for the alarm that goes off early in the morning, because it means you are alive.*

Jesus told us to be grateful. To help us along the way He said, "**Ask, and you will receive, knock and the door will be opened**" (Mt 7:7). Keep asking for the fullness of gratitude and

Joy will follow. No matter how bleak things may seem at any given moment you can ask for relief. Peace will come, and so will an abundance of joy. Believe this with all your heart. Persevere in your efforts to be grateful in all circumstances, even when you are in danger of death. Pray for the grace to accept your death peacefully, and be grateful for all you have received.

From Robert Mueller here are some inspired words on gratitude:

> *Thank the Lord for His truth.*
> *Thank Him for your wonderful body, mind, heart, and soul.*
> *Thank Him for our beautiful planet,*
> > *for the stars and the sky,*
> > *for our human brethren and sisters,*
> > *for our friends and the animals,*
> > *for our sisters the plants and flowers.*

COURAGE

"Do not let your heart be troubled. Keep trusting in Me" (Jn 14:1).

Jesus laid down His life for you. There is no greater love than this. You too can lay down your life for Him. When the time of death finally comes, stay focused, and rejoice in the knowledge of His love. Be a good patient when sickness comes. Be patient with God as well. Everything begins to make sense when you have the courage to be patient.

Joy enters the soul through faith, prayer, and the will to bear discomfort as peacefully, and as courageously as possible.

Father James Keller was the founder of The Christophers, and I had the great privilege of following him as the executive director of this New York based multimedia organization. I served in that capacity from 1978 until 1995.

In searching through the archives one day, I found the fol-

270 ENJOY YOUR PRECIOUS LIFE

lowing spiritual testament which Father Keller wrote on August 14, 1972. He wrote it while he was suffering from Parkinson's disease:

"Throughout my life I have looked forward with joyful anticipation to the 'homecoming' day when I will meet my Savior face to face and hear him say: 'Come, blessed of my Father, possess the kingdom prepared for you from the foundation of the world.'

The nearer I get to that glorious occasion, the less worthy I feel. I find myself counting more than ever before on the mercy of the Lord to make up for my defects and shortcomings.

But willing and generous as God is to forgive, He decreed that we do some penance for our sins. It seems sensible to do all the cleansing we can during our brief sojourn on earth, rather than wait for it to be done in the hereafter.

Through prayer and good works during my short life span I can do penance for my imperfections and prove that I am truly sorry for any and all of my offenses against a loving God; for example,

+ *by increasing my prayers for the work of The Christophers, for numerous intentions involving the eternal salvation and human well-being of many friends and acquaintances, as well as the poor people of the earth;*
+ *by accepting cheerfully the handicap of my physical ailments;*
+ *by welcoming rather than evading any suffering that the Lord allows to come my way, and by doing this in honor of His passion and death on the Cross;*
+ *by striving to bring Joy, not gloom, into the lives of others;*
+ *by avoiding all forms of self-pity;*
+ *by fulfilling more devotedly all daily spiritual exercises;*
+ *by endeavoring to be so conscientious about all my obligations as a priest that under all circumstances I may be a humble witness of the holiness, devotion, generosity, detachment, and purity that most people associate with a good priest;*
+ *by continually thanking God for the countless blessings He sent me throughout my life;*
+ *by recalling frequently St. Paul's reminder:* **"By God's favor**

you were saved. This is not your own doing; it is God's gift" (Eph 2:8); and

+ *by faithfully living up to the spiritual goal set by the prophet Micah:* "This is what the Lord asks of you, only this: to act justly — to love tenderly — and to walk humbly with your God."

Father Keller died a holy death on February 7, 1977. He was humble and uncomplaining to the very end.

Courage implies a willingness to stand up to fear. "**Be not afraid**" (Mt 14:27). The thought of death can be unsettling. Don't let it be. Face it, and live your precious life courageously right up to the end. Jesus wants you to be free from fear so that you can learn to enjoy your life both here and in eternity. He loves you. Do not be afraid.

Jesus said, "**Do not be afraid... do not worry about anything.**" He urged us not to fret about the future. Never doubt your own salvation. Jesus died to save you. You honor Him by accepting the gift of salvation. If you are a sinner — and who isn't? — then say you're sorry and know that you are saved by His death on the cross.

All you have to do is say yes to the Lord as your Savior. When you ask for forgiveness, believe that you have been forgiven. Let go of your petty doubts and fears. No sin is too great for His mercy.

The Lord is nothing but love and mercy. Say no to fear. Let your joy be full.

Ask for the grace to teach others to trust God's love and mercy. If you have any children under your care, it is important to protect them from needless fear. Many children develop fears and insecurities from childhood. Needless anxieties can be avoided if children are taught to trust God at an early age.

Parents are the first teachers of their children, "**Teach your children to choose the right path and when they are older they shall remain upon it**" (Pr 22:6).

The right path includes faith in God's merciful love. Youngsters need love, acceptance, and validation. They need things to do, and places to visit. They need people to care for them, and give them healthy experiences. Teach them to stay away from the drug subculture. Teach them to put their trust in God.

The ability to stand up to your fears in little things can make a great difference in your life. Take it one day at a time: **"Sufficient unto the day are today's troubles"** (Mt 6:16). Jesus tells us not to be afraid of the future. Do not sabotage your spirit of Joy. Joy is possible even in difficult times, but you must cancel your fears to possess Joy fully. Needless anxiety only saps your energy. Joy is not the same as happiness. There can be great sadness all around you, but still there is within the deepest part of your soul a fountain of Joy. This may not be apparent at first, but listen to the Apostle James: **"Consider it Joy when you fall into various trials, knowing that the testing of your faith begets perseverance"** (Jm 1:2-3).

Joy prevails over sadness. The wonderful movement called Alcoholics Anonymous spawned all the other 12-Step Programs: Gamblers Anonymous, Narcotics Anonymous, and Over-Eaters Anonymous, to name a few. These self-help movements teach their clients how to avoid self-destructive behavior.

Those who stay faithful to the program, become more serene and more joyful. When they depend on their Higher Power, instead of themselves, their joy increases, and their will becomes strong in His strength. They learn to admit that without their Higher Power they are lost. They put on the will to bear discomfort, and plug ahead as best they can. They know that the severe discomfort of withdrawal will eventually fade. They know that all they have to do is stay sober one day at a time. The will to bear discomfort for one more day leads to total freedom.

They persevere and learn the wonderful lesson that: **"Those who sow in tears shall reap in Joy"** (Ps 126:5).

People in recovery no longer dwell on the past, and all terrible things they lived through. They try living in the present moment, and letting go of the past. You can do that too, if you keep on keeping on. Do it one day at a time. Millions do it, and so can you.

CHEERFULNESS

"A cheerful glance brings Joy to the heart" (Pr 15:30). Cultivate a joyful smile. You can do this more easily if you cultivate clean and healthy thoughts. These bring Joy to the soul.

The poet Yeats once alluded to a moment of joy in his life: *"My body, of a sudden, blazed."* Such moments come rarely, but they do come. We know by faith that there is an eternal furnace of Love burning within the soul of each one of us. Occasionally it erupts. We see the supernatural more clearly than ever before. We feel safe, and joyful.

Good cheer fills us when we remember the joys of life. Joy makes us smile. We can learn to practice smiling before the mirror. Look and see what the other person sees when you smile. This is a gift you can give away any time. Your smile might be the very spark that will awaken joy in the heart of a desolate person.

Tap into that spiritual reservoir within your soul. You can do it at will.

Robert Mueller said it best:

> *Decide to be cheerful.*
> *Render others cheerful.*
> *Praise the whole Creation with your cheers.*
> *Be a rock against sadness, pessimism, and hopelessness.*
> *Switch on and keep on in yourself the cheerful buttons:*
> *Joy, laughter, happiness, love, passion for life, and*
> *gratitude.*

Pope John Paul II put it in perspective: *"True, you cannot always be healthy or successful, but you can always be with Christ, and find strength at His side."*

CARE OF THE BODY

"There is no treasure like a healthy body, no happiness like a joyful heart" (Si 30:10).

Self-love, among other things, means taking good care of your body. In a true sense your body is your best friend. Keep it fit. Make good choices about your diet, and don't neglect your exercise program. It will make a great difference when you grow older, if you take good care of your body along the way. You may live a lot longer, and be able to help many more people as you do.

All the medical studies show that eating properly, taking vitamin supplements, and exercising regularly will help enormously in keeping you healthy well into your 50's, 60's, 70's, and beyond. The aging process doesn't have to slow down the metabolism, and make you put on weight. If you eat less and exercise more you can live longer. The simple fact is that you need more nutrients as you get older. In order to compensate for the wear and tear, you should eat more raw foods, like fruits and vegetables every day.

Remember, fresh food is always better for you than processed foods. This is true because fresh foods contain antioxidants. Those are chemical compounds that fight against the destruction caused by the natural aging process. Our bodies tend to lose free radicals over time. These are oxygen molecules with an extra electron. Dr. Julian Whitaker, M.D., author of the newsletter "Health & Healing" (Warner Books), says, "Without adding more antioxidants to your diet, you increase the chances for serious conditions like heart disease."

Whitaker also recommends that older people limit their dairy products by cutting milk from the diet. Cataracts and other degenerative diseases related to aging are associated with an increase of fat. Another way to cut fat is to limit meat to two servings a week.

Vitamin and mineral supplements are also important. See that you get some added vitamins E, C, and A, and some folic acid, magnesium, selenium, and beta-carotene. Vitamins E, C, and A, and beta-carotene are all antioxidants. Consult your doctor for the right amounts of each for your age.

Exercise is not easy, but it is necessary. Start slowly. Walk briskly for ten minutes a day. Soon it will be a Joy, and you'll want to spend more time doing it. The body needs exercise. Try to break a sweat when you exercise. It helps build muscle tone, and it wards off osteoporosis in both men and women. Joy increases with a healthy body.

Last, but not least, get your annual flu shot. Nearly 20,000 people die, and over 100,000 are put in the hospital for flu every year in the United States alone. The federal Center for Disease Control and Prevention (CDC) recommends that everyone over 50 get a flu shot each fall when the flu season begins. Influenza and pneumonia rank as the fifth leading cause of death in those over 65.

GENEROSITY

Generosity is more than charitable giving. We have talked earlier about giving of your time, talents and treasures. You have to do it in a way that enables you to take care of your own family's needs first. Generosity is also about sharing the Faith. This is a higher kind of generosity because the Faith is a higher kind of treasure.

Why not keep a journal of all the joyful things that happen to you each day? Call it a gratitude journal. The idea is not original. Connect with that underground stream of Joy within your soul by consciously writing about your awareness of God's Presence. Thank the Lord, and keep a record of the major Joys in your life, and the little ones as well.

"If you love me, feed my lambs, feed my lambs, feed my little sheep" (Jn 21:17). These words of Jesus had a powerful influence on me. When I was ordained I made a resolution never to turn anyone away anyone who came to me for help. By God's grace, I have tried to be totally faithful to that holy promise, but it wasn't easy. The flame of Christ's love burning within me attracted quite a few mosquitoes over a lifetime.

To my surprise, most of them brought me unexpected joys. When everyone else turns a person away, they are humbly grateful to the one who gives them time. I must confess there have been some sick people who are prone to manipulating everyone they meet, and I do not recommend indulging them, but for the most part people in need are deserving of whatever love and attention you can give.

Many encounters, which began with difficulty and annoyance, end with joy and gratitude. So many people need someone to listen to them. Giving them time is such a sacred gift.

Even though I have often been impatient, I have always tried to be accessible. When I was a young boy my mother used to say, "Why are you always available for everyone who calls?"

I don't know why to this day. It just comes naturally to me. It was a gift. I'm happy and grateful to be who I am.

Grace builds on nature. My willingness to give of my time in later life was somewhat natural for me. I have learned that Joy comes to those who follow their grace. If you do your best to help others, even if you feel someone might be taking advantage of you, extend yourself anyway. Your generosity will be rewarded.

Jesus said to Peter, **"Feed my lambs."** These words were spoken three times after Peter's threefold denial, and they encouraged me to use my talents to spread the Good News. I felt that I could prove my love for God by feeding others intellectually and spiritually. By giving them guidance and direction I was fulfilling my mission in life. And it has become the supreme Joy in my life.

I use the printed word, radio and television to reach millions of readers, viewers and listeners every month. My radio ministry has been heard on over 1025 stations from Maine to Hawaii, on a monthly basis since 1995. I purchase the air time with money from the Koch Foundation and others. At first CBS wouldn't take my spots because they were faith based, and therefore too religious for their network.

The Westwood One Network did decide to sell time to me. Then a few years later, CBS bought Westwood One. Instead of dropping me, CBS for some reason changed their mind and allowed me to continue running my inspirational spots. The Lord works in marvelous ways.

It has been thrilling for me to receive thousands of letters from people who benefited from something I might have said or written. The basic message is based on the idea that Jesus is Lord, and that you are precious to Him. You can trust Him to help you carry the burdens you must bear.

I have known my share of hardship in this life, but it is nothing compared with the Joy the Lord has sent me. The happiness of being a priest has far outweighed all the sacrifice.

Today, I look back with no regrets about my vocational decision. I would gladly do it all over again.

Holy Desires

One of the interesting things about the experience of Joy is the relationship it has with holy desires. These always make the soul happy, whereas unholy desires make the soul sad. St.

Ignatius Loyola was wounded in battle and had to stay on a hospital bed for a year. He discovered that whenever he thought of worldly things he became sad, but when his imagination went in the direction of the heroic actions of the saints, his spirit brightened.

He developed a whole system of meditations on the life of Christ, and passed his time away lifting his soul to heights of idealism.

Eventually his holy desires led him to found the Society of Jesus, a religious order of men, better known as the Jesuits.

Holy desires bring us closer to the glory of God. A human being fully alive is God's greatest glory. Dreaming great dreams is also a way of being fully alive. Even before you accomplish anything, the very process of dreaming about good deeds brings them to life, and in the process delights the soul.

Many years ago I wrote the following piece to bolster my desire to be a more loving priest. It is adapted from St. Paul's wonderful passage in his First Letter to the Corinthians, Chapter 13:1-4.

> *If I were to preach like a prophet and impress everyone with my flair for story telling, but have no love in my heart for those who hear me, my words would be like spoiled seed buried in good soil.*
>
> *If I were to administer a huge parish complex with expert skill, but have no real love for those under my care, my talents would be squandered and my people denied.*
>
> *If I were to visit the sick and bury the dead with meticulous fidelity to liturgical rubrics, but have no compassion for those who are grieving, I would be nothing but a hired professional, light years removed from the heart of Christ.*
>
> *If I were to be loyal to my bishop while others criticized his faults, but have no feeling for him as a human being, overwhelmed with responsibilities, I would be a mere functionary, not a true friend.*

If I were elected to offices in the Church, and dignified with honors and titles, but be lacking in humility and love, I would be a vain actor on an empty stage.

If I were to remain faithful to my vocation, surmounting all temptations, yet show nothing in the end but a cold and intolerant nature, I would be a living monument to human pride, and my perseverance would count for little.

If I were a popular priest, who never challenged anyone to do his or her best, I would not possess the loving heart of Christ.

Love does not depend on good feelings or popular opinion.

Love prevails against all odds.

Love does not see the difference between attractive or homely faces.

Love bears the cross in times of trial and turmoil.

Love persists in moments of fear and confusion.

Love endures all things.

On the last day, we will all be judged on love. Our worldly accomplishments will count for little.

These holy thoughts have helped me to keep my Joy and my ideals high. Why not write your own set of goals?

Once a year on Holy Thursday, the anniversary of the institution of the priesthood at the Last Supper, priests everywhere unite with their bishops to renew the promises they made on the day of their ordination. The bishop asks the priests assembled:

Are you resolved to unite yourself more closely to Christ, And try to become more like Him by JOYFULLY sacrificing your own pleasure and ambition To bring His Peace and Love to Your brothers and sisters?

The priests all respond, "I am!"

I love the word "Joyfully" standing out so boldly in the words of the ritual. This is not merely acceptance or doleful resignation to God's will. This answer **"I am!"** is a joyful acquiescence in God's plan for the life of each priest. We become what we want to be. Holy desires form character and create destinies.

Why not write a statement of your own, to celebrate your own life commitment? Or perhaps you can keep a spiritual journal, an extension of your gratitude journal. Think about it. Write about your own desire to bring Christ's peace and love to your brothers and sisters.

Don't let that inner tyrant, that demon within, who judges you so harshly, take control of your mind. Love yourself. Accept the Joy within you and celebrate it. Never enter anything negative in your journal. If someone annoys you, just mention that you said a prayer for him or her.

Never correct or criticize yourself in your journal. Don't write those little doubts that may come to mind. Don't think: "If anyone finds this book they'll think I'm nuts. What I'm writing isn't very profound, I am being silly here."

Just be joyful and remind yourself how much you've been blessed in life. The advantage of writing about your heartfelt Joy is that you can read it when you are down. You can see how radiant your spiritual life really is.

Many of the saints did this. My favorite saint was "The Little Flower," better known as St. Thérèse of Lisieux. She had a great desire throughout her entire life to make God happy.

As she lay dying, she said, *"Everything I have ever done was to make God happy."*

She knew she had the power to please the Lord.

St. Bernard had the same insight: *"When God loves me, He desires nothing else than to be loved by me. He loves me in order that I may love Him, because he knows well that all who love Him find in that love, their joy and happiness."*

St. Elizabeth of the Trinity wrote, *"Love God as a friend. This is the secret of happiness and the secret of all the saints."* God thinks of Himself as your best friend. Why not agree with Him?

FORGIVENESS

The spirit of forgiveness implies humility. Forgiveness purifies the soul, and brings relief to the spirit. Mind and heart are reconciled with God, with neighbor, and most of all with self.

"The forgiven penitent is reconciled with himself in his inmost being, where he regains his own true identity. He is reconciled with his brethren whom he has in some way attacked and wounded. He is reconciled with the Church, and he is reconciled with all creation" (Pope John Paul II).

The idea of being reconciled with all creation is awesome. Real sin, which is mortal sin, involves a deliberate turning away from God. This is a willful violation of the Golden Rule: **"Do unto others as you would have them do unto you"** (Mt 7:12). To be in disharmony with the Divine order is a tragedy. The only good thing about it is that you can come back to God in the wink of an eye. If you ask for forgiveness, He will forgive.

"Forgive us our trespasses as we forgive those who trespass against us." These words from the Lord's Prayer tell us all we need to know. A true Christian is ready to forgive even when the one who has offended him or her has not asked for it. You can forgive a person without ever going through a painful confrontation. You can cleanse yourself of all the grudges and resentment by just willing it. Do not wait until you feel like it. Feelings will follow in time, but you must do it now. To forgive another is good for your mental health, as well as your spiritual well being.

HUMILITY

"The meek shall increase their joy in the Lord" (Is 29:19).

The willingness to forgive is the *sine qua non* of all spiritual progress, and it takes humility. Live your life as though you were the extension of the Holy Spirit, and do everything in your daily life with an eye to pleasing the Lord. Let Him lead you. Sometimes we forgive, not because we want to, but because God wants us to be humble enough to obey Him. He wants to shower more gifts upon us, but He can't find an opening if we cling to our petty hatreds.

The beautiful prayer attributed to St. Francis of Assisi describes the majestic process of living a life filled with holy desires.

Repeat this prayer often, and with God's help you will learn to become a saint. Right now you are only a joyful saint-in-training, but soon you will be with God, a saint for all eternity.

> *Lord make me an instrument of your peace;*
> *where there is hatred, let me sow love,*
> *where there is injury, pardon,*
> *where there is doubt, faith,*
> *where there is despair, hope,*
> *where there is darkness, light, and*
> *where there is sadness, joy.*
> *Divine Master grant that I may not so much seek*
> *to be consoled, as to console,*
> *to be understood, as to understand,*
> *to be loved, as to love.*
> *For it is giving that we receive,*
> *it is in pardoning that we are pardoned, and*
> *it is in dying that we are born to eternal life.*

EPILOGUE

"For this Joy is close to you, it is in you. None of you
has a spirit so heavy, nor an intelligence so feeble, none of you is
so far from God not to be able to find Joy in Him."
(Meister Eckhart)

Jesus Christ came to bring Joy to the world. His teachings were designed to help us see beyond legalism. **"I have told you all these things that your Joy may be full"** (Jn 14:11).

Pope John Paul II said, *"Christ came to bring joy to all people.... Go, therefore, and become messengers of joy."* That is precisely what I have tried to do.

The first book of my Joy Trilogy, *Enjoy the Lord*, was written at the request of a publisher who asked me to produce a collection of my syndicated columns. It was not conceived as the beginning of a trilogy, not at all. I gathered articles from the past five years, and realized it would be a boring book if I didn't arrange the material around a central theme.

I chose the topic of joy, and began writing new material. It always gave me great comfort to know that my holiness as a priest depended more on God's love for me than on my love for Him. I love God, but my feelings are not always in an affectionate mood when I come to pray.

It seemed to me that the knowledge of God's unchanging love is reason **"to rejoice always and in all circumstances,"** as St. Paul puts it (1 Th 5:16). Enjoying the Lord because of His

283

love took all the tension out my prayer life. It also facilitated my personal relationship with the Lord. So I decided to write about enjoying the Lord.

I realized that many good people sabotage their chances for joy by allowing fear and guilt to dominate their thoughts. When you think that your relationship with God depends on your moral exactitude you are in trouble.

But when you understand that holiness a gift, which has more to do with God dwelling in your soul, than on your moral perfection, you become liberated, and prayer becomes a joy not a burden.

Contemplation is wordless prayer. It is found in the awareness of God's loving presence. He is always within you, loving you with an infinite love. Why would anyone fear God? The Book of Proverbs speaks of "fear of the Lord," and we have come to understand these words as referring to the spirit of awe and wonder we experience in the presence of the Divine Majesty. They do not refer to the servile fear one might have in the presence of a slave master.

In the Bible, as I have often mentioned, we find the words, "Do not be afraid," repeated 365 times. Jesus instructs us over and over again, not to be afraid. **"Fear is useless,"** He says, **"what you need is trust."** In that first book, I wanted to promote a spirit of trust. When it comes to prayer, I want people to enjoy the Lord, and be at peace with Him. Fearing Him is useless.

My second book, *God Delights In You*, was written ten years later. It was not conceived as book two of the trilogy, but as a necessary follow-up to *Enjoy the Lord*. I felt it was important to understand that God not only loves us, He delights in loving us. It is as simple to understand as the delight you feel when you snuggle a newborn infant. Love and joy go hand in hand.

God looks upon each one of us lovingly. He delights in our response. He is Divine Joy Itself. This is a mystery as deep as the mystery of the Trinity, and all anyone can do is to describe the facts that surround the mystery. We all see "through a glass darkly" when it comes to the mysteries of our faith. Nevertheless, we know with certainty that our destiny is with God in heaven. One day we will luxuriate in His happiness for all eternity.

Jesus came to tell us this. He wanted to give us His Joy so that our joy may be complete, full, abundant, and satisfying.

The third book, *Enjoy Your Precious Life,* came ten years later, and a full twenty years since I penned *Enjoy the Lord.* I felt the Holy Spirit urging me to complete what I had begun, and was halfway into the book when I decided to call it a Joy Trilogy. I wanted to be more practical in the third book. Living the Gospel joyfully day by day is a way of life, not merely a way of conceptualizing Christianity.

I wanted to teach my reader not only what to do, but how to do it. Achieving a joyful spirit is the work of a lifetime. A journey of a thousand miles begins with the first step. In this case, the first step comes when you choose Joy as a way of life. "All the way to heaven is heaven." For this to be true in your life you must will it.

First you must will to become a loving person, and when the crosses come, you must put on the will to bear discomfort. Love leads to service and service introduces you to selflessness. There is so much discomfort in taking care of children, the elderly and the sick that people tend to run away from it. The saints experienced Joy in the very service that robbed them of freedom.

The final paragraph of the prayer attributed to St. Francis of Assisi contains the words, "For it is in giving that we receive." These words are true. It is in giving that we find Joy.

It takes great faith to understand this simple idea. I have stressed the importance of faith many times. This trilogy will only appeal to those who have the faith to see what others might think of as only pious drivel.

The title, *Enjoy Your Precious Life*, came from C.S. Lewis. He was an intellectual who in later life experienced Joy through a love relationship with his wife. Her name was Joy. Lewis had a spiritual awakening. He had never known the kind of Joy he experienced when he surrendered his life to Joy, in both senses of the word. Love and Joy brought him out of the caverns of intellectual faith, into the sunlight of heavenly grace.

For generations Christians have been trained to live in the climate of fear. So much so that even today the call to joy is looked upon by some with grave suspicion. These folks see the pursuit of joy as self-serving, but God wants us to enjoy our precious lives by loving Him and one another.

Living joyfully doesn't mean that we should give ourselves over to selfish indulgence. Anything that harms our neighbors or ourselves is against the Supreme Law. However, we can and we should seek our own happiness, which can only come about when we are faithful to the will of God.

We have been so conditioned by earlier heretical, negative influences. The Manicheans held that Satan created the world of matter, which is evil, while God created the spirit world, which is good. This dualistic view sees "eating, drinking and being merry" as sinful. People who believed this fell into self-distrust, thinking that they were essentially corrupt. The things of the "flesh" were seen as evil.

The 12th century heresy of Albigensianism carried this distortion of the truth to new generations. They declared that all bodily pleasures are sinful. A spiritual person therefore should not enjoy food, sexuality or any human delight. This heresy has ruined many lives.

Albigensianism spread through Europe. It influenced the Christian heresy of Jansenism, which had a harmful effect in France and which tainted the spiritual attitudes of many Catholics. In time, the heresy eventually made its way to America, and we have been infected with it ever since. We need to reject it without throwing out the baby with the bath. We need to cling to God, and love our neighbors as we love ourselves. Jesus wants us to love ourselves. He wants our Joy to be full. He does not want us to live under the shadow of fear. Yes we should eat, drink and be merry, but not in a mindless way. We have a right to enjoy the company of family and friends, and we have a right to celebrate our precious lives as long as we keep in mind our duty to help others.

Love is the supreme law, and our highest goal. Once you discover the magical connection between love and joy, you can begin to enjoy your life as never before. Love and joy are two sides of the same coin.

Jesus introduced us to a life of Joy when He commanded us to love one another. In writing this trilogy, I can look back and see how I was an instrument of the Holy Spirit in this undertaking. I didn't even think of it as a trilogy until I was well into the third volume. All I knew was that I wanted to be a messenger of Joy.

The late Thomas Merton, a Trappist monk who became the most important American spiritual writer of the 20th century, wanted this too. He had much to say about the importance of meditation in the process of becoming a light to the world.

"Meditation is for those who are not satisfied with the merely objective and conceptual knowledge about life, about God, about ultimate realities. They want to enter into an intimate contact with Truth itself, with God. They want to experience the deepest realities of life by living them."

Believing in God's Joy in a cognitive way is not enough. You need to experience Joy. The question I often pose to my audience when I am lecturing is this: "If you know that you have God's Joy in your heart, why don't you notify your face?"

Every one of us has to bring God's Joy up to the surface.

To live our Joy mindfully means that we consciously let go of our fears, our guilt and our nervous symptoms.

Faith is a necessary beginning, but our task is to cooperate with God's plan of bringing Joy to the world. The Eastern Church calls this the divinization process. It requires both faith and will training. You pray as if everything depended on God, and you act as if everything depended on you.

To bring the Joy from the center of your soul to the surface of your smile, you need to exercise your joyful muscles. Meditation is one of the best ways to do this. You can learn to experience Joy by practicing meditation every day.

My final gift to you therefore is a simple meditation technique.

Take a sitting position with your back erect, or if you prefer lie down with your hands at your side. Focus your attention on your breathing, three beats in, and four beats out. Feel your tummy expanding and contracting with each breath.

When your mind wanders, and it surely will, refocus your attention on your breathing. The mind jumps all over the place. Just learn to laugh at it. Don't judge yourself for failing to stay focused, but begin again, and pay attention to your breathing. Feel the air entering your lungs. Then let it go. Say "Thank you, Jesus," as you exhale.

This exercise keeps you locked into the present moment. You will be casting aside memories, and any bad feelings surrounding them. They will want to intrude, but you will refuse to let the past drag you down. Stay in the present moment. If you are angry about past injustices, accept your anger as a simple fact. Observe it. Do not try to make it disappear. Simply return to your breathing.

The same is true of fear about the future. If your mind begins worrying about the future, just laugh at yourself. The worries may be legitimate, but now is the time to give yourself to the present moment.

After ten or twenty breaths, begin saying the word "Joy," every time you inhale. Silently, receive the gift of Joy from Jesus. Say "Joy" as you breathe in, and as you exhale slowly say, "Thank you, Jesus."

Do this over and over again.

It is that simple. You are meditating. You are controlling your thoughts and inviting Joy into your conscious mind.

You may want to do this for ten or twenty minutes at a time. Add your own imaginary scenes of happy places you have been. See the faces of people you love. Enjoy your precious life, as you breathe in God's Love and Joy.

By conditioning your mind and memory in this way you will be willing to live in the present moment. Reject the idea of living like a puppet, being pulled this way and that by uncontrolled thoughts and instincts. Negative thoughts and desires will lose their power over you, as you gradually take more control of your life.

You will enjoy the Lord more, and you will experience the amazing realization that He is enjoying your company in return. Drink in His Joy. Live in His Joy, and you will find peace of soul.

More importantly, you will begin to project a joyful presence wherever you go.

Go then and become a messenger of Joy, for this is the will of God for you.

ST PAULS

This book was produced by ST PAULS/Alba House, the Society of St. Paul, an international religious congregation of priests and brothers dedicated to serving the Church through the communications media.

For information regarding this and associated ministries of the Pauline Family of Congregations, write to the Vocation Director, Society of St. Paul, 2187 Victory Blvd., Staten Island, New York 10314-6603. Phone (718) 982-5709; or E-mail: vocation@stpauls.us or check our internet site, www.vocationoffice.org